Dark Eagle

Book VI

Silures

by

K. M. Ashman

Copyright K. M. Ashman, January 2025

All rights are reserved. No part of this publication may be reproduced, stored, or transmitted in any form or by any means without prior written permission of the copyright owner. All characters depicted within this publication are fictitious, and any resemblance to any real person, living or dead, is entirely coincidental.

Keep up to date by subscribing at:

KMAshman.com

Character Names

The Occultum

- **Seneca** - Tribune, Leader of the Occultum
- **Marcus** - Former Centurion
- **Falco** - Former Gladiator
- **Sica** - Syrian Assassin
- **Decimus** - Veteran Member of the Occultum
- **Talorcan** - Belgic Scout
- **Veteranus** - Re-joined Member of the Occultum

Roman Command and Support

- **Claudius** - Emperor of Rome
- **Lepidus** - Senator, Controller of the Occultum and imperial liaison.
- **Maxima** - Decurion, Commander of the Exploratores
- **Adgennus** - Gallic Trader from the Aedui tribe

British Druids and War Leaders

- **Mordred** - Powerful Druid from Isla Mona
- **Caratacus** - British War Leader and Resistance Fighter

The Brigantes

- **Cartimandua** - Queen of the Brigantes
- **Rhiannon** - Daughter of Cartimandua

The Ordovices

- **Bodvoc** - Chief of the Eagle Clan
- **Einion** - Son of Bodvoc

The Silures

- **Belenos** - War Chief of a Silures Settlement
- **Cadoc** - War Chief of the Shadow Walkers, Silures Elite Warriors
- **Bran** - Son of Cadoc, Young Silures Warrior
- **Kynan** - Silures Warrior and Raider

Refugees and Guides

- **Maelon** - Former Slave, Guide and Scout

Map

Britannia

Prologue

Terra Siluria

The rain fell in cold sheets, hammering through the branches and sluicing down ancient trunks to soak the black loam of the forest floor. The oaks here were older than memory, twisted, moss-draped, and vast. Their roots coiled like serpents beneath the sodden earth, and their gnarled limbs clawed at the sky like the hands of drowned men reaching for breath and beneath them, crouched low among the wet bracken, a man worked in silence.

He was wrapped in a thick cloak of stitched fur, the hide of a mature hart darkened by the endless downpour. Beneath the cowl, his face was shadowed, only a sliver of cheek and a narrow, calloused mouth visible under the dripping hood, his breath forming a mist in his urgency. A long-bladed knife moved in practiced arcs through the steam-rising carcass of a deer, its blood mixing with rainwater in the leaves.

Each cut was carefully guided, the flesh carved with the efficient rhythm of a man who had done this a hundred times before and would do it many times again before winter's end.

His breath came in misted bursts now and around him, the forest groaned under the weight of wind and water, alive with the low whispers of hidden things. He worked fast, placing each chunk of bloody flesh into a rough linen sack, darkened from many seasons of use. No wasted motion, no reverence, just the grim urgency of hunger under a sky that offered no warmth. He slid the blade beneath the ribs with a sharp, practiced thrust, then wrenched them apart with both hands, the brittle cartilage cracking under pressure.

Steam rose from the cavity, and he reached in with both

hands, slick with blood to the wrists, and pulled the heart free, quickly raising it to his mouth as he looked around nervously.

The flesh tore between his teeth with a faint snap, and the hot taste of copper filled his mouth. He chewed quickly as he looked around, eyes flicking through the trees, ears straining against the roar of rain.

After a few more bites, he added what was left of the heart the sack and returned to the work, his breath hissing through clenched teeth as his knife carved through sinew and fat.

It was a good kill, a young doe, fat with acorn and autumn moss. The meat would last three weeks or more, longer if his woman boiled the sinew and dried the offcuts by the hearth. He could already see her face when he returned, could feel the little ones pawing at his knees. Gods, he missed them.

He tugged the last haunch free and slid it into the coarse sack, already heavy with good flesh. Blood soaked the cloth, thickening in the seams and the smell of it hung like a fog beneath the trees. He paused and straightened, his knees cracking in protest. He knew he had been too long and needed to get moving.

A crow lifted from a branch with a rough caw, then silence returned, no birdsong, no movement, just the cold creeping into his bones.

He slung the sack over his shoulder and turned to head back the way he had come… and froze. There, just two paces away, where no one had been just a few heartbeats ago, stood his worst nightmare. A Ilures tribesman.

The warrior was tall, and draped in heavy furs against the worst the weather could throw at him. Wolf across the shoulders, bear over the back, crudely stitched but heavy with age and use. His beard was thick, and beneath the animal hood, his face was daubed in whorls of blue woad that curled around his cheekbones and slid down one side of his neck like veins carved in ink. His eyes, piercing and ringed in soot, held the hunter without blinking. No sound. No breath. No warning.

The hunter's bow remained strapped across his back and his knife sat bloody in its sheath at his belt. He hadn't heard the warrior approach, hadn't smelled him. It was as if the forest had made him appear from thin air.

The pain didn't register at first. Just a jolt, like someone punching him in the stomach. Then the warmth bloomed across his belly, sudden and obscene and he looked down as if in inevitable acceptance.

The blade was already there, sunk deep, the hilt resting against his tunic, pressed into his gut. The hand holding it was steady and calm. The hunter looked up, his eyes meeting the warrior's again and something passed between them, not hatred, not anger, just the grim acknowledgement of a truth both men understood. The hunter shouldn't have been here. He knew the risks, but his family's hunger had meant he had no choice. Now he had paid the ultimate price.

The warrior twisted the blade and his victim's knees folded as the forest floor rose to meet him, his sack tumbling from his shoulder. As he lay on the floor, his blood turning the wet foliage red, he looked across to the nearby trees where a male child stood, watching coldly as his father killed a man.

He was no more than ten summers, wrapped in a fur cloak too large for his shoulders. His face was streaked with ash, his eyes fixed on the dying hunter with the same flat stillness of his father. The warrior grew weaker as his blood saturated his furs, but his eyes stayed on the boy. He was about the same age as his own son, and the heartbreaking realisation brought rare tears to his eyes. How would he survive now?

The warrior walked over and placed the sack into the young boy's arms.

'Dobunni,' he said, and turned to spit in the dying man's direction before turning away and vanishing back into the trees. His son looked at the dying man one more time before following his father, the pines swallowing them like ghosts returning to the mist.

Behind them, the hunter lay still. The rain fell on his face, merging with the tears as he thought of his children. His blood pooled around him, still warm for a little while longer. Then it too turned cold

----

Chapter One

Camulodunum

Maps and scrolls littered the rough-hewn table in the briefing room of the temporary fortress outside the walls of Camulodunum, held down by daggers and wine cups, the ink on some still wet with annotations.

Seneca stood with his back to the door, waiting for Lepidus to arrive. His weathered face betrayed nothing, but the tension in his shoulders spoke of sleepless nights and difficult decisions. The loss of Cassius still haunted him, a wound too fresh to have formed a proper scar.

The door opened without ceremony, admitting a gust of cold air and the imposing figure of Senator Lepidus. The older man's toga was spotted with rainwater, and his sandals were caked with the mud of Camulodunum. He nodded curtly to Seneca before moving to warm his hands over the brazier.

'A bitch of a day,' he said over his shoulder. 'Are your men joining us?'

'Not yet,' said Seneca. 'I thought it would be better to thrash out the details before sharing the burden. Besides, they need rest.'

Lepidus reached inside his toga and produced a sealed scroll.

'This contains all we know of the western territories, but it isn't much.'

Seneca took the scroll but did not break the seal.

'Is there anything I should know that isn't written here?'

'Actually, there is.' replied Lepidus. 'I know that I said Veteranus is going with you but there's been a last-minute change of plan, he has already gone.'

'Gone where?' asked Seneca.

'Into the lands of the Ordovices,' said Lepidus. 'The Brigantes are sending a trading caravan deep into their territory. Apparently it's a regular occurrence and they have some sort of treaty that guarantees safe passage.'

'And Veteranus is going with them?'

'He is,' said Lepidus. 'Under the guise of a Roman trader seeking to establish new commerce. He's travelling with another trader who knows these people intimately.' He stared at Seneca for a moment, knowing the history between the two men. 'I accept you still have bad blood between you, Seneca,' he continued, 'but he was once one of us, and a good one at that. Besides, he's already been in their territory before.'

'When he was a captive with the druids,' Seneca pointed out. 'It's hardly the same as going in pretending to be a Roman trader.'

'A fair point,' said Lepidus, but he knows the terrain, the settlements, perhaps even some of their customs and language. This was an opportunity we couldn't afford to waste.'

'So what exactly is he going to do down there?'

'Mainly gather intelligence on the Ordovices. Their settlements, fighting strength, their attitudes toward Rome, that sort of thing. It's completely separate from your mission to the Silures, parallel efforts, different targets.'

'And what happens if our paths cross?' Seneca asked, his eyes narrowing.

Lepidus shook his head firmly.

'They won't. The Ordovices territory is extensive, and you have no reason to venture that far north. Your mission is to find Mordred among the Silures, not to range across half of western Britannia.'

'I'm still not sure about this, Lepidus,' said Seneca.

'How do you know we can trust him? For all we know, he still has loyalties to Mordred. He was with him long enough.'

'His warning saved Claudius's life during the ceremony,' Lepidus countered. 'Without that intelligence, the Emperor would be dead.'

'That could have been to save his own skin,' said Seneca. 'He admitted himself he almost converted to Mordred's cause.'

'I don't think it was,' said Lepidus. 'But that's beside the point. Veteranus will focus on the Ordovices while you and the Occultum concentrate on the Silures. Two separate missions with different objectives. Rome needs intelligence on both tribes if we're to secure this island.'

There was an awkward silence as both men considered the implications. Seneca was not comfortable with the situation but knew the wisdom of gathering intelligence from multiple sources.

'Very well,' he said eventually. 'We each have our missions. Let's hope they both bear fruit.'

'There is one more thing,' said Lepidus, breaking the silence. 'The Silures.'

'What about them?' Seneca asked.

'They're not like any other tribes you've encountered.' Lepidus moved to the map, his finger tracing the boundary of the unmarked western territories. 'They don't fight in open battle. They don't respond to displays of force or negotiate in good faith. They kill from the shadows and vanish before you can respond.'

'Sounds familiar,' said Seneca.

'This is serious, Seneca,' said Lepidus. 'You haven't fought men like these before. The Occultum needs to be at their best to even survive.'

'Let me worry about the men,' said Seneca. 'You just make sure we have whatever we need.'

'It's already been authorised by Claudius,' said Lepidus. 'How soon can you move?'

'At least ten days,' said Seneca. 'My men need to rest and gather their strength. Not a moment sooner.'

Lepidus grimaced. He had wanted them moving within the week but knew better than to override Seneca's judgement. He knew what his men were capable of.

'Ten days it is,' he said eventually and started walking towards the door before pausing and looking back. 'The emperor doesn't care how much it costs or how you do it, Seneca, he just want's Mordred's head on a spike. Make sure he gets it.'

Up in one of the forests outside Camulodunum, the rest of the Occultum went about their business in their temporary camp.

'Are we going to stand here freezing our bollocks off all morning?' Falco rumbled, his breath rising in misty clouds.

Sica didn't respond. He crouched beside a weathered rock at the edge of the clearing, slowly dragging a whetstone along the curved edge of his blade. The scrape of steel on stone was soft, precise, and unhurried, the sound of someone preparing not for the day, but for what might need doing at the end of it.

'He's brooding again,' Decimus muttered, looking over. 'Every time Sica starts sharpening before breakfast, someone ends up dead before supper.'

'Let him brood,' said Talorcan. 'It keeps him out of trouble.'

'Watching him sharpen that bloody thing makes me

13

feel like he's plotting against me,' said Falco.

'Everything's plotting against you, Falco,' said Marcus, emerging from a tent with a handful of dried meat. 'Especially your liver.'

'My liver's done me proud,' said Falco, snatching a strip from Marcus's hand. 'I can still drink more than you lot put together and fight ten men before breakfast.'

Sica shook his head silently without looking up.

A breeze stirred the canvas of the tents and somewhere nearby, a hawk shrieked above the trees. Camulodunum was just over the rise, a newly created grid of Roman pride and marble ambition, but out here, in the woods, the ground still belonged to the old gods. The land was scarred, not conquered and many of the locals had not surrendered; they had simply gone quiet.

'How long do you think we'll be kept waiting?' asked Talorcan.

Marcus shrugged his shoulders as he placed some of the dried meat into the pot hanging over the fire.

'Seneca wouldn't have told us to wait here unless something was brewing.'

Falco pulled his cloak tighter and sighed loudly.

'When this is over, I'm going to Sicilia, buy a vineyard, raise pigs and grow fat.'

'The pigs or you?' Sica asked, without looking up.

'Both. Side by side. We'll toast the Empire with sour wine and eat figs until we forget our own names.'

'A tempting vision,' Decimus murmured.

'Only because it involves not freezing your bollocks off,' replied Falco.

For the next hour or so, the men of the Occultum sat in

silence around their fire, each lost in his own thoughts yet bound by the shared weight of their recent mission. Dirt and exhaustion were etched into their faces and steam rose from the crude platters balanced on their knees, boiled meat providing little pleasure but necessary sustenance. Decimus broke the silence first.

'To Cassius,' he said simply, raising his waterskin.

'To Cassius,' echoed the others, the name hanging in the air like smoke.

Falco, picked at his meat with uncharacteristic restraint. The former gladiator's usual bombast had dimmed in the days since they'd lost their brother-in-arms.

'Saved the Emperor and died a hero's death,' he muttered quietly. 'The crafty bastard always did like to make an impression.'

'Lepidus will ensure his family is taken care of,' said Marcus, 'it's the proper Roman way.'

Their silence was broken by the sound of footsteps climbing the hill toward their position. As one, their postures shifted almost imperceptibly, hands drifting closer to weapons even as they continued to eat and drink with apparent nonchalance.

'Just a messenger,' said Marcus, as they all relaxed again.

'Ten sestertii says we're being sent somewhere worse than this gods-forsaken island,' said Falco.

'Not taking that bet,' replied Marcus, spearing another piece of meat.

The men watched the messenger's approach with studied indifference, though each was already mentally preparing for whatever new mission might tear them from their brief respite.

The man approached their fire with visible apprehension, his steps slowing as he drew near. The men of the Occultum continued eating, acting as though they hadn't noticed his arrival, though each was acutely aware of the intruder in their midst.

'A message from Tribune Seneca,' he announced, standing stiffly at attention. 'You are to meet him at the fortress tomorrow at dawn for a mission briefing.'

Marcus gave a curt nod, the only acknowledgment the messenger would receive. Decimus continued chewing his meat, eyes fixed on the fire while Sica didn't look up at all, his knife scraping against the wooden platter as he gathered the last scraps of his meal.

The messenger shifted uncomfortably, waiting for a more substantial response. When none came, he turned to leave but paused after a few steps, gathering his courage.

'Perhaps,' he said, his voice wavering slightly, 'you men might consider taking a bath before the meeting.' He wrinkled his nose. 'You stink.'

With that, he hurried down the hill, glancing back over his shoulder as if expecting a knife in his back for the impertinence.

The Occultum watched him go with the same indifference they'd shown upon his arrival. When he was out of earshot, Falco broke the silence.

'A bath?' he scoffed, tearing another chunk of meat with his teeth. 'What does he think we are, senators? I washed in a horse trough not three weeks past.' He sniffed at his armpit demonstratively. 'Still fresh as a Gaulish spring.'

Marcus shook his head.

'We do smell, Falco. And you worst of all.' He eyed the former gladiator with weary disgust.

'Dawn at the fortress,' said Decimus, drawing them back to the matter at hand. 'It looks like we may have to do more of the emperor's glorious work.'

Falco grunted, stretching his massive frame.

'Another mission, another chance to die gloriously for Rome.' He raised his waterskin in mock salute. 'But this time, they want us to die clean.'

Chapter Two

Camulodunum

The fortress outside Camulodunum's walls buzzed with activity despite the early hour. Inside one of the newly built wooden buildings, Seneca stood hunched over a large map spread across the rough-hewn table. Their fingers traced potential routes through the unfamiliar terrain of southern Britannia.

The door swung open bringing with it a gust of cold morning air and the unmistakable presence of the Occultum. Seneca looked up, a greeting dying on his lips as he took in the state of his men.

Falco and stood at the front, soaking wet from head to toe, water pooling beneath his feet on the packed earth floor. The massive ex-gladiator wore an expression of subdued defiance, like a scolded child who wasn't entirely sorry for his mischief.

Behind him, Decimus sported a spectacular black eye, the purple bruise a stark contrast against his weathered skin while Marcus's face was stained crimson from what appeared to be a recent nosebleed, dried blood crusted around his nostrils and a swollen upper lip. Sica and Talorcan seemed physically unaffected though their clothing suggested there had been quite a struggle. He shook his head, his expression hovering between exasperation and amusement.

'Do I really want to know?' he asked finally, his gaze settling on Marcus, the most likely to provide a reasonable explanation.

The former centurion gave a small shrug of his shoulders.

'Falco wouldn't bathe,' he stated simply, 'so when we crossed the river, we... um... gave him some encouragement.'

Seneca's eyes moved from Marcus to Falco, who attempted to stand at attention despite the water dripping from his baldhead, then again to the rest and he suspected it had taken them all to subdue him.

'Some stories are better left untold,' he said with a sigh and gestured to the map with a sweep of his hand. 'Gather round, we have work to do.'

The Occultum members arranged themselves around the table and Marcus leaned forward, absently touching his bloodied nose as he studied the familiar parchment.

The map of Britannia lay before them, remarkably detailed for a land still largely unconquered. The invasion's progress was clearly marked, the landing site at Rutupiae where the legions had first set foot on British soil, the decisive battles at the Medway and Tamesis rivers where Roman discipline had overcome Celtic fury, and the temporary fortresses established to secure their advance toward Camulodunum.

'This map represents years of careful work,' said Seneca, gazing at the map, 'traders' routes, Caesar's expeditions and our own scouts. The tribal territories are well documented in the south and east.'

Decimus, squinting through his swollen eye, nodded in appreciation.

'Caesar's commentaries were useful,' he said, 'despite being decades old. The tribes haven't changed their territories much since his time.'

His attention turned to the conspicuous blank spaces on the map, the far northern reaches beyond the lands of the Brigantes, and the western territories stretching toward the setting sun. These regions remained stubbornly empty of

Roman markings, symbols, or notations, terra incognita, unknown and potentially hostile.

Falco grunted and tapped a finger onto the empty western section.

'Nothing there but savages and druids.'

Seneca waited as the men studied the map, their eyes drawn to the vast unexplored regions.

'The Emperor is safely on his way back to Rome,' he continued eventually, 'but he is livid that he came so close to death, and he wants Mordred killed. He doesn't care what it takes what it costs, he wants him dead, and he wants the Occultum to do it.'

The men exchanged concerned glances. They had barely recovered from their last mission, and the loss of Cassius still weighed heavily upon them.

'Do we know where he is?' Decimus added, the veteran's practical mind already turning to logistics.

'Lepidus has had word that he has fled back to the west,' said Seneca.

Falco's face darkened.

'We've just come from Isla Mona,' he pointed out, 'are we going back there?'

For a moment, Seneca stared at him, then shook his head, leaning over the map and placing his finger much further south of Isla Mona, deep in the heart of an unexplored region.

'Terra Siluria,' he said simply, his finger resting on the blank expanse of the western territories. 'We saw it from the fishing boat when we circumnavigated the island a few months ago but this time we are going in.'

Marcus stared at the map before looking up at Seneca.

'Everything we've heard about Terra Siluria is bad,' he said. 'Even the other tribes of Britannia fear to go there.'

'They do,' said Seneca, 'and this mission will take every skill we have if we are going to have a chance of pulling it off.'

'What about allies?' asked Marcus, 'are there any friendly chieftains to provide us sanctuary if it all goes wrong?'

'Not that I'm aware of,' said Seneca. 'We'll be on our own on this one.'

'So,' said Falco, 'we're to hunt a druid in unknown territory, among a tribe of savages who hate Rome, with no allies and no intelligence.' He grinned suddenly, his teeth pale against his dark beard. 'Sounds like a normal day for the Occultum.'

'I know it's a lot to ask,' said Seneca 'but it is beyond the capabilities of anything Rome has to offer at the moment so that's why Claudius has asked us to do it. He's becoming very aware of what we are capable of. He also provides the coin to keep us going and now he wants his pound of flesh.'

'Can't he send a legion?' asked Marcus.

'It will be quite a while before Plautius turns his attention on Siluria,' replied Seneca. 'His priorities are the east coast and the south at the moment, and it could be a year or more before he is in a position to take on the Silures. No, we are the only ones who have the slightest chance of finding Mordred. This will be a mission of stealth, not strength. We find Mordred, we eliminate him, and we get out as quickly as we can. We've done it before and this is no different.'

'When do we go?' asked Marcus.

'We leave in ten days,' said Seneca as his gaze swept around the table, meeting each man's eyes in turn. 'You know how this works, if any of you wish to be omitted from this mission, speak now. It will not reflect on your commitment or affect your place in this team. We have all been through a lot these past few weeks so I will support any man who feels they need to sit this one out.'

The room fell silent but despite their exhaustion, despite their wounds, not one man spoke up. They had lost Cassius; they would not abandon each other now.

'Very well,' said Seneca, satisfied but unsurprised. 'Let's discuss our approach.'

They gathered closer around the map, their bodies casting long shadows across Britannia's uncharted territories.

'First of all,' he began, 'I'm assuming nobody supports the idea of another sea approach?'

'No,' came several immediate responses.

Falco shook his head emphatically.

'Absolutely not,' he said. 'I've had my fill of the sea, in more ways than one.'

'Whatever way we approach,' said Marcus. 'How do we find Mordred once we're there? The Silurian lands are vast. He could be anywhere.'

'The presence of such a powerful druid would quickly become common knowledge among the locals,' replied Seneca.' All we need to do is question the right people.'

The men exchanged knowing glances. *'Questioning'* often meant killing in their line of work. It was an unpleasant fact, but necessary.

'I've no problem with that,' said Falco. 'After what the Wraith did to Cassius...'

'This isn't about revenge,' Seneca cut in sharply. 'It's about completing the mission. Mordred is a threat to Rome's stability in Britannia. Nothing more, nothing less.'

'And yet,' Marcus observed quietly, 'the Emperor seems to be taking this very personally.'

'The Emperor's motivations are not our concern,' said Seneca. 'We all know how dangerous Mordred is, so we do this to stop fellow Romans being killed later in the campaign. We find him, kill him and get back here as quickly as we can.'

The men of the Occultum stood in silence for a moment, contemplating the deadly simplicity of their task and the near-impossible complexity of its execution.

Seneca looked around the group again, knowing he had the finest group of men he could possibly hope for.

'Right,' he said, 'how do we do this?'

'A straight march is suicide,' said Falco. 'We'd draw eyes by the second day and be dead by the third.'

'We can't march in,' Seneca agreed. 'Not on our own and certainly not with any of the cohorts. Caratacus will have eyes beyond the border and any large movement west will give him a warning.'

'There's no route that gets us close without being seen,' said Marcus, 'not on horseback. But a mounted support column could ride us out as far as that river that forms a natural border.' He pointed at the location on the map. 'Then we go to ground.'

'Deep insertion,' agreed Decimus quietly. 'They take us in as far as they can and leave us there. We can place supply caches on the way, in, just enough to get out if it all goes to shit.'

Marcus turned slowly to look at him.

'You've done this before?'

'Standard Occultum procedure,' said Decimus. 'The trick is to stop any watchers realising there are riders missing when the mounted escort returns.'

'And how do we do that?'

'When we go to ground, the support column splits up in the dark and return via different routes. Anyone watching will be caught between two options and unable to confirm the final numbers.'

'Agreed,' said Seneca. 'But we need good support. Fighting men who won't talk about numbers or names when they return.'

'We use the legion's exploratores,' said Marcus. 'They are used to operating behind enemy lines and can keep their mouths shut.'

'I agree,' said Seneca. 'I'll arrange the support, you lot start gathering supplies. Apart from the caches, everything gets carried in our sarcinae so try to keep your loads as light as you can. We've got ten days, so let's use the time well.'

It took Seneca a full day to convince the command to release the Exploratores but eventually they arrived in silence with patched leather jerkins and cloaks cut short to ride clear of the knees. Each looked weather-beaten and rangy, the kind of men who stared through you rather than at you.

Their commander, a square-jawed Decurion named Maxima, gave Seneca a half-hearted salute.

'I was told this would be quiet work,' he said without blinking. 'So tell me, Tribune… just how loud is it likely to get?'

'If we do this right,' Seneca replied, 'you'll be back at Camulodunum within days. If we do it wrong… well, you'll know it when it starts.'

For the following few nights, Seneca met with his men in a forest clearing west of the Roman stockade. Maps were studied over and over, and the men practised their patrol skills in detail, refreshing their memories on the best tactics to move as silently as possible through enemy territory.

They rehearsed the cache routine by moonlight. Two stops in total, one in the eastern side of the river boundary, the second on the western side, deep in enemy territory. Each cache would include medical supplies, salt meat, water skins, flint, weapons and coiled rope.

'Feels like preparing for our own funeral,' muttered Falco on the third night as he sealed a wax-cloth bundle.

'Speak less,' Sica hissed beside him, 'and work faster.'

'You're welcome to prepare your own gods-damned cache next time,' Falco snapped, but the bite was half-hearted.

In the days, Seneca drilled the team without mercy. Silent hand signals, emergency regroup procedures, march order, scatter-and-hide drills. Talorcan was fairly new to the skills, but as a man used to hunting prey through the forests of Germania, the methods came naturally, and he learned quickly.

By the sixth day the men no longer joked and by the tenth, they were as prepared as they were ever going to be. The Exploratores escort were already saddled, fifty strong and their leader rode up to Seneca, his face unreadable beneath his hood.

'There are an extra six horses waiting for you and your men,' he said. 'I don't know why you are going or what you are going to do, but whatever it is, we'll do our best to give you a head start. We should be at the river in five days.'

Seneca nodded and looked across the men he was going behind enemy lines with, Marcus, Falco, Sica, Decimus and Talorcan. They had prepared as well as they could and now it was time to put it all into practice.

'Mount up,' he said. 'Let's get this done.'

Chapter Three

The Western Road

For three days, the trading caravan had been rumbling westward, the long serpentine procession stretching across the rough track that couldn't rightly be called a road. Veteranus shifted uncomfortably on the hard wooden bench of the wagon, his back aching from the constant jarring motion as the wheels found every rut and stone the ancient path had to offer. The smell of oiled leather, sweat-dampened wool, and the earthy perfume of the trade goods surrounded him. It was not unpleasant, merely foreign, like so much in this strange island.

'The Ordovices will kill any stray Roman they find on their lands,' said the man sitting beside him. 'Cut their throats and leave them for the crows.'

Veteranus glanced at his companion. Adgennus was a Gallic trader from the Aedui tribe, a people who had been allied with Rome since before Caesar's conquest. His weathered face spoke of decades spent travelling the wild borderlands of the empire, and the silver peppered through his neatly trimmed beard marked him as a man in his fifth decade. Though he wore the practical garb of a merchant, sturdy wool tunic, leather breeches, and a heavy cloak against the British damp, the quality of the fabric and the gold ring on his right hand betrayed his considerable wealth.

'Then it's fortunate I don't plan to die just yet,' Veteranus replied, flicking the reins to urge the sturdy mountain ponies forward as the wagon ahead began to pull away.

'Nor I,' said Adgennus with a wry smile. 'I've been crossing to these shores for fifteen years now, and I find breathing far more profitable than the alternative.'

The Gaul had been assigned to the Brigantes column as both a translator and diplomat, his years of experience trading with the British tribes making him invaluable to Rome's ambitions. He spoke several tribal dialects fluently and understood their customs and taboos well. More importantly, he had been granted authority by Aulus Plautius himself to negotiate a tentative truce with the Ordovices chieftains, with the specific aim of preventing them from joining forces with Caratacus, should the elusive British leader seek their alliance.

The trading column was an impressive sight, particularly in a land where commerce usually consisted of a few men with packhorses or simple carts. Over fifty wagons trundled along the ancient trackway, each drawn by teams of four or six small, hardy horses bred for the northern hills. The vehicles themselves were masterpieces of tribal carpentry and unlike the box-like Roman carpentum, these were shallow, boat-shaped affairs with high, curving sides of bent ash and oak, lashed together with strips of rawhide and sealed with pine pitch. Their wheels were solid discs of wood reinforced with iron bands, better suited to the boggy ground than the Roman spoked variety.

Between and around the wagons trudged a small army of donkeys, over twenty of the creatures, laden with goods too delicate or too awkward to be trusted to the jolting wagon beds. The patient beasts were festooned with wicker baskets, leather sacks, and clay amphorae secured in wooden frames, their handlers walking alongside with long sticks to guide them.

All of this mercantile wealth moved under the watchful eyes of the Brigantes warriors. Over a hundred mounted men flanked the column, their small, shaggy ponies moving with sure-footed confidence across terrain that would have broken a

Roman cavalry horse's leg. The warriors wore iron helmets adorned with boar crests or raven feathers, and their bodies were protected by leather jerkins stiffened with strips of iron. Each carried a round shield of lime wood covered in oxhide, painted with spiral patterns in red and black. Their weapons were varied. Some bore long slashing swords, others thrusting spears with iron heads as long as a man's forearm. All had at least one knife at their belt, and many carried slings coiled around their waists, the simple weapon devastating in skilled hands.

'What's in that wagon?' Veteranus asked, pointing ahead to a vehicle piled high with large, clay vessels.

'Salt,' replied Adgennus. 'From the coast. The tribes in the mountains need it for preserving meat through the winter. It also some has spices from the east. The Ordovices have little access to such things.'

Veteranus nodded. Salt and spices were valuable currency in most cultures, and worth its weight in tin or silver to people who had no ready access to the eastern trading routes.

'And that one?' Veteranus pointed to another wagon.

'Glass vessels from my homeland,' said Adgennus with undisguised pride. 'For chieftains to drink their mead from instead of cow horns. The prestige of such items can sometimes sway a council vote more effectively than any argument.'

'I think mead tastes better from a horn,' said Veteranus.

'Perhaps,' Adgennus chuckled, 'but you and I are practical men. Chieftains must consider how they appear to their followers. A man who drinks from Roman glass is a man with connections to the wider world, something not to be underestimated among these isolated tribes.'

The column was indeed a treasure house of goods that

rarely made it to the western reaches of the island. There were amphorae of wine from the continent, the clay vessels packed in straw and secured with rope to prevent breakage on the rough terrain. Several wagons carried textiles, not the rough wool and linen produced locally, but fine cotton from Egypt and even small bolts of Chinese silk that had passed through countless hands on its journey from the far east.

Other wagons carried pottery, ranging from simple cooking vessels to elaborately decorated ritual items, but the finest pieces came from Gaul and Hispania, their glossy red surfaces adorned with moulded scenes of hunts and harvests.

'What about this one?' asked Veteranus. 'What do we carry?'

'Mainly Roman goods,' said Adgennus. 'Silver cups and platters embossed with wolf legends. Glass vessels that would make a senator envious, tools of iron with olive wood handles and a few swords of the finest steel. There's even a complete set of mail armour with a bronze helmet, the sort Roman officers wear.'

'A varied selection,' said veteranus.

'It is, but these are not just bribes, they're carefully chosen items that speak to their values. The weapons show respect for their martial culture. The textiles appeal to their desire for comfort in their harsh climate. The drinking vessels acknowledge their love of feasting and ceremonial hospitality.'

'You seem to understand these people well,' Veteranus observed.

'I've traded with them many times in the past decade,' Adgennus confirmed. 'They're cautious but not unreasonable. Their chieftains understand the value of trade, even if their warriors prefer the glory of battle.' He paused, stroking his beard thoughtfully. 'The key to our negotiations will be

29

convincing them that neutrality serves their interests better than alliance with Caratacus.'

'Is there talk of such an alliance?'

Adgennus nodded grimly.

'Rumours only, but persistent ones. Caratacus's name carries weight among the western tribes. His resistance to Rome has elevated him to near-mythic status in some quarters. If he were to appear among the Ordovices, seeking allies...' He left the implications hanging.

'And your task is to ensure that doesn't happen?' said Veteranus quietly.

It is,' said the Gaul. 'I may speak their language, but Roman silver speaks even more persuasively.' He gestured toward the wagon. 'That's why we're here, after all.'

As their conversation continued, Veteranus studied the landscape around them. For the past two days they had been travelling through lands that grew increasingly unfamiliar. The eastern territory, with its chalk downs and open fields, had given way to rolling hills covered in ancient forests. Now those hills were rising, becoming the foothills of mountains that loomed blue and forbidding in the west.

The land felt older here, somehow. More primal. The forests were not the managed woodlands of the eastern tribes, selectively cut for agriculture and fuel. These were primeval stands of oak and ash, yew and rowan, their massive trunks testament to centuries of undisturbed growth. Between these wooded slopes lay hidden valleys where mist gathered even on clear days, and streams ran crystal clear over beds of stone worn smooth by millennia of flowing water.

Few settlements were visible from the trackway for unlike the eastern tribes who built their roundhouses in villages or fortified enclosures, the western peoples preferred to build their dwellings in strongly defended hillforts, some of which could be occasionally seen in the distance.

'The Ordovices learned to protect their homes centuries ago,' Adgennus remarked, noting Veteranus's scanning gaze. 'The Silures have traditionally raided from the south, the Deceangli from the north, and sometimes, even the Dobunni from the east.'

'Tell me more about the Silures,' Veteranus prompted. 'You must have gathered stories in your years of trading here.'

Adgennus's expression grew serious.

'I've never traded with them directly, nor has any merchant I know. They are... different. They keep to themselves, hidden in forests so old the druids say the trees remember when the mountains were young.'

'But they must trade sometimes?' Veteranus pressed. 'They must need things they cannot make themselves.'

'Rarely,' said Adgennus. 'And never directly. There are neutral grounds where goods are left for exchange. Iron for silver, mostly. They have mines in their mountains that produce silver and lead, but little good iron ore.' He paused. 'They take slaves sometimes.'

'Slaves?'

The Gaul nodded gravely.

'From raids on neighbouring tribes. Or from travellers who stray into their territory. They use them to work their mines, but no one who enters Silures land uninvited returns to tell of it.'

'What of their druids?' Veteranus asked casually. 'I've heard the western tribes still follow the old ways.'

'The western druids are more secretive than those you encountered in the east,' Adgennus replied. 'They shun outsiders entirely. There are rumours that many of the older sects retreated to the Silurian mountains years ago, seeking places where they could preserve their rituals undisturbed.' He eyed Veteranus with sudden interest. 'Why do you ask about their druids?'

'Just curious,' Veteranus replied with deliberate lightness. 'I've had some run-ins with one or two so best to understand all the players on the board.'

Adgennus seemed to accept this explanation, though his eyes lingered on Veteranus a moment longer than necessary.

By late afternoon, the column began to slow as scouts returned with news of a suitable camping place ahead. The lead wagons were already turning off the track into a broad meadow beside a small river. By nightfall, they had arranged the vehicles in a rough circle, creating a makeshift fort with the animals and people sheltered inside. Fires were lit and carefully placed to avoid silhouetting the guards who patrolled the perimeter.

Adgennus secured his wagon near the centre of the encampment, before preparing a simple meal of dried meat, hard bread, and a handful of early autumn apples they had purchased from a small settlement the previous day.

'Tell me more about the Ordovices chieftains,' said Veteranus as they ate beneath the canvas awning stretched from the side of the wagon. 'Who holds the real power among them?'

'Three main clans control their council,' Adgennus replied between mouthfuls. 'The Bear Clan of the northern valleys, the Wolf Clan from the central forests, and the Eagle Clan who hold the mountain passes. Of these, the Eagle is currently ascendant, their chieftain Bodvoc having won several victories against the Deceangli last summer.'

'And what do they value most?' Veteranus pressed. 'What arguments would sway them toward neutrality rather than alliance with Caratacus?'

Adgennus considered this, stroking his beard thoughtfully.

'The Ordovices are practical despite their fierce reputation. They value their independence above all else. If we can convince them that allying with Caratacus would inevitably lead to Roman retaliation, and the loss of that independence, while neutrality would bring trade and prosperity...' He shrugged. 'Then we might succeed.'

'And the gifts we carry? Will they help?'

'They'll get us a hearing,' the Gaul replied. 'Particularly the weapons. The Ordovices respect strength and craftsmanship. Those Roman swords will be coveted.'

'Yet we give them weapons that might one day be used against Roman troops,' Veteranus observed.

Adgennus smiled thinly.

'A handful of swords won't tip any balance of power. But they demonstrate respect, and respect is what we need to open negotiations.' He looked directly at Veteranus. 'I've negotiated many such arrangements in my years of trading. Sometimes a small risk now prevents a greater one later.'

They continued their meal in comfortable silence, each man absorbed in his own thoughts. Around them, the camp settled into its nighttime routine, traders securing their goods, warriors establishing watches or preparing their bedrolls beneath their wagons. The low murmur of conversation in various dialects created a gentle hum that seemed to merge with the night sounds of the forest.

As darkness fell completely, the camp quieted. The guards maintained their vigilant patrol of the perimeter, but most of the traders and settled into sleep, wrapped in wool blankets and furs against the cooling night air.

33

Adgennus retreated to his own bed space inside his wagon, while Veteranus made a simple bed beneath the vehicle, preferring to remain outside where he could move quickly if needed.

He lay awake for a long time, listening to the night sounds slowly return to the forest around them. But as his eyes traced the patterns of stars visible through breaks in the clouds, Veteranus couldn't shake the feeling of being watched. Tomorrow they would press deeper into Ordovices territory, and with alliances already forming that could determine the future of Rome's hold on Britannia, his task… their task, was to ensure those alliances favoured the empire.

Chapter Four

Terra Siluria

The temporary camp nestled between ancient oaks, its makeshift huts built not in the open as other tribes preferred, but scattered among the trees, half-hidden by the forest itself. Smoke rose in thin tendrils from hidden hearths, barely visible against the grey sky.

Blood-red streaks tore through the morning cloud as Cadoc stood at the edge of the camp, a broad-shouldered figure wrapped in the pelt of a massive grey wolf, the top half of its skull still attached and forming a formidable hood above his own. The beast's fangs framed his face, its empty eye sockets lending him an otherworldly appearance. His face, lined with the scars of countless battles, remained impassive as he watched the camp stir to life. The blue woad patterns that marked his cheekbones and forehead had been renewed the previous night, the spiral designs marking him as a killer of renown among the Silures.

Three weeks had passed since he'd gutted the Dobunni hunter in the eastern woods. A necessary death, but one he had savoured, nonetheless. The man had trespassed on Silures hunting grounds, taking game that belonged to Cadoc's people. The memory of the man's final moments still brought a cold satisfaction.

'Father.'

Cadoc turned to find his older son, Bran, standing behind him. The boy had grown tall over the summer, his frame beginning to fill out with the promise of the warrior he would become. At fourteen summers, he already wore the marks of his first blood, a small pattern at his temple that would grow more complex with each life he took. In his belt hung the teeth of the first man he had killed, a Cornovii trader who had wandered too far from his usual routes.

'The scouts returned before dawn,' Bran said, his young voice deliberately deepened to match his father's rumbling tone. 'They bring news of Romans.'

Cadoc's expression didn't change, but his eyes narrowed slightly.

'Where?'

'Approaching from the east. Six horsemen, moving along the riverbank.'

'The same route they've been using for a month,' Cadoc said dismissively. 'They never cross the water.'

'This time they might,' Bran insisted, the excitement of youth edging into his voice. 'Bedwyr says they're different. 'Scouts, perhaps.'

Cadoc studied his son, noting the barely contained eagerness in his stance. Bran had yet to shed Roman blood, and he hungered for it with the fervour of youth.

'Bedwyr sees Romans in his dreams,' Cadoc said flatly. 'He would attack shadows if they were cast by Roman arms.'

'And what's wrong with that?' came a new voice, sharp with challenge.

Bedwyr emerged from between two huts, a wiry figure whose lean strength belied his twenty-five summers. His hair was cropped short except for a single braid that fell over his right shoulder, dyed red with ochre and lime. At his neck hung a necklace of human knucklebones, clicking together as he moved. The blue patterns on his face were still fresh, likely applied after dawn, and far more aggressive than tradition demanded, jagged lines that made his face appear cracked like ice, a warning to all who beheld him.

'The only good Roman is a gutted one,' Bedwyr continued, his hand resting on the bone hilt of his knife. 'We should attack them before they grow bolder. Their screams would be a worthy offering to the old gods.'

Cadoc turned his gaze to the younger warrior, his silence more powerful than any rebuke. After a long moment, he spoke.

'We will wait, watch and learn,' he said. 'That is the way of the Silures.'

'That was the old way,' Bedwyr countered, stepping closer. 'Before the Romans came in their ships with their iron and their arrogance. The council listens to you, Cadoc. If you spoke for war...'

'I speak for survival,' Cadoc cut him off. 'We are not the Catuvellauni or the Trinovantes, parading in open fields with painted shields. We are not the Iceni with their golden torcs and their meaningless boasts. We are Silures. We look after our own unless threatened. Then we kill without warning and vanish before the blood cools on our blades.'

Bedwyr's eyes flashed with barely contained frustration, but he did not argue further. Even he knew better than to challenge Cadoc directly. Too many men had died trying.

'Then at least let us follow them,' Bran suggested, looking between the two men. 'If they cross the river, we should know where they go, what they seek.'

Cadoc considered his son, not missing the eager gleam in the boy's eyes. The bloodlust was rising in him, as it should in any true Silurian warrior, and it needed to be nurtured. He nodded once.

'You may go with Bedwyr but watch only. No blood.' He paused and looked across at the warrior, then added coldly, 'not yet.'

'As you wish,' said Bedwyr, but his tone betrayed his true feelings. The younger warrior held Cadoc's gaze for a heartbeat longer, before turning away, fingering the knife at his belt as though imagining it between a Roman's ribs.

Cadoc watched them go, before walking deeper into the camp. Men sharpened blades with rhythmic strokes of stone against iron, the ringing sounds echoing through the trees while others applied fresh woad to their bodies, preparing for hunting or raiding, the blue paste turning their human forms into something more primal, more terrifying. Unlike the bustling villages of the eastern tribes, there was little chatter and no idle gossip. The Silures did not waste words.

Young boys were already being trained in the arts of the hunt and of war, learning to move silently through the undergrowth under the watchful eyes of the older warriors. Several practised with small knives, their hands and arms already marked with scars from where they had cut themselves during training. The weak did not survive long among the Silures.

Women were few in the camp, kept separate in their own enclave deeper in the forest. They emerged only to deliver food or to take away bloodied weapons for cleaning. Their faces were unmarked by woad, but many bore tattoos that spiralled across their shoulders and down their arms, marks of their status and the warriors whose beds they shared. They moved with downcast eyes, knowing their place in the rigid hierarchy of the tribe.

Cadoc approached the most important place in the settlement, not a chief's hall as other tribes might have, but a narrow opening in the cliff face, its entrance facing east toward the rising sun. Two warriors stood guard, their bodies painted entirely blue, their eyes rimmed with black ash. They carried spears tipped with iron, the points stained a permanent rusty-brown from frequent use. They nodded to Cadoc as he ducked through the entrance.

Inside, the narrow passage widened dramatically, revealing a vast natural cavern that penetrated deep into the hillside. The air was thick with herb-smoke and the smell of rendered fat mixed with something more coppery, more vital. Water dripped from limestone formations overhead, each drop echoing in the primal silence that seemed to absorb all sound beyond the immediate space.

Along the walls, illuminated by the flickering light of fat-burning lamps set in carved niches, stretched paintings of breathtaking antiquity and power. Ochre, charcoal, and bloodstone images of massive beasts, some recognisable, others from a world long vanished, danced across the living rock. Hunters with spears pursued aurochs and elk across sweeping panels that disappeared into the darkness above while spirit creatures, half-human and half-animal, presided over scenes of ritual and sacrifice. These images had been ancient when the first Silures arrived in these hills, attributed by tribal lore to the old gods themselves.

In the centre of the cavern, a natural depression in the floor held a hearth of banked peat, casting ruddy light across the faces of the two men and one woman who sat facing the fire. Each bore the marks of their station, complex whorls that spiralled from temple to jaw, down their necks and across bare shoulders, recording victories, visions, and losses. Their shadows stretched grotesquely up the cavern walls, merging with the painted figures above, as though the ancient hunters and the present council were one continuous thread in the fabric of Silures existence.

The constant drip of water, the ancient paintings

watching from above, and the weight of the mountain pressing down created a sense of timelessness, as if anything that happened here connected directly to similar occurrences held centuries before. Here, in this space between worlds, the Silures leadership made their most important decisions, guided by both the pragmatic concerns of survival and the ancient wisdom that seeped from the very stone around them.

Before the three elders, a shallow stone bowl contained fresh blood, still steaming in the cool air. The sacrifice had been recent.

'Cadoc,' greeted the oldest among them, the woman whose white hair contrasted sharply with the blue patterns that covered almost every inch of her visible skin. 'You have heard of the Roman patrols.'

It wasn't a question. Nessa heard everything that happened in Bryn Caer. Some said she walked in dreams; others believed she could speak with ravens. Cadoc knew only that her counsel had saved the Silures more than once, and that she took great pleasure in personally wielding the blade when Dobunni slaves were offered as sacrifice during the rituals of the full moon.

'It is not the first time,' he replied, taking his place at the fire, 'their successes in the east make them braver but so far they have not set a single foot on our soil. I have sent Bedwyr and my son to watch them,'

A murmur passed between the elders. Not approval, not censure. Acknowledgment.

'These are not ordinary Romans,' said Mabon, a one-eyed warrior whose beard hung down to his knees. 'Their movements are different. They travel in smaller numbers but penetrate deeper, perhaps looking for weaknesses.'

'Or for someone,' Nessa interjected, her pale eyes fixed

on Cadoc. 'The whispers from the north speak of a great druid who escaped their blade on Mona. One who seeks sanctuary among the free tribes.'

Cadoc's expression remained unchanged, but his hand tightened imperceptibly on his knee.

'We have granted no sanctuary,' he said carefully.

'Not yet,' Nessa agreed. She dipped her finger in the blood bowl and drew a symbol on her forehead, a crescent that mimicked the new moon. 'But the druid approaches. His followers say he brings ancient power, knowledge that could drive the Romans back into the sea.'

'Or bring their full wrath down upon us,' Cadoc countered. 'We have remained free because we remain hidden. The forests are our strength, the mountains our shields. If we join this druid's rebellion...'

'Yet if we do nothing, we will just be the last to die instead of the first,' said Mabon. 'The Romans will not stop until all of Britannia bends the knee or lies in ashes. I say we kill every Roman who dares set foot on our soil, and send their heads back on spikes as warnings.'

The second man grunted his approval.

'The earth thirsts for Roman blood,' he said. 'I have heard it cry for such in my dreams.'

The debate continued as the morning wore on, voices rising and falling like the tide. Cadoc listened more than he spoke, weighing each argument against the cold calculus of survival. The Silures had outlasted invaders before, waves of tribes pushing westward, traders seeking tin and silver, petty kings expanding their territories. They had survived by melting into the landscape rather than challenging their enemies directly, before striking without mercy when it was least expected, descending on their enemies like a tidal wave of

41

violence, sparing no one and nothing. Men, women, children and even animals were slaughtered without mercy, but they always ensured at least one man survived to tell the tale.

But Rome was different. Rome did not simply raid or trade. Rome *consumed!*

As the council came to an end, Nessa caught Cadoc's arm, her bony fingers surprisingly strong, her nails digging into his flesh like talons.

'Your son grows restless,' she said, her voice pitched for his ears alone. 'And Bedwyr feeds that restlessness. Watch them both closely, Cadoc for Bedwyr would see himself in your place, with your son as his blade.'

'Bran is my blood,' Cadoc replied. 'He knows where his loyalties lie.'

'Does he?' Nessa's eyes seemed to look through him rather than at him. 'He hungers for glory and blood. Bedwyr offers him both. These are days for the blade, Cadoc, for the spear and the arrow. We are Shadow Walkers and whether we wish it or not, war is coming.'

She released his arm and shuffled away, leaving Cadoc standing alone in the smoky dimness of the cave. He remained there for a long moment, his thoughts as dark as the shadows that gathered in the corners.

A few days later, Cadoc found himself pausing often to scan the tree line for signs of his son's return. The sun had passed its zenith and begun its descent when he heard the soft bird call that signalled a returning scout. He moved swiftly to the eastern edge of the settlement, where Bedwyr emerged from the underbrush, his expression taut with excitement.

'Where is Bran?' Cadoc demanded, noting his son's absence immediately.

'Following them still,' Bedwyr replied. 'The Romans have crossed the river, Cadoc. Six of them and they're heading straight for the sacred grove.'

'You left my son to watch them alone?' Cadoc's voice was dangerously quiet.

'He insisted on continuing. I came back to report.'

Cadoc seized the younger man by the throat, lifting him to his toes despite his substantial weight. His fingers closed around Bedwyr's windpipe with practiced precision, not enough to kill, but enough to remind the younger warrior of the difference in their strength.

'If any harm comes to him, you will beg me to kill you, such will be your pain.'

'I told him not to engage,' Bedwyr gasped, not struggling against Cadoc's grip. 'He promised to observe only.'

Cadoc threw him to the floor.

'Go back to him and protect him with your life. Let them continue on their path but do not show yourselves. We will see where this leads.'

As Bedwyr darted away, Cadoc strode toward his own hut, catching the eye of one of his lesser chieftains, along the way.

'Gather a war party,' he ordered. 'Have them meet me at the eastern edge of the camp.'

The man nodded once and disappeared to carry out the command.

Inside his hut, Cadoc moved to the weapons rack mounted on the central post, each piece earned through combat or traded at great cost. His favoured weapon was a short, broad-bladed sword of superior iron from the northern smiths, its edge honed to a blue-black gleam that could split a man from neck to navel with a single stroke. Next came his yew bow, standing taller than himself, its pull so strong that few besides Cadoc could draw it to full extension. Finally, he selected a quiver of arrows fletched with raven feathers, their iron tips coated with a paste extracted from the roots of certain plants that grew only in the deepest parts of the forest, a poison that caused slow and agonising death.

He checked each methodically, then applied the blue woad to his face once more, not the elaborate patterns of council meetings, but the stark, practical designs of war. Three stripes across each cheek, extending back toward his ears and a single line bisecting his forehead and nose. The marks of the Shadow Walkers, the sub clan of the main Silures tribe that kept their lands safe.

When he emerged, the warriors were already gathered, grim-faced men daubed in blue, armed with spears and bows. Each carried at least one trophy from previous kills, an earring, a finger bone, a strip of tanned skin. This was not the jubilant war-lust of the eastern tribes, with their songs and boasts. This was the cold, methodical preparation for slaughter, the ritual that preceded spilled blood and taken lives.

As they prepared to depart, Nessa appeared at the edge of the gathering, her ancient frame bent like a wind-twisted hawthorn. She had been communing with the old gods and blood was smeared across her forehead in a fresh pattern.

'The patterns align, Cadoc,' she called. 'Change comes, whether we invite it or not. I have read it in the entrails.'

'And what else do the entrails tell you, old one,' he asked. 'Do they foretell my fate?'

The woman paused but he could see in her eyes that something caused her concern.

'Tell me,' he said.

'They say to beware the hairless man,' she said

eventually.

Cadoc waited for further explanation but when none was forthcoming, he nodded and turned away to his men. He had learned long ago that the gods were always ambiguous in their advice with nothing ever making clear sense. They had been so when his wife died birthing their third child. Again when that child followed her mother to the otherworld a day later, and silent again when the eastern tribes fell one by one to Roman swords in the east. The gods he worshipped spoke only in blood and death, and he had long since learned to speak back to them in the same tongue.

He rejoined the warriors, and as one, they melted into the forest, the trees closing around them like the slow current of a river, and soon the Shadow Walker camp was behind them, silent and hidden as it had been for generations.

Chapter Five

The Lands of the Ordovices

Three days had passed since they had entered the territory of the Ordovices and with each mile westward, Veteranus sensed the subtle changes in the land and its people. Their fourth night found them camped in a broad meadow beside a swift-flowing stream, the surrounding hills rising higher and more rugged than before. The sense of being watched had intensified; no longer did the Ordovices scouts merely shadow them from distant ridgelines, now they rode openly alongside the column, a dozen warriors with elaborate spiral patterns painted across their chests and faces.

'We're close,' Adgennus said, joining Veteranus beside his wagon as darkness settled over the camp. 'Tomorrow, by midday, we'll reach the hillfort.'

Veteranus nodded.

'Is there anything I need to know?'

'Yes,' said Adgennus. 'The Ordovices value two things above all else, strength and respect. Show too little of the former, they'll dismiss you as weak. Show too little of the latter, they'll take it as an insult.' He gestured to the Ordovices scouts who had established their own fires in the distance. 'They're already assessing us and reporting back to their chiefs.'

'And what are they reporting, do you think?'

'That we bring valuable goods, and that we travel with a wagon driven by a man who sits too straight to be a mere trader.'

Veteranus's hands paused momentarily in their work. 'Am I so obvious?'

'To me? Yes. To them?' Adgennus shrugged. 'Perhaps

not. But they can smell a warrior even when he wears a merchant's clothes.'

'And you? What do they make of you?'

'A familiar face. One who has traded fairly before and not broken faith. That carries weight here.' Adgennus lowered his voice. 'Which is why I must be clear about tomorrow. When we reach the hillfort, I will do the negotiating. You will be introduced as my associate, nothing more. Only when I give the signal will you present your gifts.'

'I understand,' Veteranus replied. He had played subordinate roles before when the mission required it. Pride had no place in intelligence gathering.

Adgennus nodded, seemingly satisfied.

'There's something else you should know,' he added, his tone shifting. 'It's not merely a fortress. For the Ordovices, it's a sacred place as well. The central hill was an ancient meeting ground for druids long before the ramparts were raised.'

'You think there are still druids there?'

'I know there are,' Adgennus replied. 'Though they keep to themselves, away from traders' eyes. But they influence the council deeply, especially in matters concerning Rome.' He studied Veteranus's face in the fading light. 'Should you encounter any, show appropriate deference. They can be powerful allies or deadly enemies.'

Veteranus absorbed this information silently. The presence of druids complicated matters but might also provide opportunities.

'I'm told the hillfort is impressive,' he said, deliberately shifting the subject.

'Like nothing you've seen before,' Adgennus confirmed. 'Not even the great strongholds of the Catuvellauni compare. The Ordovices had centuries to perfect their defences, and the

47

natural terrain gives them advantages your Roman engineers would envy.'

They talked a while longer about what to expect, the steep approach road, the multiple gates, the inner sanctum where the clan chiefs held council. Gradually, their conversation drifted to less consequential matters, and eventually, Adgennus took his leave, retiring to his own tent for the night.

Veteranus remained awake long after the camp had quieted, mentally preparing himself for what lay ahead. Tomorrow would bring new challenges, new information, and perhaps new dangers. This night might be his last opportunity for undisturbed reflection.

The morning dawned misty but promised fair weather as the sun began burning through the haze. The column set out earlier than usual, a sense of anticipation evident in the brisk pace and minimal delays at stream crossings. The Ordovices scouts now openly led the way, occasionally conferring with the trading master at the head of the procession.

By mid-morning, they entered a long, winding valley that curved between increasingly steep hillsides. The path narrowed, forcing the wagons into single file and Adgennus manoeuvred his mount beside Veteranus's wagon as they negotiated a particularly rough stretch.

'The final approach lies just ahead,' he said quietly. 'There's a ridge to climb, and then you'll see it.'

Even with this warning, Veteranus found himself unprepared for what awaited them and as his wagon crested the ridge, the valley beyond opened before him like a vast natural amphitheatre. At its centre rose a perfect conical hill, its sides terraced with concentric rings of earthworks and wooden palisades, creating a formidable, layered defence that spiralled from base to summit.

The hillfort dominated the landscape completely, its outermost defences encircling the entire hill, while higher ramparts creating inner rings of protection, each more formidable than the last. The approach was a single track that wound upward around the hill like a snake coiling toward the central plateau, passing through no less than four wooden gates, each capable of being closed against attackers.

At the summit, behind the highest and thickest palisade, rose an entire settlement, not just of the expected roundhouses, but structures of surprising sophistication. Some were built partially into the ground with turf roofs that made them nearly invisible from a distance. Others stood tall on timber platforms, with elaborate carved posts supporting high-peaked thatch roofs.

Around the base of the hill, the valley floor was a patchwork of cultivation, fields of grain, vegetable gardens, and pasturage, all neatly divided by low stone walls. Small clusters of roundhouses dotted these fields, satellite settlements supporting the main hillfort. People moved throughout this landscape, tending crops, herding livestock and carrying water from a stream that curved around the base of the hill.

'Impressive?' asked Adgennus noting Veteranus's carefully controlled expression. 'Over a thousand people live here, maybe more. Three major clans sharing the hillfort, each with their own section. And this is just one of three such strongholds in this part of the Ordovices territory.'

Veteranus nodded slowly, his mind calculating the military implications. A legion might take this place, but at terrible cost. Even with siege engines and superior numbers, the Romans would face a protracted and bloody campaign. Better, far better, to secure these people as allies than enemies.

'We've been spotted,' Adgennus observed, pointing to movement along the highest palisade as signal horns sounded, their hollow notes echoing across the valley.

Below the fortifications, a party was already emerging from the lowest gate. At their centre rode a figure distinguished by a cloak of beaver fur and a torque of twisted gold around his neck.

'Bodvoc,' Adgennus murmured. 'Eagle Clan chief and current voice of the council. His greeting party is an honour, usually they send lesser representatives.'

The caravan halted at the ridge while the Ordovices escort approached. Adgennus moved forward to join the trading master and two other senior merchants, leaving Veteranus with his wagon.

The meeting was brief but formal and Veteranus watched as they exchanged ceremonial wooden tokens carved with tribal symbols,. Adgennus spoke with practiced ease in what must have been the Ordovices dialect, occasionally gesturing back toward the caravan.

After several minutes, the trading master and Adgennus returned to the column while the Ordovices escort formed up at its head.

'We're welcomed,' Adgennus informed Veteranus as he passed. 'But only ten wagons may ascend to the hillfort today. Ours is among them. The rest will camp in the lower valley. Remember what I told you, let me lead the negotiations. Speak only when addressed directly, and keep your responses measured. These people value restraint almost as much as courage.'

With that final counsel, Adgennus returned to his position near the head of the column and the caravan reorganized itself, the selected wagons forming a separate group that would proceed to the hillfort while the remainder prepared to make camp below.

As he joined the smaller procession, Veteranus felt the weight of the moment settle upon him. Beyond the immediate mission, securing potential allies, and gathering intelligence on the Silures, lay a rare opportunity to document a culture and fortress that few Romans had ever seen.

Chapter Six

The Western Road

The Exploratore column wound its way through the rolling countryside like a serpent, fifty mounted men spread out in a disciplined formation that spoke of years of frontier service. They rode in a loose pattern, never bunching too closely together, always maintaining sight lines to the men ahead and behind. Their leather jerkins had been darkened with oil and mud to reduce their visibility at distance, and their short cloaks were the colour of autumn leaves, perfectly suited to blend into the landscape around them.

In the centre of this protective shell rode the six men of the Occultum. They too were dressed for discretion rather than display, their Roman gear long since abandoned in favour of clothing that would not immediately mark them as foreign in these hostile lands.

As they rode westward, the land began to change, the gentle hills giving way to more rugged terrain. They had passed through the lands of several tribes already, moving along the boundaries where possible, avoiding settlements and the curious eyes of local chieftains. Now they approached the territory of the Dobunni, the last semi-friendly tribe before the more hostile lands beyond.

'How much further to the river?' Seneca asked, drawing his mount alongside Maxima.

Maxima squinted at the horizon, his weathered face creasing further as he looked for recognisable landmarks.

'Two days,' he said, 'perhaps three if the weather turns. The Dobunni should leave us be, but I've posted outriders half a mile ahead. No point taking chances.'

Seneca nodded, appreciating the man's caution. The Exploratores were Rome's eyes and ears in this new province, men chosen specifically for their ability to move swiftly and undetected through enemy territory. They weren't legionaries, with their rigid discipline and regimented tactics, these were hunters and scouts, selected for their initiative as much as their fighting skill, and he had once been one of them.

'It sounds like you've led men through these lands before,' Seneca observed.

'I have,' he said. 'Ever since we landed at Rutupiae, I have done little else. Plautius needs information before the legions can expand outward and it is men like me who are deployed to get it.'

'What about before this?' asked Seneca.

'I've been with the Exploratores since Gaul. Before that, eight years with the auxiliaries on the German frontier.'

'You don't sound Roman,' Seneca noted.

'I'm not. Helvetian by birth. My father traded with your people and learned your ways. When your legions came, he knew enough to negotiate rather than fight. That got me a place in the auxiliaries instead of a blade across the throat.' Maxima adjusted his position in the saddle, easing the pressure on his lower back. 'It was the best thing that ever happened to me, though I didn't see it that way as a young man.'

They rode in companionable silence for a while, the only sounds the soft thud of hooves on the earth and the creak of leather. The sky was overcast, threatening rain, but for now, it held off, allowing them to make good progress along the ancient trackway.

Behind them, Falco was engaged in what appeared to be a one-sided argument with Sica, the Syrian assassin maintaining his characteristic silence in the face of the ex-gladiator's complaints. Marcus rode alongside Decimus, the two veterans discussing something in low tones, while Talorcan brought up the rear, his eyes constantly scanning the treeline to their left.

'Your men,' said Maxima eventually, turning back to Seneca. 'They're not like any unit I've seen before.'

Seneca smiled faintly.

'They're not a unit in the traditional sense.'

'I figured as much,' said Maxima. 'Each of them moves differently as if trained in different disciplines.' His gaze settled on Sica. 'That small one, he's from the east, yes? And the big one behind him looks like he spent time in the arena.'

'You have a good eye,' Seneca acknowledged.

'It's why I'm still alive,' Maxima replied simply. 'Out here, you learn to read men quickly or you don't go home.' He paused, then added, 'Whatever your mission is, I don't understand what it is that these men bring that makes them so important to the outcome.'

'Let's just say they have certain skills that makes success a little more likely.'

Maxima nodded, understanding the limits of what could be shared.

'Well, we'll get you where you need to go. After that, only the gods go with you.'

As the day wore on, the column maintained its steady pace, and by mid-afternoon, they had crossed into Dobunni lands, the transition marked only by a subtle change in the landscape, fields giving way to more wooded terrain.

'We'll make camp there,' Maxima said, pointing to a small rise ahead where a copse of beech trees offered some shelter. 'Good visibility, defensible if needed.'

Seneca nodded his agreement and within the hour, the

Exploratores had established a well-ordered camp. Unlike a legionary force, they didn't build a palisade or dig ditches. Their security came from careful positioning, multiple sentries, and the ability to mount up and move at a moment's notice if threatened.

The men ate in shifts, those off duty keeping watch while others took their meal of hard bread, dried meat, and a thin porridge cooked in iron pots.

Seneca found Maxima seated on a fallen log at the edge of the camp, his meal balanced on his knees as he studied the darkening landscape.

'May I join you?' asked Seneca.

Maxima gestured to the space beside him, and Seneca sat, stretching his legs before him. His muscles ached from the day's ride, but he didn't let the discomfort show.

They ate in silence for a while, each man lost in his own thoughts. The sounds of the camp settled around them, men talking in low voices, the occasional laugh quickly stifled, the soft whinny of horses being tended by their riders.

'So, how did you end up with the Exploratores?' asked eventually.

Maxima chewed thoughtfully before answering.

'After my time in the auxiliaries was up, I was offered Roman citizenship. I could have gone back to civilian life, maybe set myself up as a trader like my father. But I'd seen too much by then. The ordinary world felt... too small.' He shrugged. 'The Exploratores were just being formed, and they needed men who knew the frontier, who could move quietly and think for themselves. It suited me.'

'And the scar?' Seneca gestured to the old wound on his head.

Maxima's hand went to the mark reflexively.

'An ambush in southern Gaul, twelve years ago. A Gallic chieftain decided to make an example of a patrol that strayed too close to his territory. Most of my men died and I took an axe to the head but killed the bastard who swung it before I passed out.' His voice was matter of fact, without bravado. 'When I woke up, I was being dragged behind a cart, headed for slavery or sacrifice. I managed to get free in the night and made my way back to Roman lines. It took me six days, moving only after dark.'

'It's a wonder you survived,' Seneca observed.

'The gods weren't finished with me,' Maxima replied with a thin smile. 'Or perhaps they just enjoy watching me suffer.' He set his empty bowl aside. 'What about you? You don't have the look of a man who's spent his career in comfortable garrisons.'

Seneca weighed his response carefully.

'I've served in various capacities,' he said eventually. 'Most recently in Egypt, before being assigned to the Britannic campaign.'

'Various capacities,' Maxima repeated, amusement in his tone. 'That's a nice, meaningless phrase. I've heard rumours about your group, you know. Nothing specific, just whispers. Men who appear where they're least expected, who handle problems that can't be solved by marching a cohort up to the gates.'

'Rumours are often exaggerated,' Seneca replied neutrally.

'True enough.' Maxima stretched, rolling his shoulders to ease the stiffness. 'But I've been a soldier long enough to know when I'm escorting men who are more than they appear.' He glanced at the Occultum members, gathered around their own small fire. 'Take that one, for instance,' he nodded toward

Marcus. 'Moves like a legionary though no legionary I've ever met carries himself quite like that. He's watching everything, all the time, even when he seems relaxed.'

Seneca followed his gaze.

'Marcus has seen his share of campaigns.'

'And the Syrian,' Maxima continued. 'Where did you find him? He makes my scouts look clumsy, and they're the best in the province.'

'Sica found us, in a manner of speaking,' said Seneca. 'As for the rest, let's just say each man brings particular skills that complement the others.'

Maxima nodded, accepting the deflection.

'Fair enough. We all have our secrets.' He leaned forward, lowering his voice. 'But I need to know one thing, Seneca. When we reach the river, how likely is it that your departure will be noticed? My men will be riding back through these same lands, and I'd rather not have angry tribesmen hunting us because of whatever you're planning.'

'By the time anyone knows we are there, you'll be long gone,' said Seneca. 'The plan is for your men to drop us off at night before splitting into two groups and heading back to Camulodunum as fast as you can. That way, nobody watching will realise that we are missing.'

'I can't see you staying hidden for long,' said Maxima. 'It's hard to keep horses quiet in those forests.'

'We are not taking the horses,' said Seneca. 'They'll be going back with you.'

Maxima stared at Seneca in silence as the revelation sunk in.

'You are walking into Terra Siluria?'

'We are,' said Seneca.

'And if it goes wrong?' asked Maxima. 'If you're spotted crossing into Silurian territory?'

'We won't be,' said Seneca simply.

Maxima nodded, seemingly satisfied.

'Good enough.' He rose to his feet. 'We should get some rest. I want to break camp before dawn and be moving by first light.'

As Maxima walked away, Seneca remained seated, his eyes drawn to the western horizon where the last faint glow of sunset was fading. Somewhere beyond those distant hills lay their objective, a mission that seemed more daunting with each passing day.

Marcus approached, settling onto the log beside him.

'Maxima seems capable,' he observed.

'More than capable,' Seneca agreed. 'He already has a strong suspicion of who we are and what we do.'

'Is that a problem?'

Seneca considered the question.

'I don't think so. He strikes me as a man who understands the value of discretion.' He glanced at Marcus. 'How are the others?'

'As good as can be expected,' replied Marcus. 'Falco's complaining about the rations, but that's nothing new. Sica's been quiet, even for him but I think he's just focused on what's ahead. Decimus and Talorcan are checking our gear again, making sure everything's in order for when we separate from the column.'

Seneca nodded, his mind already turning to the challenges that lay ahead.

'A few more days,' he said quietly. 'Then we're on our own.'

The next morning dawned grey and misty, the landscape shrouded in a damp haze that limited visibility and muffled sound. Maxima ordered the column to move out, using the conditions to their advantage.

'The weather's a gift today,' he explained to Seneca as they mounted up. 'It limits what we can see, but also what others can see of us. We'll keep tight formations until the mist burns off, then spread out again.'

Seneca nodded his agreement.

'Are the Dobunni patrols likely to challenge us?'

'Not if we stay away from their settlements,' Maxima replied. 'They're cautious but not openly hostile to Rome.'

'And the river crossing?'

'We need not worry about that yet. It's days away.'

'But is it fordable?'

'On the route we are taking, yes. But it quickly opens up into a tidal river that feeds a navigable estuary depending on the tide. Beyond the ford, we enter the lands of the Silures and they're a different breed entirely. The Dobunni will posture and threaten before they attack. The Silures will simply kill you and leave your body for the ravens.'

'Cheerful assessment,' Seneca observed dryly.

Maxima gave a short laugh.

'Just being honest. I've already lost good men in those hills. The Silures don't fight like other tribes, they're ghosts, appearing from nowhere, striking, and vanishing again. You don't even see the arrow or the blade that kills you.'

'It sounds like they've learned the value of stealth,' Seneca mused.

'Perhaps,' Maxima conceded. 'Though I suspect they were fighting this way long before Rome ever heard of Britannia. It's in their blood, just as formation fighting is in ours.'

As they rode, the mist began to thin, revealing more of the landscape around them. They were passing through a region of rolling hills and scattered woodlands, the terrain becoming increasingly rugged as they moved westward. Small streams cut across their path occasionally, necessitating brief detours to find suitable crossing points.

By midday, they had covered a substantial distance, making good time despite the challenging conditions and Maxima called a halt in a sheltered valley, allowing the men and horses a brief rest.

'We're making better progress than I expected,' he told Seneca as they shared a simple meal of hard cheese and dried fruit. 'If we maintain this pace, we'll reach the river by tomorrow afternoon.'

'Earlier than planned,' Seneca noted.

'Yes. Does that present a problem?'

'No,' said Seneca, 'it's actually advantageous. The sooner we cross, the more time we'll have to establish our position before pushing deeper.'

The rest period ended, and the column resumed its journey. The afternoon brought clearer skies and warmer temperatures, the landscape slowly revealing more of its character as they penetrated deeper into Dobunni territory. They passed occasional signs of habitation, distant hillforts perched on prominent rises and small clusters of roundhouses tucked into sheltered valleys, but maintained their distance from these settlements, preferring to avoid unnecessary interactions with the locals.

As evening approached, they made camp in a defensible position atop a low ridge, with good visibility in all directions.

The men went about their duties with the same quiet efficiency as before, establishing a perimeter, caring for the horses, and preparing the simple evening meal.

Falco approached Seneca as he was conferring with Maxima about the watch schedule.

'Seems quiet,' the big gladiator observed, his eyes scanning the darkening landscape. 'Too quiet, maybe.'

'You'd prefer a fight?' Seneca asked, a slight smile playing at the corners of his mouth.

'At least then we'd know where we stand,' Falco replied with a shrug. 'All this riding day after day... it wears on a man.'

'Patience, Falco,' said Seneca. 'I suspect there'll be plenty of fighting before this mission is finished.'

'I'm counting on it,' Falco muttered, and moved away to join the others around their small fire.

Maxima watched him go, then turned to Seneca.

'Interesting man, your gladiator. I watched him train before we left Camulodunum. It's not often you see that combination of size and speed.'

'Falco has many qualities,' Seneca agreed. 'Patience, unfortunately, isn't one of them.'

'A common affliction among warriors,' Maxima observed. 'The waiting before battle is often harder than the fight itself.' He glanced toward the western horizon, where the sun was setting in a blaze of red and gold. 'Tomorrow we reach the river. After that, you and your men are on your own.'

Seneca nodded, feeling the weight of responsibility settle more heavily on his shoulders.

'We've prepared as best we can.'

'Preparation only takes you so far,' Maxima said quietly. 'Beyond that, it's in the hands of the gods.' He hesitated, then added, 'Whatever or whoever you're hunting in those hills,

Seneca, I hope it's worth the risk.'

'It has to be,' Seneca replied simply. 'Too many lives depend on our success.'

Chapter Seven

Terra Siluria

The mist clung to the valleys as Titus led his five-man patrol along the ridge, their breath forming small clouds in the cool morning air. The lone scouting party moved with quiet efficiency, their leather-wrapped weapons making little sound against their bodies. They were Exploratores auxiliaries, men selected for their woodcraft and ability to move silently through enemy territory, and although they were not supposed to be in lands that belonged to the Silures, they felt a certain professional satisfaction in having come this far undetected.

Two days earlier, they had been following the river that marked the boundary between Dobunni and Silures lands, mapping potential crossing points, when they spotted the deer. The herd had been moving parallel to the river on the Silures side, and the sight of fresh venison had been too tempting to resist for men who had subsisted on dried meat and hard bread for nearly a fortnight. Raurica had suggested crossing the river and Titus, after only brief hesitation, had agreed. They were scouts, after all, their job was to venture into dangerous territory. The crossing had been simple enough, a shallow ford that barely reached their knees and they'd moved swiftly, spreading out to encircle the herd. All were accomplished hunters, but the deer knew the danger of men and had long gone by the time they arrived.

'How much farther, Titus?' muttered Geta, the youngest of the scouts. He was Thracian by birth, with dark hair cropped close to his skull and a perpetual furrow between his brows. 'We crossed the river boundary two days ago. We're well beyond our orders.

Titus glanced back at him, his weathered face betraying little emotion.

'Those deer can't be far ahead,' said Titus. 'We need meat so will keep going.'

'We need to go back,' said Geta. 'We were told just to observe the river crossings, not to venture into Silures territory.'

'I don't think there's anything to be worried about,' said Titus. 'We have seen not a single soul since coming here. It's as if the lands are deserted.'

'And that alone is worrying,' said Geta, 'just because we haven't seen them doesn't mean they haven't seen us.'

"We've been two days in their territory now,' said Titus, 'and not a single sign of life. If they knew we were here, we'd have felt their presence by now. We keep going.'

Decision made, the patrol kept to the higher ground as they made their way northwest, maintaining good visibility of the terrain around them. The land here was wild and largely untouched, primal in a way that even the forests of Germania were not. Ancient oaks stood like sentinels, their massive trunks wider than two men could encircle with their arms and between them grew yew, rowan, and hazel, creating a complex undergrowth that could conceal an entire war band. The forest floor was carpeted with ferns and mosses, thick and springy underfoot, occasionally revealing the tracks of deer, boar, and other game that had not yet learned to fear human hunters.

'This would be good settling land,' observed Rullus, one of the other riders, as they paused to drink from their waterskins. 'Rich soil, plenty of game. No wonder they defend it so fiercely.'

'All of Britannia has good land,' said Titus dismissively. 'That's why Rome wants it.'

'Not like this,' said Geta, his eyes scanning the

surrounding forest. 'This is old growth. Sacred, probably, to their druids.'

They continued in silence for a time, each man lost in his own thoughts. The sky above was a clear, pale blue, visible in patches through the forest canopy, but the air beneath the trees remained cool and damp. As they pressed on, Vindex noticed something that made him pause.

'The ground,' he said, gesturing toward their feet. 'Look at the path we're on.'

What had begun as little more than a game trail was now visibly widening, the earth packed firm by the passage of many feet.

'Someone uses this trail,' Geta observed, his voice dropping to just above a whisper. 'We should leave it, find another way.'

Titus studied the path, then the surrounding forest. The undergrowth on either side had grown thick and thorny, as if deliberately left untended.

'It's the clearest way forward,' he said after a moment. 'And it must lead somewhere, perhaps to a river crossing we don't know about yet.'

'Or to a Silures settlement,' countered Rullus. 'Where we'd be greatly outnumbered.'

'We've seen no one since crossing the river,' Titus pointed out again. 'Not a single warrior, not a single herdsman. Perhaps they've abandoned this region.'

'The Britons don't abandon anything,' Geta muttered, but the others were already following Titus along the path, and he had little choice but to join them.

The trail wound deeper into the forest, growing more defined with each passing mile. Small white stones now marked its edges every few paces, and occasionally, they passed wooden

65

posts carved with spiral patterns whose meaning none of them could decipher. The forest itself began to change subtly, the trees grew with more space between them, their lower branches cleared away, the forest floor swept free of debris.

'Someone tends these trees,' Rullus observed, running his hand along the smooth bark of an oak. 'This no ordinary forest, this is…'

'Sacred ground,' said Geta, finishing his thought. 'We're walking through a temple, you fools. We should turn back.'

Titus slowed, clearly weighing their options, but as the path curved sharply, it opened into a sight that left them all momentarily breathless.

Before them lay a perfect circular grove, perhaps a hundred paces across, ringed by the tallest and most ancient oaks they had yet encountered. The trees formed a living wall around the space, their branches reaching toward each other high above to create a natural canopy. Shafts of golden sunlight broke through in places, illuminating the grove floor in dappled patterns that shifted with the gentle breeze.

Around the perimeter, spaced at regular intervals between the great oaks, stood a series of standing stones, each twice the height of a man and covered in elaborate symbols. The stones were of a pale grey granite not native to these forests, and their surfaces polished smooth by uncounted years of reverent hands.

But it was what lay at the centre of the grove that truly captured their attention. A flat stone altar, as broad as three men lying side by side, and upon it, arranged with careful precision, was a feast that made their mouths water in anticipation.

Apples, pears and dried berries were piled high in woven baskets. Beside them lay loaves of dark bread, and wooden platters holding roasted joints of venison while clay pots brimmed with honeycomb, and several leather skins suggesting wine or mead.

The six men stood frozen at the edge of the grove, torn between caution and the primal hunger that surged through them at the sight of such abundance.

'It's an offering,' Rullus whispered. 'To their gods, perhaps. Or to the spirits of the forest.'

'Or to travellers,' Titus suggested with a grin. 'Perhaps the Silures are more hospitable than we thought.'

He approached the altar slowly, his eyes scanning the treeline for any sign of those who might have prepared this feast, but the grove appeared deserted, the only movement the gentle sway of branches far above.

'I see no one,' he said at last. 'And we've had nothing but dried meat for days.'

'You can't seriously be considering eating their offerings?' asked Geta incredulously.

'Why not?' said Rullus, moving past Titus toward the altar. 'The gods have no need of mortal food, and if this was left for travellers, then we qualify.'

'And if it's a trap?' Geta persisted.

'A trap baited with food?' Titus scoffed. 'Why not simply ambush us on the trail? No, this is either an offering or hospitality. Either way, I intend to partake.'

With that, he stepped forward and picking up a leg of venison, took a bite, groaning with pleasure at the taste.

That broke the spell of caution and within moments, the rest of his men joined him at the altar, helping themselves to the feast. Only Geta held back, his gaze sweeping around the grove for signs of activity.

'To unexpected hospitality!' said Rullus, raising one of

the skins in a toast.

'To our safe return,' countered Titus, sitting on the edge of the altar with a chunk of venison in one hand and a pear in the other.

'Perhaps the Silures aren't the savages everyone says,' said Rullus. 'Anyone who prepares food this good must have some civilisation.' He turned towards Geta who was still standing a few paces away. 'Come and join us,' he laughed, 'or I swear we'll eat it all.'

But Geta didn't respond. He simply stared, his mouth slightly open, his body gone rigid with what could only be described as primal terror.

The others turned to follow his gaze, their hands instinctively moving toward weapons but what they saw froze the blood in their veins.

From between the ancient oaks and standing stones, silent as shadows, emerged dozens of Silures warriors. They moved with deliberate slowness, materialising from the forest as if born from the trees themselves.

These were not the usual tribesmen the Romans had encountered in the eastern territories, these men were giants, broad-shouldered and powerfully built, towering over even Raurica, the tallest among the patrol. Their hair hung wild and adorned with bones and feathers and thick beards gave them the appearance of creatures half-human, half-beast.

They wore the skins of wolves and bears, and their faces were covered in intricate spiral patterns of blue woad, hypnotic whorls that transformed their features into masks of otherworldly menace.

But what struck Titus most, however, was their utter silence. No war cries, no shouted challenges, not even the expected sounds of men moving through a forest. They simply appeared, encircling the grove in a perfect, unbroken ring, their eyes, rimmed in black ash that made the whites stand out with unnerving clarity, fixed on the Romans with cold, implacable hostility.

Titus assessed their situation quickly. The Silures had them completely surrounded, at least ten warriors for each Roman. The grove offered no cover, no escape route, and he knew their weapons would be useless against such overwhelming numbers.

'No sudden movements,' he murmured to his men, just loud enough for them to hear. 'Follow my lead.'

With deliberate slowness, Titus reached down to his belt, carefully drew his knife, and lowered it to the ground.

Rullus began to protest.

'Titus, we can't just…'

'Do it,' hissed Titus.

One by one, the others followed suit until finally, Rullus drew his knife and dropped it with barely disguised contempt.

Titus straightened and took a single step forward, hands still raised.

'We come in peace,' he said in the trading tongue that most British tribes understood to some degree. 'We only seek safe passage back to our lands.'

The Silures remained motionless, their faces betraying nothing. Whether they didn't understand his words or simply chose not to acknowledge them was impossible to tell.

Titus tried again, this time in the dialect of the eastern tribes.

'We meant no trespass. We will depart and never return.'

Still nothing. The warriors might have been carved

from the same stone as the monoliths that ringed the grove, for all the reaction they showed. Only their eyes moved, studying the Romans with focussed interest.

Then, from among the ranks, a warrior stepped forward. He was taller than the rest, his shoulders broader, his beard plaited into three distinct forks that reached to his chest. The woad patterns on his face formed a great spiral that began between his brows and wound outward across his cheeks and forehead. At his neck hung a necklace of what appeared to be human finger bones, clicking softly with each step.

He approached Titus directly, stopping so close that the Roman could feel the heat radiating from his body and smell his scent, a mixture of meat and blood that seemed to seep from his very pores. For a long moment, the warrior simply stared, his eyes taking in every detail of Titus's face, as if committing it to memory.

Titus met his gaze steadily, refusing to show fear despite the hammering of his heart against his ribs.

'We will leave your lands,' he said again, enunciating each word carefully. 'We wish no…'

Without warning, the warrior lunged forward, driving his forehead into Titus's face with brutal force. Bone cracked against bone with a sickening sound, and Titus crashed backward onto the ground, blood spraying from his shattered nose. Before he could recover, the warrior was upon him, a knee pressed into his chest, pinning him to the earth.

As if this were a signal, the grove erupted into violence. The Silures surged forward as one, descending upon the remaining Romans with a calculated brutality. There were no war cries, no shouts of triumph or rage, only the dull thuds of fists against flesh, the sharp cracks of wooden clubs against bone, and the grunts of men fighting desperately against insurmountable odds.

Raurica managed to land a single punch before three warriors tackled him to the ground, one seizing each arm while the third delivered precise blows to his face and ribs. Despite his strength and size, he was clearly outmatched and the big man's roars of defiance quickly turned to gasps of pain.

Vindex tried to run, darting toward a small gap between two warriors, but a swung club caught him in the small of his back, sending him sprawling. Hands seized his hair, yanking his head back before smashing it forward into the earth until he lay still, blood pooling beneath his face.

Lentulus raised his hands in surrender, backing away, speaking rapid words of submission in every dialect he knew but a spear shaft whipped across his face, sending teeth scattering across the grass. He fell backward, arms raised to protect himself, but the blows continued to rain down, calculated, unhurried, but relentless.

Geta and Rullus tried to stand back-to-back, instinctively seeking the defensive formation drilled into them since recruitment but it made no difference. Clubs struck knees and elbows, and fists pounded ribs and kidneys, until both men collapsed, curling into protective balls that offered little salvation from the relentless onslaught.

Through swollen eyes, Titus watched his men fall. The warrior above him had ceased his attack, apparently satisfied that the Roman leader was sufficiently subdued. Instead, he now observed the systematic destruction of the intruders to their lands until finally, when all six Romans lay broken and bloodied on the grove floor, the warriors stepped back, forming their circle once more.

The silence returned, broken only by the laboured breathing and occasional moans of the battered patrol. Titus tried to rise, managing only to lift his head slightly before pain forced him back down. Through the haze of agony, he saw the lead warrior standing over him again, studying the results of his handiwork with cold satisfaction.

Darkness began to close in around Titus's vision, the pain and shock finally overwhelming his determination to remain conscious and the last thing he saw before blackness claimed him was the circle of Silures warriors, still watching, still silent, their blue-marked faces the stuff of nightmares that would haunt him for whatever remained of his life.

Chapter Eight

Terra Siluria

The wind slithered through the trees as Seneca hugged the ground at the crest of the low ridge, his body flat against the damp earth. Beside him Maxima lay equally motionless, both men studying the far bank of the river through narrowed eyes. The water gurgled and hissed a stone's throw below them, marking the invisible boundary beyond which lay the territory of the Silures.

'Nothing,' Maxima whispered, his voice barely audible over the river's flow. 'I've had men watching since noon, and not so much as a hunting party.'

Seneca nodded slightly. To their front, the far bank rose gently, covered in thick forest that extended as far as the eye could see. The trees were ancient giants, their branches interlocking to form a canopy so dense that little light would penetrate even at midday.

'Perhaps they're watching us right now,' said Seneca softly, 'deciding whether we're worth killing.'

Maxima's weather-beaten face creased into a grim smile.

'Cheerful thought.' He shifted slightly, easing the pressure on his elbows. 'What's your assessment? Do we continue as planned?'

Seneca considered the question, mentally reviewing the possibilities. The original plan called for the Occultum to cross into Silures territory under cover of darkness, with the Exploratores providing escort before returning to Camulodunum. The apparent absence of Silures patrols was unexpected but not necessarily reassuring.

'We continue tonight as planned,' he decided finally and with the decision made, they retreated behind the ridge and made their way back to the horses. Once there, Seneca walked across to his men.

'We go tonight,' he said, 'so this will be our reorg point if things go wrong. Falco, Sica, find somewhere for the first cache but return here before dark.'

Without further discussion, the two men walked over to the horses and retrieved one of the two extra sarcinae they had packed back in Camulodunum.

'The rest of us,' said Seneca as they left, 'will check all our equipment one last time. Fill the water flasks and discard any unnecessary baggage.'

'We know what to do,' said Marcus quietly, but he knew that despite his vast experience, his leader was just being methodical, finding comfort in the repetition of something they had done a hundred times before.

A few hundred paces away, Falco and Sica worked in disciplined silence. Twilight was fading rapidly, the forest floor already shrouded in deep shadows that would have rendered their task impossible for less experienced men.

Falco knelt beside the hole he had dug with his short entrenching tool, carefully patting the sides to ensure stability. The cache sarcina sat beside him, its contents meticulously packed and wrapped in heavy oiled fabric, waterproofed against the damp British climate.

The location was perfect, an unusual formation where three yew trees had grown in a tight triangle, their massive roots creating a natural hollow between them. Above, their ancient branches intertwined to form a cathedral-like canopy that was distinctive enough to locate again, yet natural enough to avoid attention. A small stream gurgled nearby, providing both a landmark and a source of water.

Falco lifted the sarcina and was about to lower it into the hole when Sica's hand touched his arm.

'Wait,' he murmured, his voice barely audible even in the silence of the forest. He reached into his tunic and produced a small earthenware bottle, tightly stoppered with a wooden plug.

'What's that?' Falco asked, eyeing the bottle suspiciously.

Sica pulled the stopper, and a foul odour immediately assaulted their nostrils, rancid fat mixed with something acrid and unidentifiable. Falco instinctively stepped back, his face contorting in disgust.

'By Jupiter's balls,' he hissed, 'what is that unholy stench?'

Without answering, Sica poured a generous amount of the foul-smelling liquid onto the oiled fabric of the sarcina, working it into the material with methodical care, ensuring every surface was treated.

'Wolf urine, badger musk, and rendered fox fat,' he finally explained, his face impassive as he continued rubbing the noxious mixture into the fabric. 'Masks the scent of food from scavengers. Prevents digging.'

Falco watched with a mixture of revulsion and reluctant admiration.

'If I were dying of hunger,' he muttered, 'I still wouldn't go near that stinking bundle.'

Sica's lips twitched in what might have been the ghost of a smile.

'We'll see.'

Once the entire package was thoroughly treated, Sica

stoppered the bottle and returned it to his tunic. Together, they lowered the sarcina into the hole, then carefully replaced the earth, tamping it down to avoid any obvious signs of disturbance.

Falco gathered the excess soil into his cloak and moved twenty paces away to scatter it widely, ensuring no telltale mound would betray their work. Meanwhile, Sica collected fallen leaves and forest debris, spreading them over the disturbed ground until it matched the surrounding forest floor perfectly.

As a final measure, they rolled a limestone boulder onto the spot, positioning it to appear naturally settled rather than recently placed and using the tip of his knife, Sica scratched a small mark into the stone, three intersecting lines forming a pattern that looked like random scratches to the untrained eye but would be instantly recognisable to the Occultum.

The two men stood back, studying their work critically. To even the most observant forest traveller, the site would appear undisturbed, just another unremarkable spot in the endless wilderness of Britannia.

The two men committed the location to memory, noting the shape of the nearby hills the strange arrangement of the yew trees, and the way the stream bent sharply just beyond their position, cataloguing every detail with the precision that had kept them alive through countless missions.

With a final glance around to ensure they had left no trace of their presence, they melted back into the forest, returning to where Seneca and the others waited. The only evidence of their visit was a lingering, foul odour that would soon dissipate into the night air, leaving their precious cache protected not just by concealment, but by nature's own deterrents.

'It's done,' Falco murmured as they arrived back at the makeshift camp.

'Marked?' Seneca asked.

'It is,' Sica replied, his voice a barely audible whisper. 'He glanced briefly towards Maxima, before returning his gaze to Seneca. 'I'll brief you about the location later.'

Seneca nodded his approval.

'Any sign of locals?' Maxima asked.

Falco shook his head.

'Nothing fresh. Some old hunting tracks, but nothing recent.'

'Good,' said Seneca. 'Now get some food.'

An hour or so later, Maxima approached Seneca again.

'My men are ready,' he said quietly. 'We'll move out on your command.'

Seneca nodded, studying the night sky. The moon was a thin crescent, providing minimal light, ideal conditions for their crossing.

'We move in one hour,' he decided. 'That will put us across the river by midnight, with several hours of darkness remaining for the insertion.'

Maxima acknowledged the order with a nod and moved away to brief his Exploratores as Seneca gathered the Occultum for a final review of their plan.

'Once across, we remain mounted until Maxima signals the separation,' he reminded them. 'At that point, we dismount, take our sarcinae and the second cache, and proceed on foot. The Exploratores will then withdraw with all horses, splitting into two groups to confuse any observers on their return journey.'

'And our approach once we're on our own?' asked

Marcus.

'West, following the course of the feeder stream. Eventually, we'll patrol south and begin searching for any signs of Mordred.'

'We still don't know if he's actually among the Silures,' Decimus pointed out. 'That's based on rumours and supposition.'

'Lepidus said he has intelligence that he definitely came south,' replied Seneca. It's not much but it's the best lead we have.'

The men fell silent, each contemplating the mission ahead. They had undertaken difficult assignments before, but this, infiltrating the territory of a tribe known for their almost supernatural tracking abilities and ruthless treatment of intruders, would test even their considerable skills.

'Questions?' asked Seneca.

There were none. Each man knew his role, understood the risks, and accepted the necessities that might arise.

'Then prepare yourselves,' Seneca concluded. 'We move within the hour.'

The time passed in silence and when Seneca finally gave the signal to mount up, the men moved to their horses with total focus.

They set out at a walk, the horses' hooves making little sound on the soft forest floor as Maxima led them along game trails, avoiding the more obvious paths where sentries might be posted. The journey back to the river crossing took longer this way, but vastly reduced the risk of detection.

When they reached the ford, the column halted. Two Exploratores dismounted and slipped forward to check the crossing, ensuring no surprises awaited them before returning minutes later, signalling the all-clear.

The crossing began with the lead Exploratores entering the water first, testing the footing before signalling the others to follow. The river ran shallow at this point, reaching only to the horses' knees, but the current was swift enough to require careful navigation. The animals moved with admirable steadiness, placing each hoof deliberately, disturbing the water as little as possible.

The Occultum crossed in the middle of the formation, their years of specialized training evident in how they guided their mounts, minimal pressure on the reins, communication through shifts in weight and pressure of legs. Falco's massive frame seemed to melt into his horse's movements, while Sica sat as if he and his mount were a single entity.

The far bank was steeper, requiring the horses to scramble slightly, but they managed without incident or excessive noise. Once clear of the water, the column reformed and moved directly into the cover of the forest, putting distance between themselves and the crossing before anyone could observe their passage.

The going was slower now, the forest denser than it had appeared from the opposite bank. Ancient oaks and yews created a canopy so thick that even the minimal moonlight was blocked, forcing them to proceed at little more than a walking pace. The undergrowth was sparse beneath these giants, their shadows having choked out most competing growth, but the darkness was nearly absolute.

They continued westward for several hours, pushing steadily deeper into Silures territory. Seneca could feel the tension in the men around him, the heightened awareness of being in hostile land. Every sense was straining for signs of danger, an unexpected sound, a movement glimpsed from the corner of the eye, the sudden silence of forest creatures that might indicate human presence.

Yet they encountered nothing, as if the forest itself was holding its breath, watching these intruders with ancient, patient malevolence.

Eventually, Maxima raised his hand, signalling a halt. The column stopped immediately, the horses standing motionless as if they too understood the need for silence.

The scout commander dismounted and approached Seneca, gesturing for him to do likewise. When both men were on the ground, Maxima spoke in the barest whisper, his mouth close to Seneca's ear.

'This is as far as we can go if we're to make it back across the river before dawn.'

Seneca surveyed their surroundings, difficult though it was in the near-total darkness. They had stopped in a small clearing where a stream cut through the forest floor, creating a narrow break in the canopy above. Through this gap, he could see stars, their cold light providing just enough illumination to make out the basic features of the landscape.

The forest here was particularly dense, the trees growing so close together that in places they appeared to form solid walls of timber and bark. The undergrowth was minimal, but the ground was soft with centuries of fallen leaves, decomposing into rich, black soil. The stream gurgled quietly, its water clear and swift, running over a bed of smooth stones.

'This will do,' said Seneca. 'We'll dismount here.'

At his signal, the Occultum slid from their horses, each man retrieving his sarcina and securing it across his shoulders. Falco also took charge of the extra sarcina containing the second cache. Despite its weight, he handled it with ease, securing it atop his own pack.

They looked at each other, their faces solemn in the fragmented starlight. This was the moment of commitment, and once the Exploratores departed, they would be on their own in enemy territory, with no immediate support or extraction possible.

Maxima approached one final time.

'The gods go with you, Tribune,' he said and without another word, returned to his men. Once mounted, he raised his hand in a final salute, then led his column away, moving back the way they had come. The sound of their passage faded quickly, swallowed by the ancient forest that now surrounded the six members of the Occultum.

Seneca gave them a moment of silence, allowing each man to centre himself for what lay ahead. Then, with a series of hand signals rather than spoken commands, he directed them deeper into the forest, away from the path the Exploratores had taken.

They moved in single file, each man carefully placing his feet exactly where the man ahead had stepped, minimizing their trail. Seneca led, with Marcus behind him, then Decimus, Talorcan, Sica, and finally Falco bringing up the rear.

For over an hour they continued, working their way through the densest parts of the forest, deliberately choosing the most difficult terrain to further reduce the chance of accidental encounters. They crossed several small streams, using the water to break their trail, and avoided any signs of game paths or human tracks.

The night was wearing on, the first faint hints of dawn just beginning to lighten the eastern sky, when Seneca finally located what he sought, a dense thicket of blackthorn and holly, providing excellent concealment from all sides. With hand signals, he directed his men to spread out and check the surrounding area, ensuring they were truly alone before committing to this position.

When they returned, each signalling the all-clear, Seneca led them into the thicket. The thorns tore at their clothing, but they ignored such minor discomforts, focused entirely on establishing their hidden base without leaving evidence of their passage.

Inside the thicket, they found a space just large enough for six men to lie flat, completely concealed from outside observation. The ground was soft with fallen leaves, providing natural padding and insulation from the cold earth. More importantly, the tangled branches and dense growth all around would muffle any necessary sounds.

With practised efficiency, they arranged themselves in a circular formation, each man's head facing outward to cover all approaches. Weapons were positioned for immediate access, sarcinae positioned to elevate their heads just enough to maintain visibility through the undergrowth.

'Three watches,' Seneca murmured, his voice barely a breath. 'Two men at a time. Marcus and I take first watch. Decimus and Talorcan second. Falco and Sica third.'

The men nodded, settling into their positions. Those not on immediate watch closed their eyes, though Seneca knew they wouldn't truly sleep, rather, they would enter the state of semi-consciousness that most experienced soldiers cultivated, resting while maintaining awareness of their surroundings.

As the first genuine light of dawn began to filter through the canopy, Seneca allowed himself a moment of grim satisfaction. He glanced around at his men, these elite operatives who had followed him into so many dangerous situations. They had achieved the first objective, penetrating Silures territory without detection, now the real work would begin.

Chapter Nine

The Ordovices Hillfort

The great timber gates of the fortress's third defensive ring swung open with a deep, resonant groan. Behind Veteranus, nine other wagons formed a line as they ascended the spiralling pathway that wound its way up the conical hill. He flicked the reins gently, urging his ponies forward through the gateway. Unlike Roman fortifications with their rigid angles and uniform structures, this hillfort had been crafted in harmony with the natural shape of the land, embracing rather than dominating the terrain.

Through each successive gate they passed, the hillfort revealed itself in layers of increasing grandeur and complexity. The outermost rings contained cattle pens, storage buildings, and workshops where artisans pursued their crafts beneath open-sided shelters. Leather workers stretched hides on wooden frames, their hands moving with practised precision as they scraped flesh from freshly cured skins and smiths hammered glowing metal, the rhythmic clanging echoing across the settlement as sparks spiralled upward.

'Keep your eyes forward,' Adgennus murmured. 'Looking about too eagerly marks you as an outsider... or worse, a spy.'

Veteranus nodded almost imperceptibly, though he continued to absorb every detail through his peripheral vision. The middle rings housed the dwellings, roundhouses of varying sizes arranged in concentric circles but unlike the crude huts of the more primitive tribes, these structures showed remarkable sophistication. Smoke rose from carefully constructed vents at their peaks, while their walls of woven withies were plastered with clay mixed with lime, creating smooth surfaces painted with intricate patterns in red, white, and black.

Between these dwellings moved the people of the Ordovices, tall, well-built men and women whose bearing spoke of fierce pride and independence. The warriors were particularly striking, their bodies adorned with spiral tattoos and their hair either elaborately braided or twisted into lime-stiffened spikes that added to their imposing height. They wore tunics of finely woven wool dyed in deep blues and greens, with leather belts from which hung knives, pouches, and various talismans. Over these, many wore mail shirts of iron rings, evidence of advanced metalworking that rivalled anything Veteranus had seen outside of Rome itself.

The women dressed with equal attention to status and craft. Their tunics were longer, reaching to mid-calf, and many wore over-dresses secured at the shoulders with elaborately worked bronze brooches. Their hair was bound with leather cords threaded with beads of amber and jet, and their arms bore silver and bronze bangles that clinked softly as they moved.

'The wealth on display is deliberate,' Adgennus commented quietly. 'They want us to see their prosperity, to understand that they trade from strength, not desperation.'

Indeed, there was little evidence of hardship within these walls. The people appeared well-fed, their clothing of good quality, their bearing confident. Even the children showed the rounded limbs and bright eyes of proper nourishment, darting between the roundhouses in games of their own invention.

As they approached the last gate, the most substantial yet, Veteranus noted the change in defences. Where the outer walls had been primarily earthworks topped with wooden palisades, this inner barrier was constructed of massive oak trunks, each easily the breadth of a man's chest, set so closely together that not even a child could slip between them. The gateway itself was a masterpiece of tribal engineering, a roofed structure with towers on either side, manned by warriors whose blue-painted faces peered down at the approaching wagons with impassive scrutiny.

'They take no chances,' Veteranus observed.

'Nor should they,' replied Adgennus. 'The wealth of three clans resides within these walls, and beyond that, their sacred places. One does not guard such treasures lightly.'

As they passed beneath the watchful eyes of the gate guards, Veteranus felt the weight of their gaze. These were not simply strong arms wielding spears; these were men trained to observe, to note inconsistencies, to smell danger before it fully manifested. He kept his posture relaxed, his expression appropriately impressed but not overly awed, playing the role of an experienced trader entering a prosperous new market.

Beyond this final gate lay the summit plateau, the heart of the fortress. Here, the structures were arranged around a central open space, a gathering place paved with flat stones fitted together with remarkable precision. At its centre burned a great fire in a pit lined with carved stones, the flames tended by white-robed figures whose shaved heads and ceremonial regalia marked them as servants of the tribal gods.

'Druids,' Adgennus whispered, noting the direction of Veteranus's gaze. 'Not the high priests, those remain in seclusion, but their acolytes. They maintain the sacred flame that has burned, it is said, since the hill was first settled countless generations ago.'

Surrounding the central space stood the great halls of the clan chiefs, structures that defied the traditional roundhouse design. These were longer buildings with straight walls and pitched roofs, more reminiscent of Roman construction though entirely executed in native materials. Their entrances faced the sacred fire, elaborately carved doorposts depicting ancestral spirits and protective deities rising nearly fifteen feet high.

'The largest belongs to Bodvoc of the Eagle Clan,' Adgennus explained as they drew their wagon to a halt in the line forming at the edge of the central space. 'The smaller two belong to the lesser Stag and Boar Clans.'

The ten wagons from the trading caravan were now arranged in a neat row along the western edge of the gathering place. Their drivers remained seated, making no move to disembark or display their goods until properly invited to do so.

A crowd had begun to gather, keeping a respectful distance but clearly curious about the new arrivals. Unlike the more excitable eastern tribes, the Ordovices maintained a disciplined restraint, their murmured conversations barely audible over the crackling of the sacred fire.

'Now we wait,' said Adgennus, settling back slightly on the wagon's bench. 'The council will send a delegation when they are ready to inspect the goods.'

The waiting stretched nearly an hour, a deliberate display of the hillfort's control over the timing of all interactions within its walls. Veteranus used the opportunity to continue his careful observation of the settlement. He counted at least sixty warriors visible around the perimeter of the central space, each armed with spear and shield, many wearing the distinctive Eagle crest that Adgennus had identified as the personal guard of Bodvoc. They were positioned not in the rigid formation of Roman legionaries, but in an apparently casual arrangement that nevertheless covered every approach to the gathering place.

'They're coming,' Adgennus murmured eventually, straightening his posture slightly.

From the largest hall emerged a procession led by warriors in full ceremonial attire. Their faces were painted with elaborate designs that transformed their features into fierce masks, while their bodies were adorned with bronze torcs, arm rings, and breast plates polished to a golden gleam. Behind them came a group of older men and women, their clothing more richly dyed and decorated with intricate embroidery, their jewellery more substantial, clearly the clan elders or advisors.

At the centre of this group walked Bodvoc himself and even without Adgennus's confirmation, Veteranus would have recognised him as the paramount chief. Everything about him exuded authority, from his height, towering at least a head above most of his warriors, to the magnificent cloak of wolf fur draped across his powerful shoulders. The gold torc around his neck was thicker than a man's thumb, its ends fashioned into a stunning Eagle's heads with tiny red gems for eyes. His beard was elaborately braided with golden threads, and the tattoos on his face formed a pattern of such complexity that it seemed to shift with each change of expression.

Beside him walked a figure whose role was equally unmistakable, a druid of high rank, his white robes embroidered with silver thread depicting astronomical symbols. Unlike the acolytes tending the fire, this man's head was not shaved but crowned with a mass of white hair that fell to his shoulders, bound at the forehead with a band of polished jet. His face was deeply lined, his eyes sharp beneath heavy brows, missing nothing as his gaze swept across the waiting traders.

The delegation approached the line of wagons, beginning their inspection at the far end. With each wagon, a similar ritual unfolded: the trader would stand, bow deeply, and await permission to display his goods. Once granted, the contents would be carefully unpacked and arranged for inspection, with the delegation examining each item with deliberate thoroughness.

The crowd grew as word spread through the hillfort and hundreds now ringed the central space, maintaining a respectful distance but clearly fascinated by the exotic treasures being revealed. Children had pushed their way to the front, eyes wide as they beheld objects unlike anything produced within their own culture.

Finally, the delegation reached the wagon immediately before theirs. Veteranus felt his muscles tense involuntarily, and Adgennus noted the subtle shift in his posture.

'Steady,' he murmured. 'You are simply a trader with valuable goods, nothing more. Let me lead the interactions.'

Veteranus gave a nearly imperceptible nod, deliberately relaxing his shoulders and assuming a more merchant-like demeanour. He watched as the trader ahead of them displayed his wares, exquisite jewellery crafted from amber, silver, and gold, each piece drawing murmurs of appreciation from the delegation. Bodvoc himself selected several items, casually passing them to an attendant without discussion of price or trade, a chief's prerogative, apparently, to claim first choice from any goods entering his domain.

Then the delegation was before them. Adgennus rose smoothly from the bench and bowed with precisely the right degree of respect, neither servile nor presumptuous. Bodvoc studied him for a long moment, recognition dawning in his eyes.

'Adgennus of the Aedui,' he said in the trading tongue, his deep voice carrying the distinctive accent of the western tribes. 'You return to our halls after many seasons.'

'Great Bodvoc, Voice of the Eagle, I am honoured to be remembered,' Adgennus replied, his own command of the dialect impressively fluent. 'I bring treasures worthy of your people's craftsmanship and standing.'

Bodvoc's gaze shifted to Veteranus, his eyes narrowing slightly as he took in the stranger's appearance. Though dressed as a trader, there was something in Veteranus's bearing that could not entirely be disguised, the watchful alertness, the balanced stance even while seated, the calloused hands that spoke of weapons rather than merchandise.

'And you bring a new companion,' observed the chief neutrally.

'My associate, Lucius,' Adgennus said smoothly. 'He is here to talk of a truce between your people and the Romans and brings you not trading goods, but gifts for you and your chosen people as a sign of respect and peace.'

Bodvoc held Veteranus's gaze for several heartbeats, his expression unreadable before turning back to Adgennus.

'Show us these Roman treasures,' he commanded.

Adgennus bowed again and gestured to Veteranus. Together, they climbed down from the wagon and moved to its rear. With deliberate ceremony, Adgennus unlatched the heavy wooden door and swung it open, revealing the carefully packed interior.

Unlike the other wagons, which had displayed their goods directly from their conveyances, Adgennus set out a trestle table to arrange their merchandise, each item removed from protective wrappings of oiled cloth and placed with careful precision.

The quality of the goods was indeed exceptional. Silver cups and platters, their surfaces embossed with scenes from

Roman mythology, gleamed in the sunlight. Glass vessels of extraordinary thinness caught the light, their colours shifting from blue to green to purple as they were turned. Iron weapons of the finest quality, short swords with olivewood handles, their blades pattern-welded with rippling designs visible in the metal itself. Most impressive was a complete set of mail armour, the thousands of tiny iron rings forming a flexible protective garment topped with a bronze helmet crested with dyed horsehair.

A murmur ran through the watching crowd as each new treasure was revealed. Even the warriors of Bodvoc's personal guard seemed impressed, their stoic expressions giving way to appreciation as they recognised the quality of the weapons displayed.

The druid moved forward, his interest caught by a set of silver writing implements arranged in a cedar box lined with purple cloth. He lifted a stylus, examining the workmanship with evident appreciation.

'Your craftsmen have skill,' he acknowledged in broken Latin, addressing Veteranus directly for the first time. 'Though they lack the sacred understanding that guides our own artisans.'

Veteranus inclined his head respectfully.

'Each people has their gifts,' he replied carefully. 'We bring these items not to claim superiority, but to offer variety and choice to those who already possess great skill of their own.'

The druid's bushy eyebrows rose slightly at this diplomatic response. He studied Veteranus with increased interest, as if reassessing his initial impression.

Bodvoc, meanwhile, had lifted one of the short swords, testing its balance with the practiced hand of an experienced warrior. He turned it in the light, examining the way the patterns in the metal shifted. With a swift motion that caught many by surprise, he swung the blade through the air, its passage making a sound like cloth tearing. He nodded in evident satisfaction.

'Good steel,' he pronounced. 'Better than the Roman blades my father took from the dead legionaries in Gaul.' He handed the weapon to one of his guards, before continuing the inspection.

For nearly an hour, Bodvoc and the elders examined each item, occasionally asking questions about its origin or method of manufacture. Veteranus let Adgennus handle most of these inquiries, speaking only when directly addressed and keeping his responses appropriately respectful and commercial in nature.

Finally, when all the goods had been displayed and the most impressive pieces claimed by the chief and his inner circle, Bodvoc stepped back and made a gesture to one of his attendants.

'You will be compensated appropriately,' he announced. 'We are not savages who take without fair exchange.' He turned to a warrior standing nearby, a man of middle years with a particularly intricate tattoo covering the right side of his face from temple to jaw. 'Lugaid will show you where the remaining goods may be stored securely. They will be traded for during the feast tonight. He speaks the Roman language.'

'A feast?' Adgennus inquired.

'To welcome the caravan,' Bodvoc explained. 'And to hear what news you bring from the eastern lands.' His gaze lingered on Veteranus. 'Your Roman companion must have many interesting tales to share.'

With that, the chief turned and strode away, his

entourage following in his wake. The crowd began to disperse, though many lingered, still fascinated by the exotic items on display.

After Veteranus and Adgennus packed away the goods, Lugaid led them across the central space toward a row of smaller roundhouses situated near the eastern edge of the summit plateau.

'These are for trading guests,' he explained, gesturing to the structures. 'You have this one.' He pointed to a roundhouse of moderate size, its entrance facing the sacred fire. 'It is a Good place. An honoured place.'

'We are grateful for the chief's hospitality,' Adgennus replied with a slight bow.

The structure was well-made, its interior clean and comfortable by tribal standards. Fresh rushes covered the packed earth floor, strewn with fragrant herbs that released their scent when crushed underfoot. A central hearth contained banked coals that could be easily stirred to life, with a smoke hole directly above to vent the fumes. Around the circumference stood low platforms covered with woven mats and furs, sleeping places for perhaps six occupants, though they were apparently being granted the entire dwelling to themselves, a mark of particular status.

Lugaid gestured around the space.

'Water is there.' He pointed to a covered clay vessel standing near the entrance. 'Rest now and we will feast when the sun touches western hills.' With that, he ducked through the low doorway and was gone.

Adgennus waited until the warrior's footsteps had faded before turning to Veteranus.

'So far, so good,' he said quietly. 'But Bodvoc is shrewd. The feast tonight will be as much about assessing us as celebrating our arrival. Every question will have a purpose beyond its surface meaning. Every cup of mead will be offered in hopes that loose tongues might reveal hidden truths. These are not ordinary waters, my friend. The Ordovices remember every slight, every lie, every betrayal. And their memories are very long indeed.'

Veteranus moved to the roundhouse's entrance and drew back the leather covering that served as a door. From this vantage point, he could see across the central gathering place to the great hall where Bodvoc and his advisors had withdrawn. Warriors still stood guard around the perimeter, their eyes constantly scanning the hillfort's interior. Beyond them, the daily life of the settlement continued, smoke rising from cooking fires, children running errands between dwellings, artisans returning to their crafts after the excitement of the caravan's arrival.

It all appeared so ordinary, so mundane, a tribal society going about its business. Yet beneath this seemingly simple exterior lay complexities of politics, belief, and ambition that rivalled anything in Rome itself. These were not the barbarians that Roman propaganda depicted. They were a people with their own sophisticated culture, their own military discipline, their own strategic thinking and whatever happened next, one thing was certain, if there were more fortresses like this, and if it came to conflict, they would certainly be a formidable enemy.

Chapter Ten

The Forests of Siluria

The soft crackle of the tiny fire was the only sound that broke the silence of the forest as the men of the Occultum huddled around the shallow pit they had excavated. The hole was several hand's depth and dug wide enough to contain a small cooking fire, the flames carefully hidden below ground level to prevent any telltale light from escaping through the trees. Above it, a makeshift grill of green branches supported a battered iron pot in which a thin broth simmered, the steam carrying the scent of dried herbs and salt meat.

Falco reached forward with his wooden bowl, allowing Decimus to ladle a portion of the steaming liquid into it. He sniffed appreciatively before taking a careful sip.

'Not bad,' he murmured, his voice barely audible even in the stillness of their hidden camp. 'Though I'd give my right arm for a decent cup of wine to wash it down.'

'You need your right arm,' Sica observed quietly, accepting his own portion. 'For killing.'

Falco conceded with a faint smile that didn't reach his eyes. The former gladiator's massive frame seemed almost too large for the small clearing, his shoulders hunched as he hungrily consumed the meagre meal. The others ate in similar silence, conserving energy and words with equal discipline. For the foreseeable future, they would subsist primarily on buccellatum, the hard biscuit that was a staple of Roman military rations, supplemented with strips of dried beef and whatever edible plants or fruits they could safely forage. Hot food would be a luxury they could seldom risk, the smoke and light of a fire too dangerous in hostile territory.

Seneca sat slightly apart from the group, his attention focused on the deepening shadows around them. His weathered face revealed nothing, but the tension in his shoulders spoke of the weight of command. They were deep in enemy territory now, where a single mistake could mean death for all of them.

As the sparse meal came to an end, he signalled his men to gather closer and
reached within his cloak to withdraw a roll of thin vellum, carefully unfolding it to reveal a crudely drawn map. In the fading light, the inked markings stood out against the finely woven material and each man studied it intently. They all carried similar maps sewn into their clothing, along with three gold coins each, insurance against the unexpected.

'I think we are around here,' said Seneca quietly, his finger resting on a point just west of a crudely drawn river line, 'approximately five miles into Silures territory.'

Marcus leaned forward, his eyes narrowing as he studied the markings that represented the treacherous terrain ahead. His years as a centurion had taught him to read landscapes as easily as most men read facial expressions, to see the tactical advantages and deadly pitfalls hidden in seemingly innocuous features.

'Any settlements?' he asked quietly.

'Few that we know of,' Seneca admitted. 'We do know however, there is at least one major one here.' He placed his finger at a point halfway between them and the western coastline.

'How do we know that?' asked Marcus.

'Let's just say that Plautius has men who can be very persuasive when it comes to extracting information from prisoners,' replied Seneca, 'and besides, there is no love lost between the eastern tribes and the Silures, so some were happy to share whatever information they had.'

'How reliable were these captives?' interjected Decimus, his eyes narrowing sceptically. 'Men will say anything under questioning.'

'Some weren't under torture,' Seneca clarified. 'They were overheard speaking among themselves, unaware they were being listened to by one of our interpreters. The information was consistent across multiple sources.'

'And you believe Mordred might seek refuge there?' asked Talorcan, his Belgic accent giving the Latin words a harsh edge.

'It's a reasonable assumption,' Seneca replied. 'A druid of his standing would seek protection among tribal leadership. And if not, the settlement may at least provide us with better intelligence on his whereabouts.'

'Druids and their damned secrets,' muttered Falco. 'I've had my fill of them after Mona.'

'We all have,' said Marcus quietly, the memory their most recent interaction with the druids and the Wraith still fresh. 'But our job is to find Mordred and end his threat to Rome.'

Decimus studied the map with a critical eye, his weathered finger tracing the vague outlines of hills and forests that stood between them and their objective.

'The terrain?' he asked simply.

'Heavily forested throughout,' Seneca replied. 'Dense undergrowth in the valleys, thinner on the ridges. There will probably be quite a few streams to cross, but we'll deal with them as we find them. The forest provides cover for us, but also for any Silures so we'll need to move with extreme caution.'

Talorcan knelt closer, studying the contours representing the hills and valleys. His people had survived for generations in the dense Germanic forests by understanding the land intimately.

'These ridge lines,' he observed quietly, 'they'll offer the best observation points but should avoid cresting them whenever possible.'

Seneca nodded in agreement.

'We'll stay in the middle elevations where possible. High enough to avoid the wetlands, low enough to remain below the skyline.'

Falco shifted his massive frame.

'And when we reach this settlement? What then?'

'We go to ground,' Seneca stated firmly. 'Find a secure position from which to observe their movements, assess their strength, and gather intelligence about Mordred's possible presence. We make no move until we have a clear understanding of what we're facing.'

'Time frame?' Marcus asked.

'We have supplies for approximately twenty days,' Seneca replied. 'After that, we'll need to rely more heavily on foraging or take whatever we can from the locals. If compromised, we make our way to the last rendezvous point. We'll agree a fresh one each day but if we get split up, each man is to stay there for no more than one day to see if anyone else arrives. If not, he is to head back to Roman territory on his own, using the caches for supplies if necessary. Any survivors will then meet back at the fort in Camulodunum.

He rolled the fabric map carefully and returned it to its hiding place within his cloak. The men had committed every detail to memory, distances, landmarks, routes. Their lives might depend on this knowledge in the coming days.

'Questions?' Seneca asked, looking around at his men.

No one spoke but their silence conveyed more than

words could. These men had faced death together too many times to waste breath on unnecessary queries.

'Very well,' said Seneca with finality. 'Complete your preparations. We move out as soon as everyone is ready.'

The group dispersed, each man attending to his final tasks with methodical precision. Nothing was left to chance; every detail was checked and rechecked.

'Talorcan takes point,' said Seneca as they formed up. 'I'll follow, then Marcus, Sica and Decimus. Falco, you're rear security. Five pace intervals and absolute silence. Let's go.'

Talorcan moved forward, seeming to melt into the darkness with each silent step and, one by one, the others followed, each man carefully placing his feet where those before him had stepped, minimizing the trail they left behind.

The ancient forest enveloped them, its towering trees standing sentinel as they had for centuries before Rome even existed. Moss-covered trunks and gnarled roots created natural obstacles while the canopy above whispered with the gentle stirring of a night breeze, masking what little sound their passage might have made.

Slowly, step by careful step they advanced into Silures territory, guided by stars and the occasional glimpse of the moon, their senses heightened as their night vision adjusted to the gloom.

Hours passed as they penetrated deeper. No words were exchanged and no unnecessary gestures made so whenever Talorcan held up a closed fist, the signal rippled back through their formation and they froze instantly, becoming as still as the trees around them.

Several times they crossed small streams, using the water to help mask their scent from dogs and to confuse any potential trackers. Each crossing was methodical, one man watching upstream, another downstream, while the others moved across one by one, careful to make as little noise as possible.

Near midnight, they encountered a game trail cutting across their path. Sica studied it carefully, noting the freshness of the tracks before signalling to avoid it entirely. They detoured a hundred paces around the trail before resuming their original direction. Such caution added time to their journey, but in hostile territory, speed was secondary to stealth.

The men of the Occultum moved through the forest like ghosts, their years of experience evident in every careful step and measured breath. To the casual observer, had there been one, they would have appeared as nothing more than slow moving shadows, perhaps imagined movements at the corner of the eye, gone when looked at directly but by the time the first hint of false dawn began to lighten the eastern sky, they had covered nearly ten miles of difficult terrain and Seneca signalled a halt. They would need to find a place to conceal themselves during daylight hours, when movement would be too risky.

Finally, a small depression covered with thick undergrowth presented itself as their best option and without a word, the men established a perimeter, checking for signs of recent human activity before committing to the location. Finding none, they slipped beneath the natural canopy of intertwined branches and once again settled into a defensive formation, their backs to one another, weapons close at hand.

They would rest here until nightfall, moving only when darkness once again provided its protective cloak, and as the forest around them stirred with the first movements of morning wildlife, the six men remained utterly motionless, their presence unmarked and unsuspected in the heart of enemy territory.

They had completed th first phase of their mission. Now came the true test, surviving l ng enough to complete the rest.

Chapter Eleven

The Sacred Grove

Consciousness returned to Geta in slow, painful waves. First came the throbbing ache that seemed to emanate from every part of his body, then the coppery taste of blood in his mouth where his teeth had cut into the inside of his cheek. His eyelids felt swollen and heavy, requiring immense effort to open. When he finally managed it, the world swam before him in a blur of green and golden light. They were still in the sacred grove.

As his vision gradually clarified, Geta realised he was bound to one of the ancient standing stones that ringed the clearing. Rough hemp rope cut into his wrists, pulling his arms back at an unnatural angle that made his shoulders scream in protest. His legs too were secured, bound at the ankles with the same coarse rope.

Turning his head, an action that sent fresh stabs of pain shooting down his neck, Geta could see that his companions had received similar treatment. Each man was tied to a separate stone, spaced evenly around the perimeter of the grove and the sight of them drove the last fog of unconsciousness from his mind.

They were alive, though some barely. Titus's face was a mask of blood from his broken nose, his left eye swollen completely shut. Vindex hung limply against his bonds, his chest rising and falling in shallow, irregular movements. Raurica's massive frame was slumped forward as far as the ropes would allow, his normally ruddy complexion now ashen. Rullus appeared the least damaged physically, but his eyes held a glazed, distant look that suggested his mind had retreated from the horror of their situation. And Lentulus... Lentulus was conscious and terrified, his body trembling visibly even from where Geta was bound.

At the centre of the clearing, atop and around the stone altar where they had found the feast, sat their captors. The Silures warriors lounged with casual indifference, helping themselves to the food that had been their bait. They passed wineskins amongst themselves, occasionally speaking in low tones that didn't carry to where the Romans were bound. Their blue-painted faces betrayed no emotion, neither pleasure in their victory nor interest in their prisoners' suffering.

These were not men celebrating a successful hunt. They were simply men sharing a meal while waiting for the next phase of a ritual to begin.

Among them, Geta recognised the warrior who had led the attack, the one with the triple-forked beard and the necklace of finger bones. He sat slightly apart from the others atop the altar stone itself, his position one of clear authority. Beside him sat a younger man, barely more than a boy, watching the proceedings with keen, calculating eyes. Several other warriors of varying ages completed the group, each marked with the distinctive blue spiral patterns of the Silures.

'Help me,' Lentulus whimpered from two stones away, his voice cracking with terror. 'Someone help me.'

'Quiet,' Titus hissed through his swollen lips. 'For Jupiter's sake, man, control yourself.'

'Control myself?' Lentulus's voice rose in pitch before dropping again to an urgent whisper. 'They're going to kill us. You saw how they appeared. Like demons from the underworld.'

'They're men,' Titus insisted. 'Just men. And men can be reasoned with.'

A harsh, pained laugh escaped Rullus at this.

'Reasoned with? Look at them, Titus. Does any part of you truly believe they took us alive to negotiate?'

Geta remained silent, watching the warriors at their meal. Unlike his companions, he had spent time in Germania before joining the expedition to Britannia. He had seen tribal warfare up close, had witnessed the aftermath of raids between Germanic clans. The careful way these Silures had incapacitated rather than killed them spoke of deliberate intent. They had been saved for something.

'Geta,' Titus called softly. 'Do you recognise any of their markings? Anything that might tell us what tribe they belong to specifically?'

Slowly, Geta shook his head, immediately regretting the movement as pain lanced down his spine.

'Not one of the tribes I know,' he said, 'so we can only assume they are Silures.'

Vindex stirred at that moment, a low moan escaping his lips as consciousness returned. His eyes fluttered open, confusion evident in his gaze as he took in their situation.

'Wh-what happened?' he slurred, blood trickling from the corner of his mouth as he spoke.

'We were overcome,' Titus said. 'But take heart. We're all alive.'

'For now,' murmured Geta.

'Yes, for now,' Titus acknowledged, shooting Geta a warning look. 'And we must focus on remaining so. The fact that they haven't killed us yet suggests they want something from us.'

'Or want to do something to us,' Rullus countered darkly.

Lentulus had begun to sob quietly, his head hanging

forward as tears mixed with the blood on his face.

'We're going to die,' he repeated like a mantra. 'We're going to die in this forsaken place.'

'I told you we should have turned back,' Geta said, unable to keep the bitterness from his voice. 'This is Silures land.'

Titus attempted to straighten against his bonds, trying to project a confidence that none of them felt.

'We are Roman scouts,' he said. 'Exploratore auxiliaries. If they understand our worth, we might be ransomed.'

At this, Raurica finally spoke, his deep voice reduced to a rasp.

'You still don't understand, do you, Titus? You led us across that river to our deaths.' He coughed, spitting blood onto the forest floor. 'No one knows we're here. No one will pay any ransom and even if they would, the Silures don't want Roman gold. They want Roman blood.'

The harsh reality of Raurica's words settled over the group and for a long moment, no one spoke.

Geta closed his eyes, feeling a strange calm settle over him. He was angry, not about his approaching death, but about the pointlessness of it all. They had crossed the river for nothing more than the promise of fresh venison when they had perfectly serviceable rations in their packs. Now they would die because Titus couldn't admit the risk wasn't worth the potential reward, a failing that Geta had seen claim the lives of too many soldiers during his years of service.

When he opened his eyes again, he found himself staring directly at the leader of the Silures warriors. The man was watching him with an unsettling intensity, as if reading the thoughts behind his eyes. Geta met his gaze unflinchingly. If he was to die, he would do so with whatever dignity he could muster.

After a moment, the warrior returned his attention to his meal, seemingly losing interest in his prisoner's silent defiance.

'We need to work together,' Titus was saying, his voice taking on the rallying tone he used when addressing his men before a dangerous mission. 'Test your bonds. Look for weaknesses. If even one of us can get free…'

'Stop it,' Geta interrupted flatly. 'Just stop, Titus. Look at them. Really look. They aren't concerned about us escaping because they know we can't. These aren't some eastern tribesmen with more courage than skill. They took us down without a single casualty. Without even raising their voices.'

'So you suggest we just accept our fate?' Titus demanded, anger briefly overcoming his pain.

'I suggest we face it with dignity,' Geta replied. 'Die like soldiers, not like frightened children.'

Lentulus's sobbing increased at this, evolving into a keening wail that echoed through the grove.

'I don't want to die,' he cried, his voice rising with each word. 'Please, gods, I don't want to die!'

His desperate pleas cut through the quiet conversations of the Silures warriors. One by one, they turned to look at the source of the disturbance, their expressions ranging from curiosity to mild annoyance.

Cadoc placed his wooden cup down on the stone beside him and rose to his feet, moving deliberately across the clearing towards Lentulus. The Roman's cries grew more frantic as the warrior approached, dissolving into incoherent begging.

'Shut up, you fool,' hissed Rullus. 'For all our sakes, shut up!'

But Lentulus was beyond reason, his panic complete. He thrashed against his bonds, babbling promises, pleas, and prayers in a desperate stream as Cadoc came to stand before him.

The Silures chieftain regarded the sobbing Roman with a detached curiosity, his head tilted slightly as if listening to an unfamiliar bird call. Lentulus's words tumbled over each other, offers of ransom, claims of important connections in Rome, assurances that he could be valuable if spared.

Cadoc watched and listened for nearly a full minute as the Roman exhausted himself. When Lentulus finally paused to draw breath, something like decision passed across the warrior's blue-marked features and with the casual efficiency of a farmer wringing a chicken's neck, he reached forward and grasped Lentulus's head between his massive hands. A simple, brutal twist followed, and the sound of the Roman's spine snapping echoed across the grove like a dry branch breaking underfoot.

Lentulus's body went instantly limp, his final breath escaping in a soft sigh that seemed to carry his soul with it into the still air of the sacred place.

Without a backward glance, Cadoc returned to the altar and his interrupted meal, stepping back up onto the stone as if he had done nothing more consequential than swat an annoying insect.

The Romans stared in horror, the swift, dispassionate killing more terrifying than any elaborate execution might have been. This was not the action of a man punishing an enemy or performing a ritual sacrifice. It was the practical elimination of an irritant, nothing more.

Geta felt the last flicker of hope die within him. There would be no negotiation, no opportunity for escape, no merciful end. He looked at his fellow prisoners, seeing the same realization dawning in their eyes. The Silures did not hate them, nor did they fear them. They simply intended to use them for whatever purpose they had been saved for, and no amount of pleading or reasoning would change that fact.

In the centre of the grove, the warriors continued their meal, passing food and drink among themselves as if nothing had happened. The young boy spoke animatedly to Cadoc, who responded with brief comments and occasional nods. Another warrior laughed at something said, the sound incongruously normal in the shadow of death that now hung over the clearing.

Geta leaned his head back against the cold stone he was bound to, feeling its ancient solidity against his skull. Above, through gaps in the great leafy canopy, he could see patches of blue sky. It was a fine day, bright and clear, a beautiful day to die. The irony was not lost on him.

He thought briefly of his family, his aging parents, his younger sister who had married a local farmer. They would never know what had happened to him. Would never have a body to burn on a proper pyre. He would simply become another Roman soldier who had vanished in the mists of Britannia, one more name added to the long list of those claimed by this unconquered island.

Across the grove, Titus had fallen silent, his earlier optimism finally crushed by the cold reality of their situation. Raurica's breathing had grown more laboured, suggesting internal injuries that would likely claim him before whatever ceremony the Silures had planned. Rullus stared blankly ahead, his mind seemingly detached from the horror around him. Vindex alone still struggled weakly against his bonds, his soldier's instinct to resist not yet overcome by reason or resignation.

The feast continued in the centre of the grove, the Silures warriors now passing around a clay vessel from which each drank in turn. Their voices remained low, almost respectful of the sacred space around them. Occasionally, one would glance toward their prisoners, but these looks held no malice, no anticipation, only the same detached assessment one might give to livestock awaiting slaughter.

Geta closed his eyes once more, seeking whatever inner peace he could find in these final hours. He had been a soldier long enough to know that death came for all men eventually. Today it would come for him in this ancient grove, beneath these towering trees that had stood for centuries before Rome was even founded, and would stand for centuries after it fell.

His only regret was that it had been such a pointless journey that had brought him here.

Chapter Twelve

The Hillfort

The interior of the roundhouse grew dim as evening approached, the fading daylight filtering weakly through the smoke hole above. Veteranus sat on one of the low sleeping platforms, his back against the curved wall, cleaning his knife with slow, methodical strokes of an oiled cloth.

Across from him, Adgennus knelt before the central hearth, coaxing the banked embers into a small flame. As the fire caught, its warm glow illuminated the roundhouse interior, casting dancing shadows on the wattle walls and highlighting the weathered lines of the Gaul's face.

'These Ordovices build well,' Veteranus observed, testing the edge of his blade with his thumb before returning it to its sheath. 'This is more comfortable than many Roman barracks I've slept in.'

Adgennus nodded as he fed small sticks into the growing flames. 'They understand the land, how to work with it rather than against it. These structures have evolved over centuries to withstand the mountain winters.'

'You seem to know a great deal about them.'

'I should hope so,' said Adgennus. 'Fifteen years of trading with the western tribes teaches a man to observe more than just potential profits.' He sat back on his heels, satisfied with the fire. 'The Ordovices are a proud people, with a complex culture that most Romans dismiss as primitive simply because they don't understand it.'

'Tell me more about them,' said Veteranus, 'their history, their alliances. The more I understand, the less likely I am to cause offence.'

'A wise approach,' said Adgennus as he moved to sit on his own sleeping platform. 'The Ordovices have inhabited these mountains for longer than anyone can remember. Unlike the tribes of the flatlands, they've never been conquered, not by other British tribes, not by anyone. The mountains protect them, and they protect the mountains in return.'

'And their relations with neighbouring tribes?'

'Complicated,' Adgennus replied with a wry smile. 'They've had conflicts with the Dobunni to the east, the Silures to the south, and most of the northern tribes including the Brigantes.'

'Yet now they trade freely with the Brigantes,' Veteranus observed.

'Indeed. That particular relationship has changed dramatically in recent years.' Adgennus paused, reaching for a small leather flask hanging from one of the roof supports. He uncorked it and took a careful sip before offering it to Veteranus. 'Mountain mead, flavoured with heather. A local speciality.'

Veteranus accepted the flask and tasted the liquid. It was surprisingly smooth and stronger than he had expected.

'Good,' he acknowledged, returning the flask. 'So what changed between the Ordovices and the Brigantes?'

'Marriage,' Adgennus said simply. 'Or more accurately, a marriage arrangement that secured peace between traditional enemies.' He settled more comfortably against the wall. 'Last year, Cartimandua, Queen of the Brigantes, offered her daughter Rhiannon to Inion, the son of Bodvoc. A political alliance sealed with blood.'

Veteranus nodded. Such arrangements were common enough throughout the world, though knowing that Cartimandua had already allied herself with Rome, this connection raised interesting possibilities.

'And the girl lives here now?' asked Veteranus.

'She does. She has adapted well to life among the Ordovices though they are not yet wed. they are waiting for the right alignment of the moon and stars before the arrangement is sealed.'

Veteranus leaned forward, genuinely curious now.

'So, what did the Brigantes gain from this alliance, apart from peace? The Ordovices are powerful, certainly, but the Brigantes territory is vast by comparison.'

Adgennus looked impressed by the question.

'You understand tribal politics better than most Romans, my friend,' he said, taking another sip of mead before continuing. 'The Brigantes gained two crucial advantages. First, the Ordovices will act as an allied buffer between them and the Silures. Secondly, and perhaps more importantly, they will gain access to the Ordovices mines.'

'Mines?'

'Yes, deep in these mountains lie some of the richest deposits of gold, silver, and copper in all of Britannia. The Ordovices guard the locations jealously, working them with their own people and selected slaves. The wealth from these mines funds their ability to remain independent and well-armed.'

Veteranus absorbed this information, seeing how it fitted into the larger picture of tribal alliances and Roman expansion.

'And what did the Ordovices gain from accepting Rhiannon?'

'Secure northern borders,' Adgennus replied promptly. 'Freedom to focus their strength on containing the Silures to the south, with whom they have a much deeper, more ancient enmity, and, of course, expanded trading opportunities through the Brigantes territory.'

'Yet Cartimandua has allied herself with Rome,' Veteranus noted. 'Doesn't that cause tension with the Ordovices?'

Adgennus nodded, his expression growing more serious.

'It does. Bodvoc and his council are not pleased with Cartimandua's Roman alliance, but they're pragmatic enough to recognise it doesn't directly threaten them, at least not yet. The mountains have always protected them, and they believe they will continue to do so.'

'And Rhiannon herself? Where do her loyalties lie?'

'That,' Adgennus said carefully, 'is a question many people would like answered. She was raised in her mother's court, aware of the benefits of Roman alliance. But she has also come to love her proposed husband and his people. She walks a difficult line.'

'And this Einion? What manner of man is the chief's son?'

'Young, barely twenty-five summers, but already a respected warrior. He led the fighting against the Deceangli raids last summer with considerable skill. He's less suspicious of outsiders than his father, having grown up during a time of increased trade with other tribes. Some see him as the future of the Ordovices, a leader who might forge new connections without sacrificing their independence.'

Veteranus nodded thoughtfully.

'A young couple with potentially divided loyalties, positioned between Rome's expansion and tribal resistance. Interesting.'

'More than interesting,' Adgennus murmured. 'Potentially crucial to how the western territories respond to

Rome's advance.' He corked his flask and hung it back on its hook. 'Of course, this is merely a trader's perspective. I observe and listen, but I am careful not to involve myself too deeply in such matters.'

'A wise policy for a man who must travel between many different territories,' said Veteranus, but before he could continue, he was interrupted by a shadow falling across the doorway as the leather covering was drawn aside.

A warrior stood there, his face painted with the distinctive patterns that marked Bodvoc's personal guard. He nodded respectfully to the occupants before speaking in the trading tongue.

'Adgennus of the Aedui, Lucius of Rome. Bodvoc, Voice of the Eagle, summons you to feast in the great hall,' and, without waiting for a response, he let the covering fall back into place and departed.

'Not an invitation one refuses,' Adgennus remarked with raised eyebrows.

'No,' Veteranus agreed, rising to his feet. 'And an excellent opportunity to learn more about our hosts.' He reached for his trader's cloak, settling it around his shoulders. 'Tell me, will Rhiannon and Einion be present at this feast?'

'Apparently not. They are attending a blessing in one of their religious centres further to the east.' Adgennus adjusted his own clothing, checking that the golden torque at his neck, a symbol of his status as a recognised trader, was prominently visible. 'Remember, observe more than you speak. Now, let's not keep the chief waiting.'

They stepped out into the gathering dusk, where the hillfort was coming alive with torches and cooking fires. The central space before the great halls was now filled with people preparing for the evening's festivities and warriors stood at attention near the entrances to the clan halls, their weapons polished to gleaming perfection for the ceremonial occasion.

Above them, the first stars were beginning to appear in the darkening sky as the sun's final rays gilded the distant mountains with crimson and gold.

For now, Veteranus focused on the immediate task, surviving a tribal feast and gathering what intelligence he could about a potential future enemy.

Chapter Thirteen

The Sacred Grove

As the sun dipped toward the western horizon, a golden light filtered through the ancient canopy, casting long shadows across the sacred grove. The feast had continued for hours, the Silures warriors sharing food and drink with the casual camaraderie of men who had hunted together for years. They spoke in low tones amongst themselves, occasionally laughing at some shared jest, seemingly oblivious to the five remaining Romans bound to the standing stones around the perimeter.

Geta's body had grown numb from the prolonged immobility, the ropes cutting into his wrists where they secured him to the ancient monolith. Across the clearing, Titus had fallen into a fitful doze, his head hanging forward, chin resting on his chest. Vindex stared vacantly into the middle distance, his mind perhaps seeking escape from their hopeless situation. Raurica's breathing had grown more laboured, a wet rattle accompanying each inhalation that suggested blood in his lungs. Rullus alone remained fully alert, his eyes tracking every movement, desperately searching for any opportunity, however slight.

Lentulus's body hung limply from its bindings, a stark reminder of the casual brutality of the Silures chieftain. No one had bothered to remove the corpse or even acknowledge it further after the killing.

Eventually, as the light began to fade from the sky, the feast drew to its natural conclusion, Cadoc rose to his feet, stretching his massive frame like a bear awakening from slumber. The movement triggered an immediate response from his warriors, who fell silent and watched their leader with expectant attention.

Without speaking, Cadoc began a slow circuit of the grove, moving from prisoner to prisoner with deliberate, unhurried steps. His son followed a few paces behind, watching intently, absorbing every aspect of what was clearly an established ritual.

The chieftain stopped first before Rullus, studying the Roman with cold detachment. Rullus met his gaze defiantly, jaw clenched, refusing to show fear despite the tremor visible in his bound hands. Cadoc observed him for a long moment before moving on without comment.

Next came Vindex, barely conscious, his head lolling to one side as blood continued to seep from the wound where his face had been repeatedly slammed into the ground during their capture. Cadoc examined him briefly before placing his hand flat against the Roman's chest, directly over his heart. The touch was neither gentle nor rough, simply assessing, feeling the weakened beat beneath the scout's sweat-soaked tunic.

Apparently satisfied with what he felt, Cadoc barked a command in the Silures tongue and immediately, three warriors rushed forward to slice through the ropes binding Vindex to the stone, catching him as he slumped forward, barely conscious.

'No!' Titus shouted from across the clearing. 'Take me instead! I am their leader!'

His words went ignored as the warriors dragged Vindex toward the central altar. Unlike Geta or Rullus, Vindex was too weak from his earlier injuries to offer even token resistance, and his feet dragged across the forest floor, leaving twin furrows in the soft earth. They forced him to his knees before the altar stone, two warriors gripping his arms while the third held his head up by the hair, ensuring he faced Cadoc.

Around them, the remaining Silures formed a loose circle, their faces expectant in the fading light. Someone had lit torches, mounting them on poles driven into the ground, creating a flickering illumination that made the blue woad patterns on their skin seem to writhe like living things.

Geta watched in silent horror, his earlier resignation temporarily overwhelmed by the immediate reality of what was about to happen. Beside him, he could hear Raurica's laboured breathing quicken with fear, while across the grove, Titus continued to shout ineffectually, demanding to be taken in place of his man.

Cadoc spoke at length, his deep voice carrying through the grove in what was clearly an address to his men, though his eyes remained fixed on Vindex throughout. Though Geta couldn't understand the words, he recognised the cadence of ritual speech, the formal tones of ceremony.

When he finished speaking, Cadoc turned to his son and gestured him forward.

'You are keen to blood your blade,' he said in the Silures tongue, his voice now pitched for his son alone. 'Now is the time.'

Bran stepped forward, his expression a complex mixture of fear and excitement. A bone-handled knife hung at his belt, smaller than the weapons carried by the adult warriors but still lethal in its design.

Vindex seemed to regain some awareness of his situation, his eyes widening as the boy approached with ceremonial slowness. A low moan escaped his lips, the sound more animal than human, as base survival instinct battled through his injuries and confusion.

Cadoc nodded once to his son, a simple gesture carrying the weight of generations of tradition. Without hesitation, Bran drew his knife and stepped directly in front of Vindex. The Roman's eyes rolled wildly, focusing briefly on the blade and as his eyes closed in terrified anticipation, Bran thrust the blade forward into his victim's abdomen, driving it in just below the ribcage with surprising strength. The Roman's body jerked at the impact, a strangled cry escaping him. With practised precision, just as he had been taught by his father, Bran angled the knife upward, slicing through vital organs in a single, deliberate movement.

Vindex's cry became a wet gurgle, blood foaming at his lips as the blade penetrated his diaphragm. His eyes flew open, unfocused with shock and agony, staring at nothing as his body registered the mortal wound.

Bran withdrew the blade and moved behind the dying Roman, and with one hand, he grasped Vindex's hair, pulling his head back before dragging the knife, now slick with blood across the Roman's throat in a single, decisive arc.

Hot blood pulsed from the severed vessels in Vindex's neck, spraying forward in diminishing spurts as his heart struggled to maintain pressure in a rapidly emptying system.

The warriors held onto him as his life drained onto the forest floor and Cadoc stepped forward, extending his right hand into the stream of blood. He allowed it to coat his palm and fingers before turning to his son and pressing his bloodied hand against the boy's face, covering it from forehead to chin in a hot, wet mask of the dying Roman's essence.

A cheer erupted from the gathered warriors, a sound of approval and acceptance as Bran stood motionless, accepting the blood blessing with appropriate gravity, his eyes now meeting his father's with new confidence. He had passed this test, had taken his first Roman life in proper accordance with tradition.

Across the grove, the remaining prisoners reacted with varying expressions of horror. Titus began reciting a soldier's prayer, the formal Latin phrases carrying clearly in the evening air. Rullus joined him, their voices twining together in the familiar ritual that had comforted countless legionaries facing death far from home. Raurica was beyond such comforts, too weak to do more than witness his comrade's end through pain-glazed eyes.

Geta remained silent, watching with a strange detachment born of shock and exhaustion. He had seen death many times death before, but never like this, never as a Celtic ritual, as ceremony.

As Vindex's blood soaked into the earth of the sacred grove, feeding roots that had drunk the offerings of countless sacrifices before him, his body gave a final shudder before going completely limp and the warriors lowered him to the ground as the last flickers of life faded from his eyes.

Bran, his face still masked with drying blood, stepped back from the body. He kept his knife in his hand, the blade glistening wetly in the torchlight. The gathered warriors approached him one by one, each placing a hand briefly on his shoulder in acknowledgment of his passage into their ranks.

Cadoc watched with obvious pride before turning his attention back to the remaining Romans. His gaze swept over them, Titus still praying fervently, Rullus now silent and white-faced, Raurica drifting in and out of consciousness, and Geta, who met his eyes unflinchingly despite the fear churning in his gut.

Darkness had now fallen completely, the torches providing the only illumination in the grove. The shadows of the warriors moved across the ground like spirits, elongated and distorted. Above, through gaps in the great leafy canopy, stars had begun to appear, cold and distant, offering neither comfort nor hope to the men bound below.

Cadoc and his son had moved to sit beside the central fire, speaking quietly together. Occasionally the boy would gesture with his hands, apparently describing some aspect of the killing he had just performed. His father listened attentively, nodding or shaking his head, clearly critiquing and teaching even in this most solemn of moments.

Geta's limbs had grown numb from prolonged immobility, the ropes cutting into his flesh with every slight movement. Across the clearing, Titus maintained his soldier's bearing despite his injuries, his face set in grim determination. Raurica hung limply against his bindings, his laboured breathing the only indication he still lived, while Rullus stared blankly ahead, his mind seemingly retreating from the horror of their situation.

Two of their number were already gone, Lentulus with his neck snapped for his incessant crying, and Vindex sacrificed in the blood ritual that had initiated Cadoc's son into manhood. The silent question that hung in the air was unmistakable: who would be next?

The answer came with a sharp command from Cadoc. He stood and called out something in the Silures tongue, his voice echoing through the forest. Almost immediately, shadows moved at the edge of the clearing, not warriors this time, but handlers leading four massive hounds that strained against thick leather leashes.

The dogs were unlike any hunting breed Geta had seen in Rome's territories, larger, with powerful chests and jaws that seemed designed for tearing rather than merely holding prey. Their coats were brindled black and brown, and their eyes reflected the torchlight with an eerie amber glow. They pulled frantically at their restraints, low growls rumbling from their throats as they scented the blood already spilled.

'They're going to hunt us,' Rullus whispered, a flicker of desperate hope animating his features for the first time in hours. 'If they cut us loose and set the dogs after us, at least we'll have a chance.'

Geta wasn't so certain. The handler made no move toward any of them, instead keeping the straining hounds at the edge of the clearing. Something in the calculated way Cadoc observed them suggested a different purpose for the animals.

Titus caught Geta's eye across the grove, a silent communication passing between them. They had both seen enough tribal warfare to know that whatever came next would be far worse than a simple hunt through the forest. The Silures had demonstrated too much ritual precision in their actions thus far to suddenly resort to something so straightforward.

Cadoc nodded to one of his warriors and the man drew a long knife from his belt before approaching Raurica, whose head lolled forward, barely conscious. For a brief, hopeful moment, it seemed he might indeed cut the scout free, as his knife moved toward the bindings at Raurica's wrists. Then, with a swift, practised motion, he swung the blade in a horizontal arc across Raurica's exposed abdomen.

The slash was deep and precise, parting tunic, skin and muscle in one clean stroke. Raurica's eyes flew open in shock and agony as his intestines bulged from the massive wound, held in only by the thin membrane that contained them. Blood poured down his legs, splashing onto the forest floor in a steaming pool.

Before the echo of Raurica's agonised scream had faded, the warrior moved to Rullus, who twisted desperately against his bonds in blind terror.

'No! Please…'

The knife flashed again, opening Rullus from hip to hip with the same terrible efficiency. His scream joined Raurica's, the combined sound echoing through the sacred grove like the wails of tormented spirits.

Only now did the true purpose of the hounds become horrifyingly clear and at a signal from Cadoc, the handlers released their leashes.

The dogs surged forward in a bounding mass of muscle and teeth, drawn unerringly to the scent of fresh blood and exposed viscera. They reached the wounded men in seconds, leaping up with savage eagerness to tear at the soft, steaming organs that bulged from the gaping wounds.

Raurica's weakened body offered little resistance and two of the hounds ripped into his abdomen, their powerful jaws shredding the membrane that contained his intestines. With wet, tearing sounds, they dragged his entrails forth in steaming coils, fighting amongst themselves for the grisly feast. His screams degraded into gurgling moans as shock pain and blood loss mercifully began to dull his awareness.

Rullus fought longer, his stronger constitution prolonging his suffering. He screamed desperately at the dogs attacking him, but bound as he was, his efforts were futile. The hounds tore through the wall of his abdomen, burrowing their muzzles into the wound to drag out loops of intestine that they shook and fought over like macabre prizes. His screams became more frantic, more animal, a sound of pure terror and agony beyond language or coherent thought.

The Silures watched impassively, neither encouraging nor restraining the hounds. This was not sport for them, but something more ritualistic, a blood offering to whatever ancient forces they believed dwelled in this sacred place.

Geta forced himself to watch, even as bile rose in his throat. Some small, detached part of his mind noted that Bran, the boy who had killed Vindex with such ritual composure, now looked distinctly unsettled. The clinical precision of the sacrificial killing was one thing; this savage tearing apart of living men was clearly another. The boy's eyes were wide, his earlier confidence replaced by shock at the raw brutality unfolding before him.

Titus had turned his face away, eyes squeezed shut, lips moving in what might have been prayer. The veteran scout, who had faced countless battles without flinching, could not bear to witness the inhuman ends of his men.

The cacophony of agonised screams gradually diminished as Raurica and Rullus finally succumbed, and the only sounds remaining were the wet tearing of flesh and the guttural growls of the hounds as they fought over the last scraps of the grisly feast.

When it was over and the two Romans hung lifeless in their bonds, Cadoc called out sharply. The handlers stepped forward, dragging the reluctant dogs away from their bloody meal and led back to the edge of the clearing, where they were again secured.

An oppressive silence fell over the grove, broken only by the dripping of blood onto the forest floor. Four of the six Romans who had entered the sacred place were now dead, each in a manner more terrible than the last.

Cadoc turned his gaze toward the two survivors, Geta and Titus. In his cold, assessing eyes was the unspoken promise that their ends would be no less agonising than those of their comrades. The only question that remained was what form their deaths would take and which of them would be forced to watch the other die first

----

Chapter Fourteen

The Hillfort

The great hall of the Eagle Clan blazed with light and warmth as dozens of torches mounted in iron brackets provided the light and multiple hearth fires burning at strategic intervals supplied the heat. Unlike the roundhouses that dominated the rest of the hillfort, this structure was rectangular, nearly a hundred feet in length and half that in width, its high-peaked roof supported by massive oak pillars carved with intricate spirals and animal forms that seemed to writhe in the flickering light.

Veteranus and Adgennus were led to their places midway down one of the long trestle tables that ran the length of the hall. Their position, neither too close to the high table where Bodvoc would sit, nor too far away to suggest disrespect, perfectly reflected their status as valued traders but still outsiders. Around them, the hall gradually filled with Ordovices nobility and warriors, each clan group distinguishable by subtle variations in their clothing and ornamentation.

'The Bear Clan is well-represented tonight,' Adgennus observed quietly, nodding toward a group of powerfully built men and women whose tunics were adorned with bear claw pendants. 'Their chief, has been challenging Bodvoc's leadership at council meetings so his presence here suggests some political manoeuvring is underway.'

Veteranus noted the information without comment, his eyes continuing to scan the gathering. He counted at least sixty warriors of fighting age, many bearing the scars of recent combat. These were not ceremonial guards but battle-hardened fighters, men who had survived the harsh realities of tribal warfare. The women, too, carried themselves with the confident bearing of those who knew how to handle weapons, a common trait among the western tribes, where necessity often required all members to defend their holdings.

Slaves moved efficiently through the gathering, carrying platters of food and jugs of drink. The feast being laid out would have impressed even Roman sensibilities with haunches of venison, roasted boar, countless loaves of dark bread, wooden bowls brimming with autumn berries, and tall vessels of what Adgennus had identified as heather mead, the potent honey-based drink that was a specialty of the region.

Before anyone started the food, a series of horn blasts silenced the crowd and all eyes turned to the main entrance, where Bodvoc now stood, resplendent in ceremonial attire. He wore a tunic of fine-woven wool dyed a deep blue, over which a cloak adorned with Eagle feathers across his massive shoulders. The gold torc around his neck gleamed in the torchlight, and his beard had been elaborately braided with threads of gold and silver. Behind him stood a line of druids in white robes, their faces solemn beneath crowns of oak leaves.

The crowd parted as Bodvoc moved through the hall to the high table. There, he remained standing, raising a drinking horn carved from aurochs bone and plated with silver.

'We welcome those who come in peace to share our bounty,' he declared in the trading tongue, ensuring all guests could understand. 'May the gods witness our hospitality and bless this gathering.'

The assembled Ordovices raised their own vessels in response and a rumble of approval rippled through the crowd. Bodvoc drank deeply before taking his seat, signalling the formal beginning of the feast.

Conversation and movement resumed immediately.

Servants hurried to fill plates and cups, while musicians in one corner began playing a rhythmic tune on bone flutes and stretched hide drums. The atmosphere was one of controlled revelry, celebratory but watchful, as befitted a people for whom feasts were not merely social occasions but political forums.

'Remember,' Adgennus cautioned quietly as he reached for his mead cup, 'drink sparingly.'

Veteranus nodded, though such advice was unnecessary. He had never been one to lose control, particularly not in potentially hostile territory and as the feast progressed, he observed the dynamics of the gathering with careful attention. The various clan factions seemed to be maintaining polite distance from each other, with occasional representatives moving between groups in what were clearly diplomatic exchanges.

After the initial courses had been consumed, Veteranus was surprised to see Bodvoc himself approaching their table. The conversations around them hushed as the chieftain stopped directly opposite them, flanked by two of his personal guard.

'Adgennus of the Aedui,' Bodvoc acknowledged with a nod. 'Your trading caravans have always brought quality goods to our hills.' His gaze shifted to Veteranus, more penetrating now. 'And your Roman companion... Lucius, was it? You are new to our lands.'

Both men rose respectfully, though Veteranus noticed that Bodvoc made no gesture for them to sit again, forcing them to remain standing, a subtle reminder of the power dynamic at play.

'Great Bodvoc,' Adgennus replied with a careful bow. 'We are honoured by your attention. Indeed, this is my associate's first journey to the western territories.'

'And what brings a Roman merchant so far from the

comforts of your eastern settlements?' Bodvoc asked, his tone conversational but his eyes sharp with assessment. 'The journey is long and not without dangers.'

'Opportunity,' said Veteranus smoothly. 'New markets and new trading partners. Rome has much to offer the peoples of the west.'

Bodvoc's lips twitched in what might have been amusement or scepticism.

'Indeed? And what does Rome offer beyond what we already possess?'

'Stability,' Veteranus replied without hesitation. 'Security of trade routes. Access to goods from across the empire, wine from Hispania, glassware from Syria, textiles from Egypt.' He paused briefly. 'And of course, protection.'

'Protection?' Bodvoc repeated, his voice cooling noticeably. 'From whom do the Ordovices need protection, Roman?'

Around them, the hall had grown quieter as nearby warriors sensed the tension in their chief's voice. Adgennus shifted uncomfortably beside Veteranus, but maintained his silence, recognising that the conversation had moved beyond mere trade talk.

'All peoples need protection in uncertain times,' Veteranus continued calmly. 'The situation in Britannia is changing rapidly. Those who align themselves with Rome prosper. Those who resist... face more difficult futures.'

The veiled threat hung in the air between them. Several of Bodvoc's warriors stiffened, hands drifting toward weapons, but the chieftain himself remained impassive.

'I have watched Rome's pattern of protection before,' he said eventually. 'First come the traders, then the diplomats, then the soldiers. Soon, those who were once friends are paying

129

tribute to foreign masters.' He shook his head slowly. 'The Ordovices have held these mountains since before Rome was a collection of mud huts on a distant river. We have no need of your protection.'

'Trade benefits all parties,' Veteranus countered. 'It need not lead to conflict.'

'Yet it so often does,' Bodvoc observed. 'Tell me, merchant, can you promise that Rome will leave the Ordovices to our own ways? That we will maintain our sovereignty over these mountains that have been ours since time beyond memory?'

This was the critical moment, the question that cut to the heart of Rome's expansion. Veteranus knew that honesty, however diplomatic, was his only viable approach. Bodvoc was too shrewd to be deceived by empty assurances.

'I cannot make such promises,' he admitted. 'I am but a trader, not a diplomat or general. But I can say this, peaceful trade is always preferable to war. For all parties.'

Bodvoc studied him for a long moment, his expression unreadable.

'At least you speak truth, Roman. Yet you must understand, paying tribute to an invader, however it might be disguised as 'trade,' runs counter to all our beliefs. The old gods would turn their faces from us if we surrendered what they entrusted to our keeping.'

'The old gods care for the prosperity of their people,' Veteranus suggested. 'Surely they would not wish to see their followers suffer needlessly.'

'You presume to know the will of gods you do not worship,' Bodvoc replied, though without anger. 'Our druids tell us the old ones value courage and independence above comfort. These mountains have sustained us for uncounted generations. They will continue to do so, with or without your Roman goods.'

The conversation might have continued in this vein, the diplomatic dance of two cultures circling each other, seeking common ground while maintaining their positions. But fate intervened in the form of a sudden commotion at the hall's entrance.

A young warrior burst through the doorway, his face flushed with exertion, his breathing laboured as if he had run a great distance. The assembled feast-goers turned in surprise, such an interruption being a serious breach of protocol. The newcomer ignored the stares, pushing his way directly toward the group of druids seated near Bodvoc's high table.

Reaching the eldest of the white-robed figures, he bent low, whispering urgently in the man's ear. Whatever message he delivered had an immediate effect, and the druid's expression transformed from mild annoyance at the interruption to stark concern.

The hall had fallen completely silent now, all eyes fixed on the unfolding scene. The druid rose slowly to his feet, his aged frame seeming to carry a new burden as he approached Bodvoc. He leaned close to the chieftain, speaking in tones too low for others to hear, but the effect of his words was visible in Bodvoc's face, first surprise, then anger, finally a cold, focused intensity that transformed his features.

During this exchange, Veteranus noticed the messenger staring directly at him from across the hall. There was something in the young warrior's gaze and a chill of premonition ran through Veteranus. Something had changed, fundamentally and irrevocably.

Bodvoc straightened, his decision made. With a single sharp gesture, he silenced the murmuring that had begun to spread through the hall.

'The feast is concluded,' he announced suddenly, his voice carrying the unmistakable tone of command. 'All will return to their dwellings until the council has met.'

Confusion rippled through the crowd, but none dared question the abrupt dismissal. Warriors and clan members began filing out, their expressions puzzled but obedient. Bodvoc himself turned without another word to Veteranus or Adgennus, striding toward a side entrance with the druids in close attendance.

Adgennus gathered their cloaks, clearly relieved that the tense conversation had been interrupted.

'Come,' he murmured to Veteranus. 'We should return to our quarters until whatever this is has been resolved.'

Chapter Fifteen

The Sacred Grove

The night had grown deeper as stars wheeled overhead in their eternal dance, visible in patches through the ancient canopy. The torchlight cast grotesque shadows across the clearing, transforming the standing stones into looming sentinels witnessing the night's horrors with impassive silence.

Cadoc stood at the centre of the grove, his massive frame silhouetted against the central fire. Blood stained his arms to the elbows, spattered across his chest and face in ritual patterns more terrible than any woad design. His eyes moved deliberately between the two remaining Romans, assessing them with the cold calculation of a butcher selecting his next carcass.

Geta and Titus stared back at him, their faces gaunt with exhaustion and terror, yet somehow defiant still. They had watched their comrades die in ways that would haunt them through whatever remained of their lives, yet somehow both men clung to the last shreds of their dignity.

Titus straightened against his bonds as much as they would allow, his jaw set in determination.

'If you're going to kill me, get on with it,' he said in Latin, his voice surprisingly steady. 'I am a soldier of Rome. I do not fear death.'

Though Cadoc couldn't understand his words, he recognized the challenge in the Roman's tone. A flicker of something like respect crossed his features before his expression hardened once more, and with a single, decisive gesture, pointed directly at him.

Two warriors immediately moved forward, drawing

knives to cut through the ropes that bound the Roman scout to the standing stone. Titus's legs buckled as he was released, the circulation returning painfully to his numb limbs. He made a half-hearted attempt to struggle, but his battered body betrayed him, and the warriors caught him easily, dragging him toward the stone altar at the centre of the grove.

Across the clearing, Geta watched in helpless horror, knowing he would be forced to witness yet another death before facing his own. Part of him wished for the mercy of unconsciousness, but some deeper soldier's instinct kept him alert, observing even now, as if by bearing witness he could somehow honour his comrades' suffering.

The Silures warriors worked with practiced efficiency. They bound Titus's ankles together with a length of heavy rope, the other end of which they threw over a thick branch that extended above the altar stone. Several men heaved on the rope, pulling until Titus dangled upside down, suspended over the stone table where the feast had been laid, his face reddening as blood rushed to his head.

Cadoc stepped forward, speaking words in the Silures tongue that rose and fell like a chant. The assembled warriors responded in kind, their voices forming a low, rhythmic backdrop to the ceremony. Around the grove, the torchlight seemed to flicker in time with their words, as if the very air responded to their invocation.

One of the older warriors, his face so heavily marked with woad that his features were nearly obscured, raised his arms toward the star-flecked sky visible through the canopy. His voice rose above the others, calling out to unseen forces in words that seemed ancient even compared to the language of his fellows.

Geta couldn't understand the words, but their meaning

was unmistakable, an offering to hungry gods, a sacrifice of enemy blood to feed powers that had dwelled in these woods since before Rome was founded.

The warrior lowered his arms suddenly, drawing a gleaming blade from his belt. The knife was unlike the iron weapons they had used before, this one appeared to be obsidian, its edge honed to a lethal sharpness that caught the torchlight in sinister reflections.

Titus made no sound as the warrior approached. His eyes remained open, fixed on some distant point beyond the physical world, perhaps already preparing his spirit for the journey to whatever afterlife awaited a Roman soldier who died far from home.

The movement when it came was swift and precise, a single, practiced slash that opened Titus's throat from ear to ear. Arterial blood erupted in a pressurized spray, splashing across the altar stone and the remains of the ritual feast. Titus's body jerked violently in its suspended position, a reflexive response rather than conscious struggle.

Without hesitation, the warrior placed his hands against Titus's shoulders and pushed, setting the dying man's body swinging in a pendulum motion. With each pass over the altar, more blood rained down, splattering the stone and food in a grotesque baptism. The warriors watched in reverent silence as the lifeblood of their enemy sanctified their sacred space.

As Titus's swinging body began to slow, his blood reduced to a weak drip onto the stone altar below, Geta watched in mute horror. The last of his comrades was gone, leaving him alone among these silent, methodical killers.

All hope had drained from him now. He leaned against the standing stone he was bound to, no longer straining against ropes that had rubbed his wrists raw. Whatever came next would come; he had no strength left to fight it.

Cadoc turned toward him, his face impassive beneath the blood and woad patterns. The Silures chieftain approached with deliberate, unhurried steps, his footfalls making almost no sound on the forest floor. He stopped directly before Geta, close enough that the Roman could smell the metallic scent of blood, the earthy musk of sweat, and something older, embedded in the wolf fur draped across his shoulders.

The chieftain's eyes bored into Geta's, studying him with the intensity of a predator. The moment stretched, seeming to Geta to last hours though it could only have been minutes. The Roman felt himself being weighed, assessed, his worth determined not as a man but as something else, a message, perhaps, or a warning.

Unable to bear the silence any longer, Geta rasped,

'What are you waiting for? Get on with it.'

Cadoc didn't respond, but instead turned and gestured to one of his warriors, a leaner man with intricate spiral patterns tracing from his forehead to jaw. This warrior stepped forward, eyes fixed on Geta with calculated interest.

'You alone did not eat from the table,' the warrior said in broken Latin, each word carefully formed as though rarely used. 'For this reason, you will live.'

Geta blinked in disbelief, certain he had misheard.

'What?' he managed, his voice barely a whisper.

'You will live,' the warrior repeated, his accent struggling with the strange words. 'Our chief has decided.'

Astonishment flooded through Geta. The gods must be watching over him after all, though what he had done to deserve their favour, he couldn't fathom.

The warrior continued, gesturing to the bodies of Geta's fallen comrades.

'You must look around. Remember everything you have seen in this grove. Every death. Every drop of blood. You will tell your people what awaits them if they come to our lands.'

Geta nodded slowly, understanding dawning through his exhaustion. They were setting him free not from mercy, but as a messenger, a living warning to Rome of what waited in these ancient forests.

'You will be cut loose,' the warrior explained, his eyes never leaving Geta's face. 'Taken to the northern border. Given food and water. Set free near a village of your kind. You will tell this tale. You must remember it all.'

Geta nodded more eagerly now, hope rising painfully in his chest. He would live. He would see the sun again, feel wind on his face without the shadow of imminent death hanging over him.

The warrior paused, studying him with unsettling intensity. Cadoc stood silently beside him, his expression unchanged, watching the exchange with the patience of a hunter.

'You were chosen,' the warrior said finally. 'Few men leave this grove alive.' He paused, his face betraying nothing. 'But there are two things you cannot take with you.'

Geta frowned, confusion cutting through his relief. 'What things?'

The warrior's expression remained impassive as he answered:

'Your eyes.'

Before the word had fully registered, two Silures warriors stepped forward, pinning Geta against the standing stone and as understanding crashed through him like ice water, the interpreter drew a long, thin knife from his belt.

'*No!*' Geta shouted, struggling uselessly against the iron grip of his captors. '*No! Please!*'

The knife moved closer, its edge gleaming in the torchlight and the last thing Geta saw was the expressionless face of Cadoc watching from behind the interpreter's shoulder, observing this final act without emotion or hesitation.

Seconds later, Geta's screams echoed across the sacred grove, rising above the ancient trees to a sky that offered neither comfort nor mercy, only the cold, distant light of uncaring stars.

Chapter Sixteen

The Forests of Siluria

Darkness enveloped the forest like a living thing, a presence that seemed to swallow light itself. The dense canopy of ancient oaks and yew blocked even the faintest starlight, creating a blackness so complete that the men of the Occultum could barely see their hands before their faces. The forest floor, treacherous with roots and hidden obstacles, became a maze they navigated more by touch than sight.

Seneca paused, allowing his eyes to adjust as much as they could to the oppressive darkness. The air hung heavy with moisture, thick with the scent of decomposing leaves and the musty perfume of fungi that thrived in the perpetual twilight beneath these ancient trees. Somewhere distant, an owl called, a lone, plaintive sound that seemed to emphasize their isolation in this hostile territory.

'Hold,' he whispered, the command passing down the line from man to man.

The navigation techniques they had relied upon in other territories, following stars, tracking the moon's position, were nearly useless here in Terra Siluria, where the forest canopy formed an almost unbroken ceiling above them. Even during daylight, the sun appeared only as occasional dappled patterns across the forest floor, offering little guidance for maintaining direction.

Necessity had forced them to adopt slower, more primitive methods. Seneca scanned what little he could see of the terrain ahead, finally selecting a distinctive tree, its trunk split near the base into two massive stems that formed a rough V-shape against the marginally lighter background.

'Reference point marked,' he murmured. 'Talorcan, advance.'

The Belgic scout nodded silently and moved forward, passing the reference tree and continuing until he was nearly lost from sight in the darkness. Seneca remained stationary, watching as Talorcan's silhouette became a barely discernible shadow. When the scout could advance no further without losing visual contact, he began carefully shifting position, moving left then right in small increments until Seneca signalled that he was perfectly aligned with the reference tree.

'Hold position,' Seneca called softly

Marcus moved past Talorcan, repeating the process, advancing, then aligning himself with both Talorcan and the reference tree as viewed from Seneca's position. It was painstaking work, each man becoming a living marker in a human chain that maintained their westward course through the trackless forest.

This leapfrogging technique was achingly slow, allowing them perhaps a mile of progress in an hour of careful movement, but it was their only reliable method in the absence of celestial navigation.

'We need to find a break in the canopy,' Decimus muttered during one such repositioning. 'Just a glimpse of the stars. Without it, we're blind.'

'The cloud cover is too thick tonight anyway,' Seneca replied. 'Even if we found a clearing, we'd see nothing useful.'

They continued their laborious progress, each man concentrating on maintaining the fragile alignment that kept them moving consistently westward, or what they hoped was westward, given the circumstances. The silence of the forest was unnerving, broken only by the occasional distant call of night creatures and the soft sounds of their own careful movements.

Hours passed in this manner, the men growing increasingly fatigued not just from the physical strain of navigating difficult terrain in darkness, but from the constant mental focus required by their navigation method. Every step demanded attention, every tree and shadow needed evaluation.

They reached a section where the undergrowth thinned slightly, allowing marginally better visibility and Seneca seized the opportunity to increase their pace, selecting reference points more quickly and allowing the men to advance with greater confidence.

Sica had moved past Decimus to establish the next position in their human chain, when he suddenly cried out, vanishing from sight as if swallowed by the forest itself.

The remaining members of the Occultum dropped immediately to one knee, lowering their profiles and drawing weapons in a synchronous movement born of years of training. They froze, listening for the sounds of an ambush, the whisper of a blade being drawn, the soft footfall of approaching enemies, but the forest remained unnaturally quiet.

'*Sica?*' hissed Seneca, his voice barely above a whisper, 'report.'

Silence answered him.

Seneca gestured for the others to follow and moved carefully forward, following the path Sica had taken. The darkness seemed to press against him again like a physical barrier, limiting his vision to mere feet ahead. He moved with exquisite care, testing each step before committing his weight.

'*Sica?*' he called again, softly.

Nothing.

He advanced further, straining his eyes against the darkness, when suddenly the ground beneath his forward foot simply disappeared. There was a moment of lurching vertigo as his body started to fall forward but instinctively he threw himself to one side and managed to stop himself from falling any further.

'Falco,' Seneca called frantically back to the following men. 'Stop. It's a cliff! I'm hanging from the edge!'

The footsteps behind him stopped abruptly, just short of the precipice.

'I can't see you. Where are you?'

'Two paces to your front on a forward slope. Reach down.'

He heard Falco lowering himself carefully to the ground.

'To your left,' Seneca directed, his voice strained as the ground began to give way under his weight. 'Slowly.'

A massive hand materialized out of the darkness, groping blindly. Seneca reached for it with his free arm, his fingers brushing against Falco's before the gladiator's grip closed around his wrist like an iron manacle.

'I've got you,' Falco murmured, and with a single powerful movement, he hauled Seneca up and over the edge to safety.

As they gathered at the edge of the cliff, the men of the Occultum tried to gauge the drop before them. The darkness was absolute, a void that seemed to continue forever below them.

Marcus lowered himself onto his stomach, inching forward until his head and shoulders extended just beyond the cliff edge.

'Sica!' he called, his voice kept deliberately low but projected downward. 'Sica, can you hear me?'

The silence that followed was broken only by small pieces of earth dislodged by Marcus's movement, tumbling into the darkness below. No sound of impact reached them, suggesting a considerable drop.

'Sica!' he tried again, desperation edging into his voice. 'Answer if you hear me!'

Still nothing.

Marcus turned his head slightly.

'I can't see anything. It's too dark to tell how far down it goes.'

'Try again,' said Seneca, his tone tight with concern.

Marcus drew a deep breath.

'*SICA!*' he called slightly louder this time despite the risk.

Just as they were about to give up hope, a faint response drifted up from below.

'*Here.*' The voice was distant, strained, barely audible.

'He's alive!' Marcus reported over his shoulder, relief flooding through him. He turned back to the cliff edge. 'Are you injured? Can you climb up?'

A moment passed before the response came, each word seemingly forced out with great effort.

'Caught... on tree. Growing... from cliff. Branch... breaking.'

Marcus visualized the precarious situation, Sica suspended in darkness, clinging to a tree that had somehow managed to grow horizontally from the cliff face, its roots now pulling free under his weight. There might be mere moments before it gave way completely.

'Falco,' said Marcus sharply, turning back to the group. 'The rope. *Quickly!*'

Falco was already in motion, shrugging off his sarcina and extracting the coiled rope they carried for just such emergencies.

'How far down is he?' asked Falco, passing it to Marcus.

'Can't tell,' replied Marcus, securing one end of the rope around a nearby tree trunk with a quick, practiced knot. 'Sica!' he called down again. 'We're throwing a rope. Can you reach it?'

The response was even fainter now.

'I'll try. You need to hurry.'

With the free end of the rope gripped tightly in his fist, Marcus positioned himself at the cliff edge.

'Ready,' he announced, and cast the rope outward and downward, letting it uncoil into the darkness below.

The men held their breath, straining to hear any indication that the rope had reached its target. Seconds stretched into what felt like minutes, the silence oppressive.

'Sica?' called Marcus. 'Do you have the rope?'

'No,' came the faint reply, followed by a cracking sound that carried clearly up the cliff face. 'Tree... giving way.'

Fifty feet below, Sica clung to the failing tree with every ounce of his remaining strength. He had landed on it during his fall, the impact driving the breath from his lungs.

The tree groaned beneath him. He could feel it shifting, the roots gradually tearing free from their tenuous hold in the rock face. Small cascades of dirt and stone showering down into the void below with each subtle movement.

His hands, normally steady even in the most desperate situations, were beginning to cramp from the sustained effort of gripping the increasingly unstable branch. Below him was only darkness, a fall of unknown depth that almost certainly promised death.

He heard Marcus's voice from above, distant but clear enough. The rope was coming again. He scanned the darkness above, seeing nothing but the faintest differentiation between the cliff face and the night sky beyond.

The tree shifted again, a more violent movement accompanied by the sound of splintering wood and tearing roots. Sica felt himself dropping several inches as the tree's anchor began to fail catastrophically.

Something whised through the air nearby, the rope descending, but not close enough to reach. He couldn't risk releasing one hand to grab for it, not with the tree on the verge of collapse.

'Missed,' he called upward. 'Further left.'

The tree gave another lurch, dropping several more inches, now angled sharply downward. Roots tore free with sounds like snapping bones, and Sica's body slid forward toward the end of the branch.

He locked his knees around the wood, using the last of his strength to maintain his position. If the rope didn't reach him on this attempt...

Something brushed against his arm, the rope, swinging in the darkness. Without hesitation, Sica released one hand from the branch, his body immediately shifting precariously with the movement and he grasped blindly in the direction where he had felt the contact and as the tree gave a final, splitting crack, the remaining roots tearing free from the cliff face all at once, his fingers closed around the rope, gripping with desperate strength as the tree fell away into the darkness below.

Above, the men felt the sudden weight come onto the rope and braced themselves.

'Got him!' Decimus called, feeling the distinctive tug. 'Pull!'

Together, they hauled on the rope, Falco's massive

strength leading the effort. The hemp creaked under the strain but held firm as they drew their comrade upward from the abyss.

Seneca and Talorcan lay flat at the cliff edge, reaching down as Sica's form finally emerged from the darkness. His face was a mask of pain and determination, both hands now locked around the rope.

They seized him under the arms, pulling him over the edge to safety and Sica collapsed onto the forest floor, his breathing shallow and rapid, his face glistening with sweat.

Seneca knelt beside him, hands moving carefully over Sica's torso, assessing the damage.

'I can't feel anything broken,' he said. 'But you're lucky to be alive.'

Sica managed a pained grimace that might have been an attempt at a smile.

'Luck had nothing to do with it. Perhaps the Syrian gods are more powerful than the roman ones.'

Falco coiled the rope with quick, efficient movements.

'That was too close,' he muttered, glancing back toward the cliff edge. 'We almost lost you.'

'We've gone far enough for tonight,' Seneca decided, looking around at his exhausted men. 'We need to find somewhere defensible and rest until dawn.' He glanced at Sica. 'Can you move?'

The Syrian assassin nodded once, though the effort clearly cost him.

'Falco, help him,' Seneca directed. 'Marcus, take point. No more than twenty paces ahead, and test every step. The last thing we need is to find another drop like this one.'

As they moved away from the cliff edge, retracing their steps with even greater caution than before, Seneca felt a chill that had nothing to do with the night air. They had been lucky, Sica could easily have disappeared into that darkness forever. In this hostile territory, where the very land seemed to conspire against them, such luck might not hold a second time.

In Terra Siluria they were intruders in an ancient domain, and whether by the hand of its inhabitants or the treacherous nature of the land itself, he sensed that the forest would exact a price for their trespass before their mission was complete.

Chapter Seventeen

The Hillfort

The roundhouse felt smaller with each passing hour, its curved walls seeming to contract around them like a slowly tightening noose. For two days, Veteranus and Adgennus had been confined to this single space, their status transformed from honoured guests to suspicious prisoners with no explanation offered.

Veteranus paced the circumference of the roundhouse for what must have been the hundredth time. Each circuit brought him past the doorway where two grim-faced warriors stood guard, their spears crossed to prevent exit. They had not spoken a single word since being posted there the morning after the abruptly ended feast.

'This is becoming intolerable,' Adgennus muttered, seated on one of the sleeping platforms, his normally composed demeanour showing signs of strain. 'They at least owe us an explanation.'

Veteranus paused in his pacing.

'Something has changed dramatically. The question is what, and why it affects us.'

'That messenger,' Adgennus said thoughtfully. 'The one who interrupted the feast. He looked directly at you after speaking with the druids.'

'I noticed that as well,' admitted Veteranus, 'but I have no idea why.'

A warrior approached the doorway, carrying a wooden tray with two bowls of stew and a small loaf of bread. One of the guards accepted it, then entered the roundhouse to deliver the food before resuming his position without a word.

Adgennus inspected the meal suspiciously.

'At least they're still feeding us. Not the fare of the feast, but adequate.'

'They need us alive for something,' Veteranus concluded, taking a bowl of the stew. It was simple fare, root vegetables and some unidentifiable meat in a thin broth, but nourishing enough. 'The question is what.'

'The Brigantes-Ordovices alliance should protect them from any northern threats,' Adgennus mused. 'And the Silures haven't mounted a significant attack this far north in years.'

'Unless something has changed the situation,' Veteranus countered. 'A new threat, or intelligence that demands immediate action.'

They fell silent as a party of warriors passed close to their roundhouse, their voices raised in what sounded like heated debate. Though they couldn't make out the words clearly, the tone suggested disagreement over some significant decision.

As evening approached on their second day of confinement, Veteranus began to consider options for escape. The roundhouse walls, though sturdy, were constructed of wattle and daub that might be breached with sufficient effort. The roof thatch could also potentially be parted to create an exit but either approach would make noise, however, and could alert the guards.

'If they meant to kill us, they would have done so already,' Adgennus reasoned, seeming to read Veteranus's thoughts. 'We have more value to them alive, at least for now.'

'As hostages, perhaps,' Veteranus suggested. 'Or as sources of information.'

'Information about what?' Adgennus asked. 'They know I'm a trader.

Before Veteranus could respond, sounds of approach interrupted their conversation. Not the usual soft tread of a single warrior bringing food, but the coordinated footfalls of multiple men. A moment later, the leather covering was thrust aside, and six warriors entered the roundhouse.

These were not the Eagle Clan guards who had watched over them for the past two days. These men bore different tattoo patterns, angular designs that covered not just their faces but extended down their necks and across their exposed forearms. Their expressions were hard, hostile, and they carried shorter, broader-bladed spears than those used by Bodvoc's men.

Without ceremony or explanation, two warriors seized Adgennus while three more surrounded Veteranus. Their grip was not gentle, fingers dug into muscle with deliberate force, a clear message that resistance would be met with immediate violence.

'What is the meaning of this?' Adgennus demanded, his trader's dignity reasserting itself despite their circumstances. 'We are guests of Bodvoc!'

The warriors ignored him completely, forcing both men toward the doorway and out into the fading evening light. The central area of the hillfort was now crowded with warriors from multiple clans, their distinct tattoo patterns and clothing styles marking them as representatives from across the Ordovices territories. All eyes turned to watch as Veteranus and Adgennus were marched across the open space toward the great hall.

The atmosphere was filled with tension, faces grim and weapons prominently displayed. Whatever gathering had been called, it was clearly not a social occasion. This was a war council, or something very much like it.

They were pushed roughly through the entrance of the

great hall, which had been transformed since the feast. The long tables had been removed, and in their place, a large circle of stones had been arranged on the packed earth floor. At its centre stood a single carved chair, more throne than seat, its oak frame adorned with Eagle heads and spiral patterns inlaid with silver.

Upon this chair sat Bodvoc, his massive frame now encased in full battle regalia, a mail shirt that reached to mid-thigh, vambraces of hammered bronze on both forearms, and a cloak of wolf fur secured with a brooch of gold and amber. His beard had been re-braided into a warrior's configuration, tight against his jaw and threaded with small iron rings.

Beside him stood the chief druid, his white robes contrasting sharply with the martial display around him. The old man's face was painted with symbols in blood-red ochre, patterns more complex than any Veteranus had seen before. In his right hand, he held a staff topped with a silver crescent moon, its surface inscribed with runes that caught the light from the hall's central fire.

As Veteranus and Adgennus were forced to their knees before this imposing tableau, the hall fell silent. Even the warriors who had brought them stepped back, forming a loose circle that effectively blocked any possibility of escape.

Bodvoc's eyes, cold and hard as iron, fixed upon them. The warmth and hospitality of the feast had vanished entirely, replaced by something ancient and implacable, the judgment of a tribal leader whose decision would mean life or death for those who knelt before him.

The druid stepped forward, his voice carrying clearly in the hushed hall.

'The gods have shown us the wolf in sheep's clothing,' he intoned, 'the trader who enters with honeyed words while

151

concealing the knife of treachery.'

The druid's piercing gaze bore into Veteranus, his voice taking on a harder edge.

'You are not who you say you are.'

Veteranus held the old man's stare, his face betraying nothing. Inside, his mind raced through possible responses, evaluating and discarding each option in an instant. He chose silence, the safest response when uncertain of the accusations.

The silence stretched, becoming a contest of wills between the Roman and the druid. Adgennus glanced sideways at his companion, confusion and growing concern evident in his expression.

When it became clear that Veteranus would not break the silence, the druid nodded to someone at the back of the hall. Footsteps approached from behind, and a man stepped into Veteranus's field of vision. With a jolt of recognition, Veteranus identified him as the messenger who had interrupted the feast, the young warrior who had stared at him with such certainty.

'Do you know who this is?' the druid asked, gesturing to the newcomer.

'No,' Veteranus replied evenly. 'I have never seen him before the feast.'

The druid's thin lips curved into a sneer.

'Tell him what you told me,' he instructed the warrior.

The young man stepped forward, his voice carrying clearly in the hushed hall.

'Many days ago, I was in the lands of the Boar Clan in the north. A delegation came from Mona and stayed outside the fort.' His eyes never left Veteranus's face as he spoke. 'They came seeking tribute for the druids, and the elders gave them two boys.'

Veteranus felt a cold weight settling in his stomach. He knew immediately where this account was leading.

'When they were taken out,' the man continued, 'their warriors lined up. This man was among them.' He pointed directly at Veteranus. 'He stood with the warriors of Mona.'

'Are you certain?' the druid pressed. 'Could there be a mistake?'

'There is no mistake,' the accuser replied firmly. 'I studied him hard, for the druid warriors never ride with foreigners. His face is unmistakable.'

The druid turned back to Veteranus, triumph evident in his ancient eyes.

'Is this true?'

Veteranus weighed his options rapidly. A direct lie would only deepen their suspicions and likely lead to more severe treatment. A partial truth might provide him room to manoeuvre.

'It is,' he admitted, his voice calm despite the growing tension in the hall.

A murmur ran through the assembled warriors as Adgennus's head snapped toward Veteranus, shock and betrayal written plainly across his features.

'Then you are a spy?' the druid pressed, his staff tapping the ground for emphasis.

'No,' Veteranus replied firmly. 'I was their prisoner, but their leader saw something in me and tried to recruit me into their clan. At first I was tempted for the life of the people in these lands appeals to me, but I was not sure. During that time they allowed me to come into the lands of the Ordovices on the day you speak of.'

'If that is true, how are you here now in the guise of a trader.'

'They allowed me to travel with a group of warriors to Camulodunum,' said Veteranus maintaining steady eye contact. 'Their task was to attack the Roman emperor, but we were attacked, and I survived. I then returned to the roman garrison at Camulodunum.'

'So why were you sent here?' Bodvoc spoke for the first time, his deep voice rumbling through the hall. 'What is your true purpose?'

'For exactly the same reasons I have already explained,' Veteranus insisted. 'To offer trade and to seek peace. They sent me because they knew I had been in these lands before and would perhaps understand your needs better.'

Adgennus stared at Veteranus in undisguised shock, the colour draining from his face.

'You never told me this,' he said, his voice barely above a whisper. 'I know nothing of this.'

The druid's eyes narrowed, studying Veteranus closely.

'I think you lie,' he said finally, his tone carrying the weight of judgment. 'You are a spy.' He turned to Bodvoc, who had watched the entire exchange in stern silence. 'He should face the wrath of the Ordovices.'

Bodvoc gave a single, curt nod, and immediately the warriors who had brought them stepped forward, dragging them both from the great hall and back toward their roundhouse prison.

This time, they were not simply deposited inside. Warriors forced them to the centre of the dwelling, where they were made to sit back-to-back. Thick hemp ropes were wound around them, binding their arms to their sides and securing them together.

As the warriors completed their task and withdrew, the last man paused at the doorway, turning back to regard the bound men with cold eyes.

'The council gathers to decide your fate,' he said in heavily accented trading tongue. 'Pray to your gods that they grant you a quick death.'

With that, he let the leather door covering fall back into place, leaving them alone in the growing darkness of the roundhouse.

For a long moment, neither man spoke. The only sound was their breathing, Adgennus's quick and shallow with shock and fear, Veteranus's measured and controlled despite their dire situation.

'You lied to me,' Adgennus said finally, his voice tight with anger and betrayal. 'All this time.'

'I told you what you needed to know,' Veteranus replied quietly. 'The rest would have only put you at greater risk.'

'And now?' Adgennus demanded bitterly. 'What risk am I at now, bound to a man they believe is a spy? A man who apparently travelled with druids from Mona, the same druids who have been calling for war against Rome across all of Britannia!'

Veteranus sighed, feeling the ropes shift slightly with the movement.

'My situation is... complicated.'

'*Complicated?*' Adgennus repeated incredulously. 'They're going to kill us both, and all you can say is that your situation is *'complicated'*?'

'They haven't decided that yet,' Veteranus pointed out. 'If they intended immediate execution, we would already be dead.'

'Small comfort,' Adgennus muttered. 'What were you really doing on Mona? And don't tell me more half-truths, I deserve the full story, given that I'm likely to die for it.'

Veteranus was silent for a moment, calculating what he could reveal that might help their situation without compromising his mission entirely. Before he could respond, however, a commotion outside the roundhouse caught their attention, raised voices, the sound of running feet, and the distinct notes of a horn call echoing across the hillfort.

'Something's happening,' Veteranus observed, straining to hear more clearly.

The sounds of activity increased, orders being shouted, the clash of weapons being distributed, the heavy tread of many feet moving with purpose. Whatever deliberations had been occurring regarding their fate had apparently been interrupted by something more urgent.

'If there's an attack,' Adgennus said, his voice lower now, 'they might kill us immediately as insurance against our escape or rescue.'

Veteranus nodded, though the gesture was invisible to his companion.

'We need to work on these bindings. Can you reach the knot?'

'I think so,' Adgennus replied, his fingers already exploring the ropes that bound them together. 'But it will take time.'

As darkness settled fully over the hillfort, the two men worked in silence at their bonds, listening to the growing sounds of preparation outside, the sounds of a people readying themselves for war.

Chapter Eighteen

The Hillfort

The hours stretched into the next day, each moment marked only by the shifting of light through the smoke hole and the increasing discomfort of their bonds. Their captors had not returned, neither with food nor water, a concerning development that suggested their status had been downgraded from valuable prisoners to forgotten inconveniences.

Thirst became their first torment, lips cracking and tongues swelling as they entered the second day of their confinement. Hunger followed, a gnawing emptiness that sapped their strength and sharpened their tempers.

'This is your doing,' Adgennus muttered during a particularly long silence on the afternoon of the second day. His voice had grown hoarse from thirst, each word seemingly painful to form. 'Your complicity has probably cost us our lives.'

'Had I told you everything,' replied Veteranus, 'you would have been complicit. Better you remained ignorant.'

'Better?' Adgennus gave a harsh laugh that dissolved into a dry cough. 'I am bound to die alongside you regardless. At least knowledge would have allowed me to make my own choices.'

Silence fell between them again, heavy with recrimination. Outside, the sounds of the hillfort continued, movement, voices, but no one approached their prison.

'What really happened on Mona?' Adgennus asked eventually, his anger giving way to a weary resignation. 'If I am to die for being associated with whatever you were doing, I deserve to know what it was.'

Veteranus remained silent, weighing how much to

reveal. His mission, even now, demanded discretion.

'Your silence confirms my suspicions,' Adgennus said bitterly. 'You were never a trader. Probably not even truly a Roman merchant. A spy, then? Or an assassin?'

'Believe what you will,' Veteranus replied neutrally. 'What matters now is survival.'

In truth, Veteranus's mind was occupied with calculations far removed from Adgennus's accusations. Throughout their captivity, he had been mapping the movements around the roundhouse, noting the changing of guards, the patterns of activity in the central area of the hillfort. He was plotting, not for explanations, but for escape.

The plan forming in his mind was desperate, with slim chances of success. It would likely cost him his life, but he had long ago accepted that possibility as an inevitable risk of his profession. Better to die fighting than be executed as a spy, his body left unburned, his spirit unable to find its way to whatever afterlife awaited.

By the morning of the third day, both men had lapsed into a state of semi-consciousness, their bodies weakened by dehydration. The ropes had chafed their wrists raw, and the cramped position had sent Adgennus's legs into painful spasms that he no longer had the strength to suppress.

Veteranus forced himself to remain alert despite his physical distress. He had identified mid-morning as the time when the hillfort's activity seemed at its lowest ebb, and if an opportunity for escape presented itself, it would likely come during those hours.

He was mentally rehearsing the sequence of movements that might break his bonds when the leather covering at the doorway was thrust aside. Three warriors entered, their expressions impassive as they surveyed the weakened prisoners.

One carried a clay jug of water and a loaf of coarse bread, items he set on the floor within reach of the bound men. Another drew a knife from his belt, approaching with obvious caution.

'If you struggle,' he said in broken trading tongue, 'you die now.' He indicated the third warrior, who had nocked an arrow to his bow, the weapon trained steadily on Veteranus's chest.

Veteranus nodded his understanding, keeping his movements slow and deliberate as the warrior cut through the ropes binding him to Adgennus. The relief of separation was immediate, blood flowing painfully back into compressed limbs. Though his arms remained bound to his sides, the ability to move independently was a significant improvement.

The warrior who had cut the ropes stepped back, gesturing toward the water and bread.

'Drink. Eat.'

Neither man needed further encouragement. They fell upon the offerings with desperate thirst and hunger, Veteranus forcing himself to drink slowly despite his body's demands for immediate relief. Too much water too quickly after prolonged dehydration could be as dangerous as none at all.

The bread was hard and simple, but felt like a feast after days without food. They ate in silence, watched impassively by their captors, who made no move to interfere or hurry them.

When they had finished, the warrior with the knife approached Adgennus, gesturing for him to stand. The Gaul struggled to his feet, his legs nearly buckling after so long in one position.

'You,' the warrior said, pointing at Adgennus. 'Come.'

Adgennus looked at Veteranus, confusion and fear evident in his exhausted features.

'Where are they taking me?'

'I don't know,' Veteranus admitted, meeting his companion's eyes directly for perhaps the first time since their capture. 'But they wouldn't have fed us if you was to be killed immediately.'

Adgennus nodded slowly, straightening his posture despite the pain it clearly caused him.

'And if I don't return?'

'Then I will remember you to whatever gods await us,' Veteranus replied simply.

The warriors retied Veteranus's bonds, checking them carefully to ensure he remained securely restrained. Then, with firm hands on Adgennus's shoulders, they guided the trader toward the doorway.

At the threshold, Adgennus paused, looking back at Veteranus.

'Despite everything,' he said quietly, 'I hope you find your way back to Rome, stranger. Whatever your true purpose here was.'

Before Veteranus could respond, the warriors ushered Adgennus out, the leather covering falling back into place behind them. Veteranus was left alone in the dimness of the roundhouse, his mind immediately returning to thoughts of escape now that he was freed from the additional complication of Adgennus's presence.

Several hours later, the leather door covering was thrust aside once more. Veteranus tensed, ready for whatever might come through, be it executioners or an opportunity.

To his astonishment, Adgennus was shoved roughly into the roundhouse, stumbling and falling to his knees on the packed earth floor. The trader's face was ashen, his eyes wide with what appeared to be shock rather than pain.

Two warriors followed him in, one keeping a spear trained on Veteranus while the other approached with a knife. Without explanation, the warrior cut Veteranus's bonds, the ropes falling away to reveal raw, bleeding furrows where they had chafed against his skin. Wordlessly, the guards withdrew, securing the leather covering behind them.

Veteranus rubbed his wrists, restoring circulation to his hands while studying Adgennus with cautious curiosity. The trader hadn't moved from where he'd fallen, his posture suggesting a man overwhelmed by whatever he had experienced outside the prison.

'I thought you were being taken to your death,' said Veteranus quietly, breaking the silence.

Adgennus looked up finally, moving with careful, pained movements to sit on the sleeping platform.

'We have a problem,' he said, his voice still hoarse from thirst despite the water they'd been given earlier. 'An important woman has been abducted.' He shook his head, still processing the information himself. 'The perpetrators were the Silures and though the Ordovices warriors followed their tracks, the trail has gone cold.'

'Why is that relevant to our situation?' asked Veteranus.

Adgennus met his gaze directly.

'Because the chieftain believes that you may be able to find her.'

'Me?'

'You,' Adgennus confirmed. 'And if you succeed, we will be allowed to live.'

Veteranus considered this carefully, searching for the trap.

'Even if I were to agree, what would prevent me from

simply disappearing into the woods and making my way back to Camulodunum once free of this hillfort?'

'Two reasons,' Adgennus replied. 'First, the rest of the trading column will be held hostage, and they'll all die if you fail to return.' He paused, his expression growing even more serious. 'But there's a far bigger reason, one that affects Rome directly.'

Veteranus waited, watching Adgennus's face closely.

'The abducted woman is Rhiannon,' said Adgennus with a sigh. 'Cartimandua's daughter. She was in the care of the Ordovices so if any harm comes to her, the Brigantes will probably declare war against them.'

Veteranus shrugged, though his mind was already racing with the implications.

'So what? Let them fight among themselves. It weakens both tribes.'

'You don't understand,' Adgennus insisted, leaning forward with sudden intensity. 'If there is war between the Ordovices and the Brigantes, as allies, Rome would have to support the Brigantes. That means the Ordovices would have no choice but to ally with Caratacus and potentially the Silures.'

The gravity of the situation became suddenly, starkly clear to Veteranus. Such an alliance would create a unified western resistance far more formidable than the isolated tribal conflicts Rome had exploited thus far.

'This would create an enormous problem,' Adgennus continued, giving voice to Veteranus's own thoughts. 'It would mean many more Romans would die in the coming months and years and the alliance could even be strong enough to drive Rome out of Britannia entirely.'

The words hung in the air between them, their weight almost palpable in the dimness of the roundhouse. Veteranus rose slowly to his feet, stretching his cramped muscles while his mind processed this new information. The strategic implications were undeniable, a war between Cartimandua and Bodvoc would reshape the political landscape of Britannia in ways profoundly unfavourable to Roman interests.

Adgennus watched him, seeming to read the calculations taking place behind his impassive expression.

'We can't allow that to happen, Veteranus,' he said quietly. 'We have to find her.'

Veteranus paced the perimeter of the roundhouse, feeling strength returning to his legs with each step. The situation presented both danger and opportunity. On one hand, venturing into Silures territory in search of the abducted woman was likely a suicide mission. On the other, it aligned perfectly with his original objective, to gather intelligence on the western tribes, particularly the Silures.

'What exactly does Bodvoc expect me to do?' he asked finally. ' I have no special knowledge of the Silures or their territories.'

'But you have operated in hostile territory before,' Adgennus pointed out. 'Your time with the druids from Mona proves that. You've demonstrated an ability to survive where others wouldn't.'

Veteranus stopped his pacing, turning to face Adgennus directly.

'And if I refuse?

'Then we die,' Adgennus said simply. 'All of us. And Rome faces a united western resistance that could cost thousands of legionary lives, possibly even the province itself.'

A tense silence filled the roundhouse as Veteranus weighed his options.

'How much time do we have to decide?' he asked.

'No time at all,' Adgennus replied grimly. 'The chieftain awaits your answer now. That's why they cut your bonds. Either you agree to attempt the rescue, or we return to our previous status as spies awaiting execution.'

Veteranus nodded slowly, his decision made. Whether by design or chance, fate had presented him with a path that guaranteed his life, at least for the immediate future.

'Tell Bodvoc I accept,' he said firmly. 'But I'll need weapons, supplies, and whatever information they can provide. I will also need a scout who knows the lands of the Silures.'

Adgennus's shoulders slumped with visible relief.

'Thank you,' he said quietly. 'I believe this is the right choice, for both of us and for Rome.'

'Don't thank me yet,' Veteranus cautioned. 'There is almost no chance I will be able to find her. But if I do, I will bring her back.'

As Adgennus moved to inform the guards of their decision, Veteranus turned his thoughts to the task ahead. The Silures were legendary for their ferocity and knowledge of the forested hills they called home, yet his years with the Occultum had prepared him for precisely this kind of impossible mission. And somewhere in those same forests, Seneca and the others might already be hunting for Mordred, creating the possibility of unexpected allies if their paths should cross.

An hour or so later, the leather covering was again pushed aside as one of the guards returned.

'It is agreed,' he said, looking at Veteranus. 'You will leave at first light.'

Chapter Nineteen

The Hillfort

Veteranus stood in the central gathering place of the Hillfort. the morning mist still clinging to its highest palisades. The Ordovices chieftain now towered before him, his massive frame draped in a battle cloak of wolf fur despite the early hour.

'You have accepted our terms,' stated the warrior beside the chieftain, his deep voice carrying across the otherwise silent space. 'You will find Rhiannon and return her to us.'

It wasn't a question, but Veteranus nodded, nonetheless.

'I will need supplies, weapons, and knowledge of the lands I'm entering.'

The interpreter gestured down to a bundle wrapped in oiled leather. Inside were: a short sword of good iron, a hunting knife with a bone handle, and a small axe suitable for both combat and clearing brush.

'These will serve you,' he said. 'Food and water will be provided.

He left the sentence unfinished, the implication clear enough.

'And guidance?' Veteranus asked. 'The Silures territories are unknown to me.'

A thin smile appeared beneath the warrior's braided beard. 'For that, Bodvoc has found you something better than maps.' He turned and made a sharp gesture toward one of the nearby roundhouses.

A boy emerged, perhaps fourteen or fifteen summers old, slender but wiry. His face was unmarked by tattoos, but a pale scar ran from his left temple to the corner of his mouth,

165

giving him a perpetually sardonic expression. He wore simple leather breeches and a tunic of undyed wool, with soft-soled boots that looked well-worn from travel.

'He is called Maelon,' said the warrior. 'He speaks your language and will be your guide in the forests of the Silures.'

Veteranus studied the boy with undisguised scepticism.

'A child? This is your solution?'

The boy's eyes flashed with sudden heat.

'I am no child,' he snapped, 'I have walked the hidden paths of Terra Siluria and lived to tell the tale. I know their ways.'

'Maelon was a slave among the Silures for three years,' said the interpreter. 'He escaped during the last winter festival and made his way to our southern border. He knows their forests, their settlements, their patterns of movement.'

'And why would he risk returning to people who once enslaved him?'

'Because if you succeed,' said the warrior, 'he will earn the right to live amongst us as a free man.'

Veteranus looked to the boy, searching for fear or hesitation and finding neither. There was only determination in those young eyes, and something harder, colder, the look of someone who had endured much and survived through sheer force of will.

'How do I know you won't lead me into an ambush at the first opportunity?' he asked directly.

'You don't,' Maelon replied with unsettling honesty. 'Just as I don't know you won't kill me once I've served my purpose. We must trust each other, or we both fail.'

Despite himself, Veteranus felt a grudging respect for the boy's directness. He turned back to the warrior.

'When do we leave?'

'Now,' he replied. 'Every moment you delay, Rhiannon moves further from our reach.' He stepped closer, looming over Veteranus. 'Remember Roman. The lives of your trading companions depend on your success. And if you attempt to flee to your own people instead of completing this task...' He let the threat hang in the air between them.

'I understand,' said Veteranus simply. He had no intention of abandoning the mission; it aligned too perfectly with his original orders to gather intelligence on the western tribes.

Within the hour they were descending the winding path that led from the hillfort to the valley below. Their packs were light, deliberately so. Each carried dried meat, hard bread, and a waterskin that could be refilled from streams along their route. Veteranus had the weapons provided by Bodvoc, while Maelon carried only a small knife and a sling tucked into his belt, its pouch filled with smooth river stones.

Neither spoke as they left the settlement behind, moving southwest along a narrow track that soon disappeared into dense woodland and only when the sounds of the hillfort had faded completely did Maelon break the silence.

'We should reach the Silures border by nightfall,' he said. 'There's a stream marking the boundary. We'll cross under cover of darkness.'

Veteranus grunted in acknowledgment, still reserving judgment on his young guide. The boy moved well, he'd grant him that much. Each step was placed with deliberate care, making surprisingly little noise despite the carpet of autumn leaves covering the forest floor.

'You still don't trust me,' Maelon observed after another long stretch of silence.

'I don't know you,' Veteranus replied evenly.

'Then ask your questions,' the boy said with a shrug. 'We have many miles ahead of us.'

Veteranus considered this for a moment. Knowledge of his guide could indeed prove valuable, particularly if the boy's story revealed anything useful about the Silures themselves.

'How did you become their slave?' he asked finally.

Maelon's pace didn't falter, but something in his posture shifted, a tightening around the shoulders that suggested the memory was not a pleasant one.

'My village was raided three summers ago,' he said. 'I lived with the Dobunni, near the eastern border of Silures territory. Our warriors were away, hunting a great boar that had been destroying our crops.' A bitter smile twisted his scarred face. 'I sometimes wonder if the boar was their doing, a way to draw our fighters from the village.'

'They came at dawn?'

'At dusk. The hour when the light plays tricks, when shadows move strangely.' Maelon pushed aside a low-hanging branch, holding it for Veteranus to pass. 'They killed the old men first. Then any young men who tried to fight. The women they evaluated like livestock, the pretty ones taken for pleasure, the strong ones for labour. Children too young to work were left behind.'

'And you?' Veteranus prompted when the boy fell silent.

'I was twelve summers, old enough to work the mines but young enough to train into obedience.' His voice hardened. 'Or so they thought.'

They walked in silence for a while after that, the forest growing denser around them. Maelon led them along game trails so faint that Veteranus could barely discern them, yet the boy never hesitated at any fork or crossing.

By midday, they had covered impressive ground, moving steadily southwest through increasingly rugged terrain. They paused briefly to drink from a clear stream and eat a portion of their rations, though Maelon insisted they did not linger.

'The Silures have hunters who range far beyond their settlements,' he explained, scanning the forest around them with quick, practiced movements. 'We must keep moving.'

'These mines you mentioned,' said Veteranus as they resumed their journey. 'Silver mines?'

Maelon nodded. 'Silver, lead, some copper. The Silures control the richest veins in the western hills. It's why they can remain independent, they trade metal for whatever else they need.'

'And they use slaves to work them?'

'Mainly slaves, yes. It's killing work. The air in the deep shafts chokes the lungs, turning them black over time. Men rarely last more than a few years.'

'But you escaped it?' Veteranus asked, noting that the boy showed no signs of the hunched posture or rasping breath common to mine workers.

'I was fortunate,' Maelon replied, a hint of pride entering his voice. 'I showed skill in hunting small game with my sling. A man called Cadoc decided I would be more valuable helping feed his warriors than dying below ground.'

Veteranus filed away the name for future reference.

'This Cadoc, was he the leader of your captors?'

'One of them. The Silures don't have single chieftains like other tribes. They have many, each responsible to a council of elders who decide together. Cadoc is what they call a Shadow Walker, a warrior who leads raids into other territories. He has killed more men than any other Silures warrior.'

This information piqued Veteranus's interest.

'Is he connected to their druids? To a man called Mordred, perhaps?'

Maelon turned, surprise evident in his expression.

'You know of Mordred?'

'I've heard rumours,' Veteranus replied carefully.

'There was talk of him even before I escaped,' said Maelon. 'He lived on the holy island of Mona though there are some who say he was recently killed by the Romans in the east. Others say he still lives and gathers strength in the west to rise again. They also speak of ancient prophecies, of a druid who will unite the western tribes against Rome.'

Veteranus didn't respond. He knew that Mordred was indeed alive, but kept the information to himself.

They continued through the afternoon, the terrain becoming progressively more challenging and as evening approached, Maelon led them to a small clearing beside a swift-running stream.

'This is the boundary,' he said quietly, crouching beside the water. 'Beyond lies the lands of the Silures. We'll cross after full darkness,' He settled against the trunk of a massive oak. 'We still need to be wary. There are no regular patrols, but hunters sometimes follow the stream looking for game.'

They ate sparingly while waiting for night to fall, speaking little. Veteranus observed his young guide carefully, noting the way the boy's eyes constantly scanned their surroundings, how his head turned slightly to catch sounds too faint for ordinary hearing. Despite his initial scepticism, he was beginning to appreciate Maelon's woodcraft.

'How did you escape them?' he asked eventually.

Maelon's fingers absently traced the scar on his face, a gesture Veteranus suspected was unconscious.

'It was during the winter solstice celebration,' he said after a long pause. 'The darkest night of the year. Even the Silures fear that night, they believe the boundary between worlds grows thin, allowing ancient spirits to walk among the living.' A ghost of a smile touched his lips. 'They were all gathered around the sacred fire, drinking mead mixed with certain herbs that bring visions. The guards were less vigilant than usual.'

'You simply walked away?'

Maelon shook his head. 'Not quite that simple. I had been planning for months, saving small amounts of food, learning which paths were least used, watching how the hunters moved through the forest.' His eyes took on a distant look, remembering. 'I took a knife from one of the drunken warriors and used it to cut through the barrier. When the alarm was raised, I was already deep in the forest.'

'They pursued you?'

'For seven days,' Maelon confirmed. 'I survived by eating berries and roots and hiding during daylight. On the eighth day, I crossed into Ordovices territory and collapsed from exhaustion.' His expression hardened. 'That's when I learned that escaping one captivity often means entering another. The Ordovices were suspicious of a Silures-trained youth suddenly appearing in their lands. They kept me confined until they determined I was no threat.'

'Yet now they trust you enough to guide me into Silures territory?'

'Trust?' Maelon gave a short, sharp laugh. 'No. They're using me, just as the Silures did. The difference is that this time, I have a promise of freedom when the task is complete.'

As darkness settled fully over the forest, Maelon rose silently to his feet.

'It's time,' he whispered. 'Follow exactly where I step. The stream is shallow here, but the stones are slippery.'

They crossed the boundary in silence, the freezing water swirling around their calves. On the far side, Maelon paused, head tilted as if listening to something only he could hear.

'We are in their lands now,' he said softly. 'From this point forward, we must move like ghosts. No fire, no speaking above a whisper, no careless steps.' His eyes, reflecting the faint starlight filtering through the canopy, met Veteranus's. 'The settlement where I was held, where Cadoc dwells, lies three days' journey southwest from here. If Rhiannon was taken by his hunting party, that's where they would bring her.'

'And if she wasn't?' Veteranus asked.

Maelon's expression grew solemn.

'Then we are both already dead men. Now come, we should put at least two miles between us and the boundary before we rest.'

They moved deeper into Silures territory, the forest seeming to close around them like a living entity. Veteranus followed his guide with newfound respect, watching as the boy selected paths invisible to untrained eyes, avoiding areas where dry leaves might betray their presence with sound.

They made camp, if it could be called that, in a small hollow. No fire was lit, and no shelter constructed beyond the natural cavity in which they huddled. They ate cold rations in silence, each wrapped in his own thoughts.

As fatigue finally began to claim him, Veteranus found himself reassessing his young guide. The boy was competent, certainly more so than he had initially assumed, and his knowledge of Silures territory might indeed prove invaluable. Whether that knowledge would be enough to locate and rescue Rhiannon remained to be seen, but for now, following Maelon seemed their best, perhaps only, option.

'Sleep,' Maelon whispered, settling himself at the entrance to their crude shelter. 'I'll take first watch.'

Veteranus nodded, though he had no intention of sleeping deeply in hostile territory. As he closed his eyes, he kept one hand on the hilt of his knife, ready for whatever the forests of the Silures might bring. If the boy's assessment was correct, they were moving toward the heart of Silures power, toward the very warrior who had enslaved Maelon and possibly now held Rhiannon captive.

Chapter Twenty

Terra Siluria

Seneca led his men forward in single file. They had been traveling for six days through the dense forests of Terra Siluria, seeing little evidence of habitation beyond the occasional hunting trail or abandoned lean-to. The land itself had become their most persistent enemy, treacherous underfoot, dense overhead, and seemingly endless in all directions.

Talorcan moved silently at point, his years of hunting in the forests of Germania serving him well in this similarly primal landscape. He paused suddenly, dropping to one knee and raising a closed fist, the signal to halt that rippled instantly back through their formation. Seneca moved forward to join him, crouching beside the Germanic scout.

'What is it?' he whispered, his voice barely audible above the soft rustle of leaves.

Talorcan pointed to a narrow gap between two ancient oaks ahead. Beyond, the forest floor dropped away sharply, revealing a sliver of open ground visible through the trees.

'The valley opens up ahead,' he murmured. 'And look there.' He indicated faint trails of smoke rising above the distant treeline, so slight they might have been mistaken for morning mist by less experienced eyes.

'How many fires, do you think?' Seneca asked, nodding toward the barely visible smoke.

Talorcan squinted, studying the distant signs.

'Many. Too regular for forest fires. Too numerous for hunters' camps.'

Seneca weighed their options. They had been searching

for precisely this, evidence of Silures habitation that might lead them to Mordred, but approaching unknown settlements in enemy territory required extreme caution.

'We need a better vantage point,' he decided. 'Somewhere we can observe without being seen.'

Talorcan nodded in agreement.

'I will go forward and check the land. The high ground to the northwest might offer a view into the valley.'

As the scout disappeared silently into the undergrowth, Seneca returned to where the others waited.

'There's a potential settlement ahead,' Seneca informed them quietly. 'We'll assess from distance first, then decide our approach.'

Falco's eyes gleamed with sudden interest.

'About bloody time,' he muttered. 'Another day of tramping through this cursed forest and I'd have volunteered to be eaten by bears.'

'No bears in these parts,' Decimus corrected automatically. 'Wolves, perhaps.'

'Whatever would tear my throat out,' Falco replied with a dismissive gesture. 'Anything to break the monotony.'

Just over an hour later, Talorcan returned, moving like a shadow through the trees.

'The forest ends a thousand paces ahead,' he reported, crouching within their small circle. 'Beyond is a wide valley with a river running through its centre. On the far side, built into the hillside and spreading around the hill's base, there's a settlement. Larger than anything we've seen in Britannia outside of Roman construction.'

This news silenced even Falco. Their intelligence had suggested scattered tribal settlements, not large, organized communities.

'How large?' Seneca asked.

'I count at least a hundred structures,' Talorcan replied, 'but there could be more.'

'Population estimate?' Marcus queried.

Talorcan shook his head.

'Difficult to say from my position. Perhaps five hundred, maybe more.'

Seneca absorbed this information, mentally recalculating their approach. A settlement of that size would have organized security and patrols, watchmen of some kind.

'We need to establish a base,' he decided. 'Somewhere secure but close enough to conduct observation. Then we determine if Mordred is among them.'

'There's a ravine system to the east,' Talorcan offered. 'Deep forest cover, defensible, with a clear stream running through it. I noticed it as we approached. It would serve for a hidden camp.'

'Show me,' commanded Seneca.

Two hours later, they stood at the edge of a steep, narrow valley that cut into the forested hillside like a wound. The slopes dropped away sharply on both sides, creating natural barriers to approach, while dense undergrowth provided visual cover from anyone passing nearby. At the bottom ran a clear stream, its quiet gurgling masking any small sounds they might make.

'This will serve,' Seneca decided, surveying the ravine with professional appreciation. 'Falco, Decimus, establish the laying-up point. Sica and Marcus, check the approaches and set perimeter warnings. Talorcan and I will conduct the initial reconnaissance of the settlement.'

They moved with practiced efficiency, each man knowing his role without need for detailed instruction and as the rest of the Occultun descended into the ravine, Seneca, and Talorcan moved along the ridgeline, using the forest cover to mask their approach toward the settlement.

They travelled in silence, communicating only with hand signals when necessary. By midday, they had reached a secure position overlooking the valley Talorcan had described and lay flat on their stomachs at the forest edge, concealed by undergrowth while observing the spectacle below.

The settlement was unlike anything Seneca had expected to find in these remote forests. It sprawled across the valley floor and up the opposite hillside, a complex network of structures arranged in concentric circles around what appeared to be a central gathering place. Most buildings were traditional roundhouses, their thatched roofs golden in the midday sun, but others were built partially into the hillside itself, with only their front facades visible.

The entire community was surrounded by a wooden palisade, as Talorcan had reported, though it appeared more ceremonial than defensive and along the valley floor stretched cultivated fields, the autumn harvest clearly underway as figures moved between neat rows of crops.

Seneca studied the settlement carefully

'No visible watch towers,' he said, 'but look there.' He pointed to groups of men moving in formation at various points around the settlement perimeter. 'Regular patrols. Well-armed. They compensate for fixed defences with mobile security.'

'And the terrain itself provides protection,' Talorcan added. 'The valley would channel any attacking force, making them vulnerable to ambush from the hillsides.'

They continued their observation in silence, noting the

patterns of movement, the apparent organization of the settlement, and any details that might prove useful in their mission. Smoke rose from numerous hearth fires, and even from their distant position, they could hear the faint sounds of communal living, hammering from what must be a forge, the distant barking of dogs and the calls of herdsmen tending sheep on the valley floor.

'Doesn't look like a people living in fear to me,' said Seneca, 'For a tribe with Rome pushing at their borders, they seem remarkably at ease.'

'Confidence is often mistaken for ignorance?' said Talorcan. 'These forests have protected them for generations. They believe they will continue to do so.'

After an hour of observation, they retreated back into the deeper forest, moving with careful precision to avoid leaving visible signs of their presence. The information they had gathered was valuable but incomplete. They needed closer observation, details that could only be obtained from proximity.

'We'll need to establish a forward observation post,' Seneca decided as they made their way back toward their ravine camp. 'Somewhere with clear sight lines to the settlement but with sufficient cover to remain hidden.'

'The western ridge would serve,' Talorcan suggested. 'It has forest cover nearly to its edge, an elevated position, and is approximately only half a mile from the settlement perimeter.'

'I agree,' said Seneca. 'Once we have gone to ground, we'll get it done.'

They returned to find the ravine camp taking shape under Decimus and Sica's skilled hands. Using only fallen timber and materials that would leave minimal evidence of human presence, they had constructed a hidden shelter nestled amongst the rubble and dead wood of a recent rockfall. It was nearly invisible unless one stood directly before it, the entrance concealed by carefully arranged deadwood that could be moved aside for access.

Inside, the space was surprisingly large, with sleeping positions for all six men arranged around a small central area.

'Impressive,' Seneca acknowledged, inspecting their work. 'How's the perimeter?'

'Secured,' Sica replied succinctly. 'There is only the one path that we used which is easily defended but we can withdraw downstream if necessary.'

'Any signs of local activity?'

Decimus shook his head.

'Nothing fresh. Some old tracks along the stream, probably deer or boar but this ravine doesn't appear to be frequently visited.'

'Good,' Seneca settled into a crouch, and with the point of his knife, began sketching the layout of the settlement into the soil, marking key features and potential approaches.

'We'll establish the forward observation post tomorrow,' he said once the map was complete. 'Talorcan, Marcus, Sica, and I will handle that. Decimus and Falco, you will remain here. Continue improving our position and conduct close reconnaissance of our immediate surroundings.'

'What exactly are you looking for when you observe them?' asked Falco, his massive frame making the shelter seem even smaller as he hunched forward. 'It's not like Mordred will be wearing a sign announcing his presence.'

'We watch for patterns,' Seneca explained patiently. 'Religious ceremonies, council gatherings, anything that might involve a druid of Mordred's stature. We observe which buildings receive the most visitors, and which individuals

179

command respect.'

'And then?' Decimus prompted.

'Then we get closer,' said Seneca simply. 'We can't complete this mission from a distance. Eventually, we'll need to enter the settlement itself.'

A heavy silence followed this statement, each man contemplating the risks such an approach would entail. Infiltrating a Roman town or even a friendly tribal settlement was challenging enough; penetrating a Silures community, people legendary for their hostility to outsiders, approached suicidal.

'We've done more with less,' Marcus reminded them, breaking the silence.

Falco grunted what might have been agreement.

'I'd prefer enemies I can fight openly. All this skulking about makes my sword arm itch.'

'You'll get your chance for action soon enough,' Seneca predicted grimly. 'For now, we observe, we learn, and we plan. Everything else follows from that.'

As evening approached, they established a watch rotation and consumed a cold meal of dried meat and hard biscuit. Fire, even the smallest and most carefully hidden, was too great a risk this close to potential Silures patrols and they ate in silence, each man lost in his own thoughts about the mission ahead.

Dawn found Seneca and his group moving carefully along the western ridgeline Talorcan had identified. They travelled light, carrying only essential weapons, water, and minimal rations. Their goal was to establish the forward observation post, a position from which they could maintain constant surveillance of the Silures settlement while remaining undetected.

The ridge offered excellent vantage points, but most were too exposed for sustained occupation. They continued along its length, searching for the ideal combination of concealment and visibility, finally discovering a position where a lightning-struck oak had created a natural blind. The massive tree had split years ago, its splintered trunk and spreading roots forming a hollow space large enough for two men to occupy comfortably. Dense undergrowth had grown up around it, providing additional concealment, while its elevated position overlooked the valley without being silhouetted against the skyline.

'This will serve,' Seneca decided after careful inspection.

Marcus nodded in agreement, already planning the small modifications they would make to improve the position.

'We'll need to clear some of the brush for better visibility, but nothing that would look deliberate from a distance.'

Sica, meanwhile, had been systematically checking the surrounding area for signs of Silures presence. He returned to their position with his characteristic silent approach, appearing beside them without warning.'

'There is a game trail fifty paces further back,' he said, 'but no sign of any Silures movement.'

Over the next few hours, they carefully modified the natural blind, improving visibility while maintaining its appearance as nothing more than a fallen tree with surrounding undergrowth. Sica placed his distinctive warning devices along the nearby game trail, arrangements of twigs and stones that would appear natural to anyone passing by, but would alert the trained eye to disturbance.

By midday, the observation post was ready. From its

concealed interior, they had an excellent view of the settlement's main entrance, the central gathering area, and much of the surrounding valley.

'We'll maintain observation in shifts,' said Seneca. 'Two men at a time, rotating every half a day but withdraw to the ravine at dark. Sica and Talorcan, you take first watch. We'll need to build a complete picture of their routines and security measures, before we do anything more.'

As Marcus and Seneca made their careful way back to the ravine camp, Seneca found himself calculating probabilities and risks. The settlement was far larger and more organized than their intelligence had suggested. If Mordred was indeed there, he would likely be well-protected, possibly housed within the structures built into the hillside, which appeared to be reserved for individuals of importance.

Extracting, or eliminating, a target from such a position would challenge even the Occultum's considerable skills. But Seneca had not led them through countless impossible missions by dwelling on difficulties. Each problem would be addressed in sequence: observation, infiltration, location of the target, and finally, execution of their orders.

For now, they had established a secure base and a viable observation post. The Silures settlement lay spread before them like a living map, and with patience and discipline, they would uncover its secrets.

Chapter Twenty-One

The Silures Village

The training ground at the heart of the settlement echoed with the sharp crack of wood against wood and the grunts of men pushing their bodies to their limits. Belenos stood in the centre of the cleared space, his massive torso gleaming with sweat despite the cool morning air. Blue woad patterns spiralled across his chest and shoulders, the pigment mixing with perspiration to create rivulets of colour that traced the contours of his muscled frame.

In his hands, he wielded a wooden sword, its blade carved from seasoned oak and weighted to match the balance of true steel. Around him, three other warriors circled like wolves, each carrying blunted spears with leather-wrapped points. The weapons might not be lethal, but they were far from harmless, and already, angry welts marked Belenos's ribs where spear thrusts had found their mark, and blood trickled from a split lip where an opponent's wooden blade had connected.

'Again,' he shouted, rolling his shoulders to loosen muscles that had begun to tighten from the sustained combat.

The first warrior lunged forward, spear point aimed at Belenos's midsection. The chieftain pivoted sideways, bringing his wooden sword down in a powerful overhead strike that would have split a real skull. His opponent barely got his spear shaft up in time to block, the impact driving him to one knee under Belenos's overwhelming strength.

Before he could recover, the second warrior attacked from behind, thrusting his spear toward the small of Belenos's back. Without turning, Belenos stepped aside and swept his leg in a wide arc, catching his attacker's ankles and sending him sprawling into the dirt. As the man fell, Belenos spun to face the third warrior, who had used the distraction to close distance.

The wooden blades met with a resounding crack, the force of the collision sending vibrations up both men's arms. For a moment they stood locked, each straining against the other's strength, before Belenos suddenly gave way and stepped aside. His opponent, overbalanced by his own momentum, stumbled forward directly into Belenos's rising knee. The blow caught him in the solar plexus, doubling him over as he gasped for breath.

Around the training ground, dozens of Silures warriors watched with keen interest, some calling out encouragement or criticism, others simply observing the techniques being displayed. This was more than simple combat practice, it was a demonstration of leadership through physical dominance, a reminder of why Belenos commanded respect among people who valued strength above all else.

The warrior Belenos had swept to the ground rolled away and sprang back to his feet, blood streaming from his nose where it had struck the earth. He grinned fiercely, apparently relishing the violence, and immediately resumed his attack. His spear work was skilful, the point weaving intricate patterns as he sought an opening in Belenos's defences.

Belenos gave ground slowly, his wooden sword working in tight defensive arcs to deflect the probing thrusts. To the watching warriors, it might have appeared that he was being driven back, but those with experience recognized the patience of a master fighter drawing his opponent into overconfidence.

The spear thrust came, a powerful, committed strike aimed at Belenos's heart, but at the last instant, the chieftain twisted aside, letting the point slide past his ribs while his left hand shot out to grasp the spear shaft. With his opponent momentarily off-balance and unable to withdraw his weapon, Belenos brought his wooden sword around in a vicious horizontal cut that took the warrior across the temple.

The man dropped instantly, his legs folding beneath him as consciousness fled but he would wake with a splitting headache and the respect of his peers for lasting as long as he had against their most feared fighter.

The remaining two warriors attacked simultaneously now, recognizing that individual efforts were futile against Belenos's skill and experience. They came from opposite sides, spears thrusting in coordinated strikes meant to overwhelm his defences through sheer numbers. For a moment, the two-pronged assault seemed to have the measure of him, sweat ran more freely down his torso, and his breathing grew laboured from the sustained effort.

Then, moving with explosive speed, he ducked under a spear thrust and drove his shoulder into one of the warrior's midsection. The impact lifted the smaller man off his feet and drove him backward into the crowd of spectators, who scattered with good-natured curses as they scrambled to avoid the collision.

The final warrior, now isolated, pressed his attack with desperate courage. His spear work was excellent, the point seeming to be everywhere at once as he sought to overwhelm Belenos through sheer aggression. But against a fighter of Belenos's calibre, courage alone was insufficient.

Belenos caught the spear shaft on his wooden blade and twisted sharply, using leverage to tear the weapon from his opponent's grasp and as the warrior reached for the knife at his belt, Belenos's wooden sword took him across the side of the head with a blow that would have been fatal with steel. The man staggered, fought to maintain his footing for a moment, then collapsed beside his unconscious companion.

The watching crowd erupted in approval, warriors shouting their appreciation for the display of skill and ferocity they had just witnessed.

Belenos raised his wooden sword to acknowledge their acclaim, his chest heaving as he caught his breath. Blood from various small wounds mixed with sweat and woad to create an intimidating sight, he looked like a war god fresh from battle, terrible and magnificent in equal measure.

'Who comes next?' he called out, his voice carrying clearly across the training ground. 'Will no one else test themselves against me?'

His words were cut short by a commotion from the far end of the settlement. Voices were raised in excitement, and he could see people moving toward the village perimeter with unusual urgency. Most curious of all, several women had broken from their usual tasks and were hurrying to join the growing crowd, a behaviour almost unprecedented in Silures culture, where the affairs of warriors were considered strictly masculine concerns.

Belenos lowered his wooden sword, his attention now focused on the disturbance. Something significant was happening, something that had captured the interest of the entire settlement. He threw his practice weapon to one of the watching warriors and began pushing through the crowd, his authority clearing a path as people stepped aside to let him pass.

The crowd thickened as he approached the settlement's edge, men and women pressed together in a way rarely seen in Silures society. Their voices created a buzz of excitement that reminded Belenos of a disturbed beehive, everyone speaking at once, speculation and rumour spreading through the gathered people like ripples in a pond.

He used his size and status to force his way through the press of bodies, ignoring the muttered complaints of those he displaced. As war leader his right to witness whatever had caused this excitement was unquestioned, even if his methods were somewhat less than diplomatic.

Finally, he broke through the front ranks of the crowd and found himself at the settlement's main entrance, where the wooden palisade opened to admit visitors. What he saw there caused him to stop abruptly, his eyes widening with surprise.

Kynan stood beside his foam-flecked horse, accepting a wooden cup of water from one of the settlement's women. Around him, his hunting party, six warriors in total, were similarly refreshing themselves after what had clearly been a hard ride. Their horses steamed in the cool air, and mud splattered their legs to the knee, evidence of forced travel over difficult terrain.

But it was not Kynan or his warriors that had drawn the crowd's attention. Mounted on one of the horses, her hands bound before her with leather cords, sat the most striking woman Belenos had ever seen.

She was young, perhaps twenty summers, with auburn hair that caught the sunlight like burnished copper. Her skin was pale but not unhealthy, speaking of noble birth rather than manual labour. She wore a dress of fine-woven wool dyed a deep blue, now travel-stained but still obviously of good quality. Gold torcs adorned her throat and wrists, their craftsmanship immediately marking her as someone of considerable importance.

What struck Belenos most powerfully, however, was not her beauty or obvious wealth, but her bearing. Despite being bound and clearly a captive, she sat straight in her saddle, her chin raised with unmistakable pride. Her eyes, a startling shade of green, surveyed the crowd of Silures warriors with no trace of fear, only a kind of regal assessment, as if she were evaluating subjects rather than confronting captors.

This was no ordinary prisoner. This was a woman accustomed to command, to respect, to deference and even in captivity, she radiated an authority that commanded attention and, grudgingly, a kind of respect from those who witnessed her defiance.

For a long moment, Belenos simply stared, struck by the unexpected sight. In all his years of raiding and warfare, he had never encountered a captive who faced adversity with such composed dignity. Most prisoners, regardless of their station in life, showed some signs of fear or desperation when faced with Silures captivity. This woman seemed almost bored by the proceedings, as if being kidnapped were merely an inconvenience in her otherwise ordered existence.

Around him, the crowd continued to murmur and speculate, but their voices seemed distant, muffled by his intense focus on the captive woman. He found himself wondering who she was, what position she held that could instil such unshakeable confidence even in these circumstances.

Gradually becoming aware of the spectacle he was creating by his prolonged staring, Belenos forced himself to look away from the woman and focus on Kynan. The younger warrior had finished drinking and was now wiping dust from his face with a damp cloth, apparently oblivious to the attention his prisoner was receiving.

With deliberate casualness, Belenos began walking toward the dismounted hunting party, his expression carefully neutral despite the questions burning in his mind.

As he approached, Kynan looked up and grinned, his face splitting in an expression of fierce satisfaction.

'Belenos!' he called out, his voice carrying clearly across the settlement entrance. 'Wait until you hear what we have accomplished. This will change everything.'

Belenos continued his measured approach, his eyes flicking once more to the bound woman on horseback. She was watching him now, her green eyes meeting his with steady assessment. For a moment, he felt as if he were the one being evaluated, weighed, and judged. It was a disconcerting sensation for a man accustomed to being the source rather than the object of intimidation.

He stopped directly in front of Kynan, close enough that their conversation would not be overheard by the still-gathering crowd.

'Walk with me,' he said quietly, nodding toward a path that led away from the main gathering. 'Leave your men to tend the horses.'

Kynan followed his war leader, his earlier excitement now tempered by the gravity in Belenos's voice. They moved perhaps thirty paces from the crowd before Belenos stopped beneath the spreading branches of an ancient oak.

'Tell me everything,' commanded Belenos eventually. 'From the beginning. Leave nothing out.'

Chapter Twenty-Two

Northern Siluria

The forest seemed to grow denser with each mile they travelled southwest, the ancient trees pressing closer together as if conspiring to block out the sky itself. Veteranus followed Maelon through terrain that would have been impassable to anyone lacking the boy's intimate knowledge of these hidden paths. They moved in single file, communication reduced to hand signals and the occasional whispered warning about obstacles ahead.

On their second day in Silures territory, Veteranus witnessed the first demonstration of his young guide's remarkable skill. They had been traveling since before dawn, following what appeared to be nothing more than a deer track through impossibly thick undergrowth, when Maelon suddenly froze, his head tilted in concentration.

'What is it?' Veteranus whispered, his hand instinctively moving to the hilt of his knife.

Maelon didn't respond immediately, instead reaching slowly for the sling tucked into his belt. With practiced movements, he selected a smooth stone from his pouch and fitted it into the leather cradle, his eyes scanning the canopy above, searching for something Veteranus couldn't see.

Then, with a movement so fluid it seemed almost casual, Maelon whipped the sling in a tight circle and released. The stone whistled upward through the branches, followed immediately by a heavy thud and the crash of something falling through leaves.

A moment later, a wood pigeon landed at their feet, its neck cleanly broken by the stone's impact.

'Food,' Maelon said simply, retrieving the bird and tucking it into his pack. 'We'll eat better tonight than most Roman soldiers.'

Veteranus stared at the boy with newfound respect. The shot had been taken at a target he hadn't even been able to see, through dense foliage, at a range that would have challenged even experienced hunters with proper bows.

'Where did you learn to use a sling like that?' he asked.

Maelon's expression darkened slightly.

'When I wasn't working below ground in the mines, I hunted for the camp. The warriors only kept me alive because I could bring them fresh meat.' His voice carried no self-pity, only the matter-of-fact tone of someone recounting simple facts. 'A slave who couldn't contribute was a dead slave.'

They continued their journey, and over the following days, Maelon's skill with the sling proved their salvation. Small birds fell to his stones with remarkable regularity, thrushes, blackbirds, the occasional wood dove. Most were too small to provide much meat, but in hostile territory where lighting cooking fires was impossible, every morsel was precious.

Their method of eating was crude but necessary. Maelon would quickly pluck the breast feathers from each bird, exposing the pale flesh beneath before biting through the skin to tear away strips of raw meat with his teeth. The meat was tough and gamey, but it provided the protein their bodies needed for the demanding journey ahead.

By their fourth day in Silures territory, the forest had begun to thin slightly, allowing glimpses of rolling hills through breaks in the canopy. Maelon led them up increasingly steep slopes, following paths so faint that they seemed more suggestion than actual trail. The air grew cooler as they gained elevation, and occasionally they could hear the distant sound of running water echoing through hidden valleys.

'We're close,' Maelon announced as they crested a particularly challenging ridge. He pointed southwest, where smoke could be seen rising above the treeline in the distance. 'The camp lies in the valley beyond that next hill.'

Veteranus studied the terrain ahead, noting the strategic advantages of the location. Anyone approaching the camp would have to cross open ground, making stealth difficult. The surrounding hills provided excellent observation points for sentries, while the dense forest offered numerous escape routes if the camp came under attack.

'How large is this camp?' he asked.

'Perhaps fifty warriors, maybe a few more,' Maelon replied. 'Not all are there at the same time, some are always out hunting or raiding. But it's enough to make a direct approach a death sentence.'

As darkness fell, they moved closer to the camp, using the cover of night to approach within observation distance. Maelon led them to a position on the hillside overlooking the valley, where gaps in the forest canopy allowed a clear view of the settlement below.

What Veteranus saw surprised him. Instead of the organized village he had expected, the camp appeared to be a collection of temporary structures scattered throughout a natural clearing. Most were simple lean-tos or hide tents, built for function rather than comfort. A few larger structures, probably communal buildings, occupied the centre of the camp, but even these looked hastily constructed and easily abandoned if necessary.

Cooking fires dotted the clearing, their orange glow providing enough light to reveal figures moving between the various shelters. Even from this distance, Veteranus could see that the inhabitants moved with the alertness of men always ready for violence. These were not farmers or craftsmen, but warriors living a semi-nomadic existence in the forest depths.

'It's not what I expected,' he murmured to Maelon.

The boy nodded. 'Most people think the Silures live in proper villages like other tribes. But the Shadow Walkers are different. They move their camps regularly, never staying in one place long enough for enemies to locate them.'

'Tell me more about these Shadow Walkers,' said Veteranus.

'They are the raiders and the hunters of the Silures. The men who strike at their enemies and disappear before retaliation can come.' Maelon's voice carried a mixture of fear and grudging respect. 'Other tribes fight in open battle, but the Silures prefer to kill from hiding and vanish like ghosts.'

They observed for several hours, noting the camp's routines and security measures. Guards were posted at regular intervals around the perimeter, and Veteranus counted at least six separate watch positions that would provide overlapping fields of observation. Anyone attempting to approach the camp would be spotted long before they could get close enough to pose a threat.

More concerning was the evident discipline of the inhabitants. Despite the informal appearance of their shelters, the men moved with military precision. Groups formed and dispersed with obvious purpose, and even casual conversations were conducted in the low tones of men who understood the value of stealth.

As the night wore on, Veteranus began to grasp the true nature of what they were observing. This wasn't a village where Rhiannon might be held as a traditional captive. This was a military camp, home to the warriors who carried out the

Silures' most dangerous operations. If the young woman was here, she was being held by some of the most lethal fighters in Britannia.

Before dawn, they withdrew to a safer distance, finding concealment in a thick grove of yew trees nearly a mile from the camp. As the first light filtered through the forest canopy, Maelon began explaining what Veteranus had witnessed.

'What you saw last night, that's not a village,' he began, settling against the trunk of a massive yew. 'The real Silures settlements are further south, hidden deep in the mountains. This is just an outpost, a camp for the Shadow Walkers who patrol these borders.'

'And you were held here?' Veteranus asked.

'Not here but nearby,' said Maelon. 'The Silures use slaves to do the work they consider beneath warriors, cooking, maintaining weapons, hauling supplies. But mostly, we were used to work the secret mines nearby.'

'What makes these different from ordinary Silures warriors?'

'Everything,' Maelon replied with conviction. 'Regular Silures fighters are fierce, but they follow traditional codes of combat. The Shadow Walkers follow no such rules. They kill without honour, strike without warning, and disappear without trace. They're the ones who taught me that survival matters more than dignity.'

Veteranus absorbed this information, recognizing the implications for their mission. If Rhiannon had been taken by ordinary raiders, there might be hope of negotiation or even rescue. But Shadow Walkers operated by different rules entirely.

'You mentioned their leader,' he prompted. 'Cadoc?'

'Cadoc is... different,' Maelon said slowly, seeming to

choose his words carefully. 'Most Silures leaders are chiefs or elders, chosen for their wisdom or their ability to speak for their people. Cadoc leads through fear and skill. He's the deadliest fighter among the Shadow Walkers.'

'What kind of man is he?'

Maelon was quiet for a long moment, his fingers absently tracing the scar on his face, a gesture Veteranus had noticed whenever the boy discussed his captivity.

'Intelligent,' he said finally. 'Brutally so. He doesn't kill for pleasure like some of the others. Every death serves a purpose, every act of violence achieves a goal. That makes him more dangerous than the ones who simply enjoy causing pain.'

'And you think he would have ordered Rhiannon's capture?'

'If she was taken by Shadow Walkers, it was probably Cadoc's decision,' Maelon confirmed. 'Nothing happens in that camp without his knowledge and approval.'

Veteranus leaned back against his own tree, contemplating the challenge before them. Rescuing a high-value captive from a heavily guarded military camp would have been difficult enough. Doing so when that camp was commanded by a brilliant tactician who knew the local terrain intimately approached impossibility.

'How many men would it take to assault the camp directly?' he asked.

Maelon gave him a look that suggested the question bordered on madness. 'A full Roman legion might succeed, if they were willing to accept massive casualties. But even then, the Shadow Walkers would likely kill their captives and escape into the deeper forests before the assault could reach them.'

'Then we need a different approach,' Veteranus concluded. 'Something that doesn't rely on force.'

'Such as?'

Veteranus smiled grimly.

'We get inside the camp before anyone realizes we're here.'

Maelon stared at him in disbelief.

'That's not a plan, that is death.'

'Only if they see us,' said Veteranus, and before Maelon could ask what he meant, Veteranus was already planning their next move. They would need to observe the camp for several more days, learning its routines and identifying potential opportunities. But somewhere in those observations, he would find a weakness they could exploit.

The Shadow Walkers might be deadly fighters operating on familiar ground, but they were still men. And all men, no matter how dangerous, had patterns and vulnerabilities that could be turned against them.

Chapter Twenty-Three

The Silures Village

Kynan straightened, recognizing the seriousness of the moment. His earlier grin faded as he began his report.

'We were patrolling the northern border, as you ordered,' he began. 'Following the old deer paths that run parallel to the Ordovices territory. Three days out, we spotted movement near the boundary stones, riders approaching from the north.'

'How many?' Belenos interrupted.

'Eight in total. Seven warriors and the woman. They were moving slowly, not like a war party or raiders. More like... pilgrims, perhaps, or traders.'

Belenos nodded for him to continue.

'We followed them for most of a day, staying hidden in the forest. They made camp near the sacred spring where the three boundaries meet. We could see they carried heavy packs, well-secured and obviously valuable.'

'So you decided to investigate,' Belenos observed, his tone neutral but his eyes sharp.

'I did,' Kynan confirmed. 'We moved closer after dark, close enough to see what they were doing. The warriors were Ordovices, I could tell by their tattoos and the way they wore their hair. But they weren't behaving like typical border patrol. They were... ceremonial. Preparing for something.'

'What kind of ceremony?'

Kynan's expression grew more animated as he recalled the scene.

'They had unpacked their goods in a careful arrangement around the woman. Fine cloth, silver cups, weapons with decorated hilts, jewellery. Everything was laid out like offerings, with the woman at the centre wearing robes I'd never seen before, a white cloak with gold stitching, like something a druid might wear for high ceremonies.'

Belenos felt a cold weight settling in his stomach, though he kept his expression carefully neutral.

'Continue.'

'We couldn't understand all their words from our position, but it was clearly some kind of blessing ritual. The woman was speaking in the old tongue, calling on the spirits of the boundary waters. The warriors were responding like they were taking sacred vows.'

'And then?'

Kynan's enthusiasm returned, apparently oblivious to the growing tension in his leader's posture.

'We realized they were carrying tribute, valuable goods being offered to secure divine favour for something important. Too valuable to let slip away into Ordovices hands.'

'So you attacked,' Belenos stated flatly.

'We did. Just before dawn, when their watch was at its lowest. We struck from three directions, using the trees for cover.' Kynan's chest swelled with pride at the tactical success. 'They never had a chance to form a proper defence. Their weapons were ceremonial pieces, beautiful but not meant for real combat. We cut down all seven warriors without losing a single man.'

'And the woman?'

'She never even tried to run,' said Kynan, shaking his head in apparent admiration. 'Just stood there in the middle of it all, watching her protectors die without showing any fear. Even when one of my men put a blade to her throat, she barely flinched. That's when we knew she was someone special.'

Belenos turned away from Kynan, ostensibly to observe the captive woman still seated on horseback near the settlement entrance, but actually to hide his expression of growing alarm. Everything Kynan was describing pointed to a situation far more dangerous than a simple border raid.

'The packs,' he said eventually. 'What exactly did they contain?'

'Like I said, tribute goods. Silver work from the northern smiths, textiles that must have come from Gaul, and weapons that were more art than steel.'

'You brought these items back?'

'Everything,' Kynan confirmed. 'It's all loaded on the pack horses. Wait until you see the quality of the metalwork.'

'Burn it,' Belenos interrupted sharply.

Kynan stared at him in shock.

'Burn it? But the value alone…'

'Burn all of it. Tonight. Everything except what the woman was wearing when you took her.' Belenos turned back to face his subordinate. 'And tell your men that if anyone speaks of what was in those packs, they'll answer to me personally.'

'I don't understand,' Kynan protested. 'Why would we destroy such valuable…'

'Because you've made a mistake,' snapped Belenos cutting him off, 'a potentially catastrophic one.'

For the first time since his return, uncertainty crept into Kynan's expression.

'What kind of mistake?'

Instead of answering immediately, Belenos gestured toward the woman.

'Look at her. Really look. Not at her beauty or her defiance, but at what she represents.'

Kynan followed his gaze, studying the captive with new attention. She sat straight-backed on her horse, her bound hands resting calmly in her lap, her green eyes surveying the crowd with the cool assessment of someone evaluating subordinates rather than fearing captors.

'Her clothes,' Belenos continued, his voice pitched for Kynan's ears alone. 'Even travel-stained, they're worth more than most warriors see in a lifetime. That embroidery work, do you recognize the patterns?'

Kynan looked more closely, his confidence beginning to waver. 'I... it's not Ordovices work. Too fine. Too complex.'

'Brigantes,' Belenos confirmed grimly. 'Royal Brigantes. And if she was participating in a blessing ceremony with Ordovices warriors, carrying tribute goods and official documents...'

Understanding dawned in Kynan's eyes, followed immediately by fear.

'A marriage alliance?'

'At minimum. Possibly something even more significant.' Belenos stepped closer, his voice dropping to barely above a whisper. 'You may have just kidnapped the daughter of a queen, interrupting a ceremony that was meant to seal peace between two of the most powerful tribes in the north.'

The colour drained from Kynan's face as the full implications hit him. 'If she's Brigantes royalty, and the Ordovices were protecting her...'

'Then both tribes will be looking for her. And when they discover what happened to their warriors, they'll know exactly who was responsible.' Belenos glanced around to ensure they weren't being overheard. 'This isn't some border skirmish or cattle raid, Kynan. This could mean war.'

'What do we do?' Kynan asked, his earlier pride

completely evaporated.

Belenos was quiet for a long moment, calculating options and consequences. Around them, the normal life of the settlement continued, warriors preparing for training, women tending to daily tasks, children playing between the roundhouses. None of them yet realized that their world might have changed fundamentally in the space of a single raid.

'First, we find out exactly who she is,' he decided. 'If she's truly royal Brigantes, we need to know her value, both as a hostage and as a target for retaliation.'

'And then?'

'Then we decide whether she's worth the war that keeping her might bring.' Belenos turned away from the settlement entrance, his mind already working through possibilities. 'Get your men settled. Say nothing to anyone about what you've told me. And burn those tribute goods tonight. Whatever was in those packs, it's evidence of something the other tribes will kill to recover or avenge.'

As Kynan nodded and moved away to carry out his orders, Belenos approached the small group of women who had been watching the proceedings from a respectful distance. These were the wives and daughters of his warriors, women who understood both discretion and authority.

'Morwen,' he called to the eldest among them, a grey-haired woman whose husband had fallen in a raid three summers past. She stepped forward immediately, her weathered face showing no curiosity about the unusual situation.

'Take the captive to the guest house,' he instructed quietly. 'Feed her, provide clean water for washing and treat her with the respect due to someone of obvious station. But watch her carefully, she's not to be left alone or allowed to speak with anyone except you.'

Morwen nodded once, understanding both the spoken and unspoken elements of her instructions.

'And if she asks questions?'

'Tell her I will speak to her when I'm ready. Nothing more.' Belenos glanced once more at the bound woman, noting how she sat with patient dignity despite her circumstances. 'And Morwen, handle her as you would handle a blade that might cut you if you're careless. She's more dangerous than she appears.'

As the woman moved to carry out his instructions, carefully helping the captive down from her horse and escorting her toward one of the larger roundhouses, Belenos found himself studying the woman's face. Even now, being led away by strangers into an uncertain fate, she showed no sign of panic or desperation. If anything, she seemed almost curious about her surroundings, taking note of the settlement's layout and defences.

That level of composure in captivity suggested either extraordinary courage or absolute confidence in her eventual rescue. Either possibility pointed to someone of significant importance, and significant danger to his people if her disappearance triggered the wrong response from her allies.

He had faced many challenges as a war leader, but few had presented such complex political ramifications. The woman was valuable, certainly, but keeping her might cost more than her worth if it brought the combined might of the Brigantes and Ordovices down upon his settlement.

For now, he would treat her as the valuable prisoner she appeared to be. But soon, he would need to decide whether that value was worth the price it might demand.

On the wooded hill overlooking the same Silures settlement, Marcus lay motionless in the concealed observation post, his eyes fixed on the village. Beside him, Sica maintained his characteristic silence

'Something's happening,' Marcus murmured. 'It looks like a patrol coming back from somewhere.'

Seneca shifted slightly, his own eyes straining to make out the details.

'How many?'

'Six, maybe seven riders. But there's something else. They've got someone with them. A prisoner, by the look of it.'

'Silures taking captives isn't unusual,' Seneca observed quietly.

'No, but this one is,' said Marcus. 'She is well dressed and not cowering or struggling. This isn't some farmer's daughter snatched from a field.'

The crowd parted as a large figure pushed through, clearly someone of authority by the way others stepped aside. The man's size and bearing marked him as a war leader, the kind of individual who commanded through personal strength and tactical skill.

'I think their leader's getting involved personally,' said Seneca.

They watched as the situation unfolded. Any unusual activity in the settlement might provide intelligence about their target or reveal patterns they could exploit in their own mission.

'The women are taking her toward one of the larger buildings,' said Marcus. Treatment looks... respectful. Not like a typical captive.'

'Whoever she is, it's none of our business,' said Seneca eventually. 'we are here for Mordred.'

They watched as the settlement gradually returned to its

normal routines, accepting the fact that whatever was going on, they could be here for quite a while. The chances of Mordred being in the first settlement they found were slim, but this was a chance for them to learn a lot of information about the Silures. How they lived, their strengths and weaknesses and their way of life, and in the sort of work the Occultum were now engaged on, all such information was invaluable.

Chapter Twenty-Four

The Camp of the Shadow Walkers

For two days, Veteranus had observed the Shadow Walker camp with the methodical patience of a predator studying its prey. Every movement and shift change had been memorized, and he knew which paths through the camp saw the least foot traffic during different times of day.

The camp followed patterns, as all military establishments did, regardless of their apparent informality. The Shadow Walkers might live in temporary shelters and move their location regularly, but they were still warriors operating under discipline and discipline, no matter how well-maintained, inevitably created predictable behaviours that could be exploited by someone with the right training and patience.

On the third night, as darkness settled over the valley and the campfires began to burn low, Veteranus made his decision.

'I'm going down,' he told Maelon, his voice barely above a whisper.

The boy's eyes widened in alarm.

'In full darkness?'

'Darkness is my ally, not my enemy,' said Veteranus, already checking his equipment. 'You'll remain here. If I'm not back by dawn, head back toward Ordovices territory and don't look back.'

'What if you're captured?'

Veteranus met the boy's worried gaze steadily.

'Whatever happens to me, your path to freedom remains the same. Help the Ordovices when you can and earn your place among them.'

Maelon nodded reluctantly, understanding that arguing would be futile. He had learned enough about Veteranus over their days together to recognize the quiet determination that preceded action.

Veteranus began his descent using every technique developed through years of infiltrating enemy positions under cover of darkness. He moved during the brief moments when sentries' attention was focused elsewhere, when they turned to speak to companions, and when they paused to scratch an itch or adjust their equipment.

His approach was not the direct path a normal person might take, but a zigzag route that utilized every piece of available cover. He moved from tree to boulder to fallen log, never crossing open ground when any alternative existed. Each movement was preceded by long minutes of absolute stillness, watching and listening for any sign that his presence had been detected.

The technique was exhausting, requiring constant mental calculation and physical control in near-total darkness. Every muscle had to be managed, every breath controlled, every footfall placed with deliberate precision. A single carelessly kicked stone or snapped twig could mean discovery and death.

Once at the camp's edge, his infiltration became even more methodical. The darkness that had aided his approach now required even greater care, as the slightest miscalculation could send him stumbling into a tent rope or alerting a hunting dog.

He had identified his target during his observations, a

roundhouse near the centre of the settlement that showed unusual patterns of activity. Unlike the other structures, which were visited only by their inhabitants or the occasional messenger, this building saw a steady stream of visitors throughout the day, obviously attending someone of importance.

More significantly, it was the only structure in the camp that Veteranus couldn't observe properly from his hillside position. The building was positioned in a natural depression, shielded from external observation by the careful placement of other structures around it. Someone had deliberately designed the camp layout to protect this particular building from prying eyes. If Rhiannon was being held anywhere in the camp, this would be the most likely location.

Moving through the settlement in darkness required even greater care than the approach. Here, the slightest sound or movement could alert inhabitants who were trained to notice such things, and the night guards would be particularly vigilant. Veteranus used every shadow, every momentary distraction, every brief gap in the patterns of movement he had memorized during daylight observations.

He timed his movements to coincide with the normal sounds of night camp life, slipping between buildings when someone stirred a dying fire nearby, using the soft crackle of flames to mask his footsteps. When warriors walked past his hiding places on their rounds, he synchronized his breathing with theirs, eliminating any sound that might alert them to his presence.

The infiltration technique was one well used by the Occultum and taught to only the most elite soldiers, requiring years of training to master. It involved reading human behaviour so precisely that an infiltrator could predict when someone would turn their head, when they would speak, when their attention would be focused elsewhere, all while navigating in near-total darkness. It was as much psychology as physical skill, understanding people well enough to move through their midst like a ghost.

Finally, he reached the rear of the target roundhouse. The structure was built into a natural hollow, its back wall pressed against a rise in the ground that created a perfect blind spot from the rest of the camp.

The building itself was more solidly constructed than most others in the camp. While the majority of structures appeared temporary, built for quick assembly and abandonment, this one showed signs of more permanent construction. The walls were thicker, the roof more carefully thatched, the foundation more substantial.

Veteranus pressed himself against the rear wall, listening intently for any sounds from within. Voices reached him, at least two people speaking in low tones, too quiet for him to make out words but suggesting the building was currently occupied.

He moved carefully along the wall toward what he hoped was an entrance, his hands guiding him along the rough timber surface. Most Celtic roundhouses had their doorways facing east, toward the rising sun, but military considerations might have dictated a different orientation for this structure.

As he reached the corner where the wall curved toward the front of the building, he could hear the voices more clearly. One was definitely male, deep, authoritative, while the other was harder to identify, but something in its tone suggested either a woman or a very young man.

Veteranus positioned himself beside the entrance, pressing his back against the wall while he listened to the conversation inside. The voices had fallen silent, which could mean the occupants had heard something, or simply that their discussion had reached a natural pause.

Taking a breath to steady himself, he reached slowly toward the edge of the leather curtain, preparing to ease it outward just enough to create a gap through which he could observe the interior by the light of whatever fire burned within, but just as his hand reached the doorway, he heard the slightest sound behind him, a sound that shouldn't be there.

Veteranus felt every muscle in his body tense involuntarily. His hand froze as his mind raced through options. He had heard no footsteps, no rustle of clothing, no indication that anyone had approached his position through the darkness. Yet someone had managed to get close without alerting any of his highly trained senses.

Slowly, he began to turn around but before he could say a word, a club smashed against the side of his head sending him crashing to the floor and into a deep pit of unconsciousness. As he lay there motionless, another figure walked out of the shadows to stand over him. He looked down and used his boot to expose his face before finally nodding in recognition.

'Hello again, Veteranus,' said Mordred quietly. 'I've been expecting you.'

Chapter Twenty-Five

The Camp of the Shadow Walkers

Consciousness returned to Veteranus slowly, like emerging from deep, dark water. His head throbbed with a pain that seemed to pulse in rhythm with his heartbeat, and his mouth felt as dry as sun-baked leather. As awareness gradually returned, he became conscious of his surroundings, rough timber bars pressing against his back, the smell of something distinctly animal, and the uncomfortable realization that he was confined in a space barely large enough for a man to sit upright.

He opened his eyes carefully, squinting against the morning light that filtered through gaps in the crude wooden cage. The construction was solid but simple, thick oak posts driven into the ground and connected with crossbeams, creating a pen that might normally house hunting dogs or valuable livestock. The spaces between the bars were too narrow for a man to squeeze through, and the timber was too thick to break without tools he didn't possess.

As his vision cleared, Veteranus saw two figures standing perhaps ten paces away, engaged in what appeared to be an intense discussion. One was unmistakably Cadoc, the massive Silures warrior who Maelon had told him about, and to his astonishment, the other was the man who Claudius himself wanted dead...*Mordred!*

'You said you knew this man,' Cadoc was saying, his deep voice carrying clearly in the still morning air. 'How?'

Mordred glanced over to the cage.

'For several months, Veteranus was my... *guest*... on Isla Mona. He had been captured at the battle where Togodumnus was killed. He is part of a group called the Occultum, Rome's own shadow warriors who operate behind enemy lines, conducting missions too sensitive for regular legions.'

Cadoc's scarred face showed interest at this revelation.

'What makes them different from ordinary scouts?'

'Everything. Training, methods, objectives.' Mordred turned slightly, his gaze briefly meeting Veteranus's through the cage bars before returning to his conversation with the war leader. 'They are assassins and infiltrators, men trained to accomplish the impossible. Where a legion might take a city through siege, the Occultum would kill its leaders in their beds. Where diplomats might negotiate, they would eliminate the opposing negotiators.'

'And this one was on your island?'

'He was. For a time, I thought I might convert him to our cause. He showed... interest in our ways, our beliefs. I even allowed him to accompany raiding parties, to see how we fought.' Mordred's voice carried a note of what might have been regret. 'It was a mistake. I believed I could turn Rome's weapon against Rome itself.'

Cadoc studied the caged prisoner with new understanding.

'But he escaped?'

'During our attack on Camulodunum, his comrades mounted a rescue operation that not only freed him but also thwarted our attempt to eliminate Emperor Claudius.' Mordred's tone hardened with the memory.

The two men fell silent for a moment, each contemplating the implications. Veteranus remained motionless, giving no indication that he was conscious or listening to their conversation. Information was a weapon, and the more he learned about his captors' knowledge and intentions, the better his chances of survival, however slim those might be.

'What is he doing here?' Cadoc asked eventually. 'These forests are far from any Roman settlement. Why would one of these Occultum come to our territory?'

'That,' Mordred replied, 'is the question that concerns me most. Veteranus does nothing without purpose. His presence here suggests a specific mission, probably one of significant importance to Roman interests.'

Cadoc's expression darkened.

'You think he's here for you?'

'Possibly. Or perhaps he seeks intelligence on your people, your defences, your alliances.' Mordred paused, his scholarly mind working through possibilities. 'What troubles me more is that he's unlikely to be operating alone. The Occultum rarely sends single operatives on missions of this magnitude.'

This observation had an immediate effect on Cadoc. The war leader's posture shifted, his relaxed confidence replaced by the alertness of a predator sensing potential threats.

'You think there are others?'

'I think we must assume there are,' Mordred replied grimly. 'And if I'm correct, they may already be closer than we realize.'

Cadoc turned sharply and gestured to one of his warriors.

'Kelm,' he called. 'Come here.'

The warrior approached immediately.

'Send out a search party,' Cadoc commanded. 'Conduct a full sweep of the surrounding forest, extending at least five miles in all directions. They're looking for signs of other intruders, tracks, camps, anything that suggests Roman presence in our territory. 'Tell them that anyone they find is to be taken alive if possible, dead if necessary. But no one escapes to report back to Roman territories.'

Kelm nodded once and departed immediately to organize the search party. Within minutes, Veteranus could hear the sounds of men preparing for an extended patrol, weapons being checked, supplies gathered, horses prepared for rapid movement through difficult terrain.

As the activity swirled around the camp, Cadoc turned his attention back to the cage and its occupant.

'We should kill him now,' he said bluntly. 'He is too dangerous to keep alive.'

'Not yet,' Mordred replied. 'First, we need to know exactly why he's here.'

'Do you think he'll tell us?'

Mordred's smile was cold and entirely without humour.

'Veteranus is a strong man. He won't break easily, but there are ways to extract information from even the most disciplined minds.'

Cadoc's scarred features showed interest in these possibilities.

'Torture?'

'Crude and often ineffective against men of his training. No, I have other methods in mind.' Mordred approached the cage slowly, his eyes fixed on Veteranus's motionless form. Sometimes the mind provides more effective torture than any physical pain.'

'And if that fails?'

'Then we explore other options.' Mordred knelt beside the cage, bringing his face close to the wooden bars. 'I know this man, Cadoc. I know his strengths and his weaknesses. Given time, I can break him.'

The two men stood in contemplative silence for several

minutes, each weighing options and considering implications. Finally, Mordred straightened and stepped away from the cage.

'Keep him secure but alive for now,' he instructed. 'Minimal food and water, enough to maintain his health but not his strength. No communication with anyone except myself. And Cadoc…' He turned to face the war leader directly. 'If your patrols encounter his companions, take no unnecessary risks. The Occultum are as dangerous as cornered wolves.'

With that, both men walked away, leaving Veteranus alone in his crude prison. The sounds of the search parties departing gradually faded, replaced by the normal activities of a military camp maintaining its routines despite the current crisis.

For the first time since his capture, Veteranus allowed himself to assess his situation honestly. The cage was solid and well-constructed, impossible to break without tools or help from outside. His captors knew exactly who he was and what he represented, eliminating any possibility of deception or misdirection but most troubling of all, they had immediately recognized the likelihood that he wasn't operating alone and had taken swift action to locate any comrades.

Maelon was obviously at immediate risk, but somewhere in these forests, Seneca and the rest of the Occultum were pursuing their own mission. But now the hunters had become the hunted, and experienced Silures trackers were moving through the woods seeking to turn their advantage against them.

Veteranus closed his eyes and leaned back against the wooden bars of his cage. He was prepared for capture, interrogation, even death in the service of Rome. But the knowledge that his presence might have compromised his comrades' mission weighed on him more heavily than any personal concerns about his own fate.

For now, he could only wait and hope that the others would complete their mission successfully. The initiative had passed entirely out of his hands, and only the gods could determine what would happen next. Time was running out for everyone involved.

Chapter Twenty-Six

The Silures Village

The roundhouse had been prepared with care befitting a guest of importance and fresh rushes covered the floor, strewn with fragrant herbs that released their scent when disturbed. A small fire burned in the central hearth, casting warm light across wooden bowls filled with the finest food the settlement could provide, roasted venison, fresh bread, autumn fruits, and honey mead in a silver cup that had clearly been plundered from some wealthy victim.

Belenos sat cross-legged on a woven mat, his massive frame somehow managing to appear relaxed despite the tension that had gripped the settlement since Kynan's return. He had exchanged his blood-stained training clothes for a clean tunic and had taken time to rebraid his beard, presenting himself as a leader rather than a warrior fresh from combat.

The leather door covering was drawn aside, and the captive was escorted in by Morwen and two other women. The transformation was remarkable. Gone were the travel-stained clothes and dishevelled appearance of the previous day. The prisoner now wore a simple but well-made dress of undyed wool, clean and properly fitted to her frame. Her auburn hair had been washed and brushed until it gleamed like burnished copper in the firelight, and her skin showed the healthy glow of someone who had been allowed to bathe and rest.

What struck Belenos most, however, was her bearing. Despite being a captive in an enemy settlement, she moved with the confident grace of someone entering her own hall. Her green eyes surveyed the interior arrangements with what appeared to be approval rather than fear, and when she saw the prepared feast, a slight smile of irony touched the corners of her mouth.

'Please,' Belenos said in the trading tongue, gesturing to a mat across the fire from his own position. 'Sit. We have much to discuss.'

She inclined her head gracefully, not a bow of submission, but the courteous acknowledgment one noble might give another, and settled onto the indicated seat with fluid elegance. Her posture remained perfectly straight, hands folded calmly in her lap, every inch the composed aristocrat despite her circumstances.

'You have been treated well?' Belenos inquired, more out of genuine curiosity than concern. Her transformation suggested his women had indeed followed his instructions to accord her appropriate respect.

'Your people have been most courteous,' she replied. 'I am grateful for their kindness.'

The formality of her response intrigued him. This was not the desperate gratitude of a terrified captive, but the polite acknowledgment of someone accustomed to receiving such treatment as her due.

They began to eat in relative silence, Belenos observing his guest carefully while she sampled the various dishes with evident appreciation. She ate with the refined manners of nobility, small bites taken with deliberate grace, nothing hurried or desperate about her consumption despite whatever hunger she might have felt.

'The venison is excellent,' she commented after several minutes. 'Your hunters are skilled.'

'They are,' Belenos agreed. 'Though perhaps not as skilled as your own warriors were unfortunate.'

A shadow passed across her features at this reminder of

the men who had died protecting her, but her composure never wavered.

'They were good men. They deserved better than death in a forest ambush.'

'All warriors deserve better than they receive,' Belenos replied philosophically. 'Yet we all know the risks when we take up the spear.'

She nodded slowly, acknowledging the truth of his observation.

'Indeed. Though some deaths serve greater purposes than others.'

This comment hung in the air between them, laden with implications about the potential consequences of her capture. Belenos continued eating while he considered how to approach the crucial questions that needed answers.

'You are not a common woman,' he said eventually, stating the obvious as a way to begin the more delicate inquiries.

'No,' she agreed simply. 'I am not.'

'Perhaps you might tell me who you are? It would help me understand the situation more completely.'

She set down her wooden spoon and met his gaze directly, her green eyes reflecting the firelight with steady confidence.

'I am Rhiannon, daughter of Cartimandua, Queen of the Brigantes.' Her voice carried no boastfulness, merely the matter-of-fact tone of someone stating an undeniable reality. 'The men your warriors killed were my escort, accompanying me to my betrothal ceremony.'

Belenos felt the blood drain from his face as the full implications crashed home. This was far worse than he had feared. Not merely a high-ranking noble, but the daughter of the most powerful queen in northern Britannia, and she had been preparing for a political marriage that would have significant strategic importance.

'Your betrothal?' he managed, his voice carefully controlled despite the alarm bells ringing in his mind.

'To Einion, son of Bodvoc of the Ordovices. Our union was to seal the alliance between our peoples.' Her tone remained calm, but something in her eyes suggested she was fully aware of the earthquake her words had just created. 'I was going to undertake a cleansing ceremony at the sacred spring where your men found us.'

The war leader set down his own eating utensils, his appetite completely vanished. Kynan hadn't simply interrupted a trading mission or captured a minor noble. He had destroyed a marriage alliance between two of the most powerful tribes in Britannia, killed the bridegroom and his escort, and kidnapped the bride herself.

'The son of Bodvoc,' he repeated, hoping he had misheard. 'He was among those killed?'

'He was,' Rhiannon confirmed, her voice carrying genuine sadness for the first time. 'Einion was a good man, brave and honourable. His death will not go unavenged.'

Belenos leaned back, his mind racing through the cascading consequences of this revelation. The Ordovices would demand either massive compensation or blood vengeance for the death of their chief's son. The Brigantes, on the other hand, would require the return of their princess or face accusations of failing to protect their most valuable diplomatic asset. Both tribes together commanded enough warriors to cause serious problems to the Silures if they chose to unite in common cause.

'You understand the position this places my people in,'

he said carefully.

'I do.' Rhiannon picked up her cup of mead and took a measured sip before continuing. 'Which is why I propose a solution that serves everyone's interests.'

'I'm listening.'

'Release me,' she said simply, 'and allow me to return to my mother's court. I will tell her that while the attack was regrettable, you personally ensured my safety and treated me with honour. The Brigantes will have their daughter back, and the Ordovices will have confirmation of what happened to Einion. Do this and the Silures will avoid a war they cannot win.'

The logic was compelling, but Belenos could see the flaws immediately.

'The Ordovices will not simply accept the death of Einion.'

'Perhaps not, but that becomes a matter between you and Bodvoc. Perhaps compensation can be negotiated.' She met his gaze steadily. 'But if I do not return to Brigantes, both tribes will assume the worst. They will believe I was murdered alongside the escort, and they will demand blood vengeance against all Silures settlements.'

Belenos considered this, recognizing the brutal accuracy of her assessment. With no evidence of Rhiannon's survival, the two northern tribes would indeed assume the worst and respond accordingly.

'And if I release you,' he asked, 'what guarantee do I have that you won't simply call for war anyway? You could claim you were abused, tortured, dishonoured. Such claims would justify any retaliation.'

'You have my word,' Rhiannon replied without hesitation. 'And the word of Cartimandua's daughter carries weight in both courts.'

'Forgive me if I find royal promises insufficient security for my people's lives,' Belenos said dryly.

A slight smile touched her lips at his scepticism.

'A fair point. Then consider this, even if I wanted to lie about my treatment here, why would I need to? The mere fact of my capture and Einion's death provides all the justification either tribe would need for war. Additional provocations would be redundant.'

Despite himself, Belenos found himself impressed by her reasoning. This was clearly a woman raised not just in luxury, but in the intricacies of tribal politics and diplomatic calculation.

'There is another problem,' he said after a long pause. 'Even if releasing you might prevent war with the Brigantes and Ordovices, it might not be sufficient to satisfy them. The death of Bodvoc's son demands more than the return of a bride who is no longer useful to either party.'

Rhiannon's composure faltered slightly at this harsh assessment of her changed circumstances, and, for the first time since entering the roundhouse, she looked like what she truly was, a young woman whose carefully planned future had been destroyed by violence.

'Perhaps,' she admitted quietly. 'But my continued captivity certainly guarantees war. My release at least offers the possibility of negotiation.'

Belenos nodded slowly, acknowledging the truth of her argument while weighing it against other considerations. The strategic situation was complex, with no clear path that guaranteed his people's safety.

'I will consider your words,' he said finally. 'For now, you will be treated as an honoured guest, but you will not leave the settlement.'

'I understand,' Rhiannon replied, rising gracefully to her feet. 'And I thank you for your consideration.'

As she moved toward the door covering, she paused and turned back to face him.

'For what it's worth, I believe you to be an honourable man caught in circumstances beyond your control. I hope you find a path that serves your people's interests without requiring further bloodshed.'

After she left, Belenos remained seated by the fire, staring into the flames while his mind worked through an impossible puzzle. Every option seemed to lead to disaster of one form or another.

If he released Rhiannon, he might avoid immediate war but would face demands for massive compensation that his people couldn't provide. If he kept her, he would certainly face the combined wrath of two powerful tribes. If he killed her, he would eliminate a potential witness but also guarantee that no negotiation would ever be possible.

And underlying all of these considerations was the uncomfortable knowledge that Kynan's raid had been unauthorized, motivated by greed rather than strategic necessity. The young warrior had created this crisis through poor judgment, but it was Belenos who would have to find a way to navigate its consequences.

Outside, the normal sounds of the settlement continued, children playing, warriors training, women going about their daily tasks. None of them yet understood that their world had changed, that a decision made in a moment of opportunistic violence might soon bring war to their hidden valley.

Belenos reached for the mead cup and drained it in a single swallow, tasting the honey sweetness while contemplating the bitter choices that lay ahead. Whatever path he chose, people would die. The only question was how many, and whether they would be his enemies or his own people.

Chapter Twenty-Seven

The Camp of the Shadow Walkers

Dawn crept across the valley like a cautious animal, its pale light filtering through the ancient canopy to dapple the forest floor with shifting patterns of gold and shadow. Maelon had not slept, his eyes fixed on the distant glow of cooking fires from the camp far below. Through the long hours of darkness, he had strained his eyes and ears for any sound that might indicate Veteranus's return, but the forest had offered only the normal chorus of night creatures and the occasional distant call of a sentry.

As the sky lightened enough to make out individual shapes in the camp below, a cold dread began to settle in his stomach. By now, Veteranus should have returned, successful or not. The Roman was many things, but careless was not among them. If he had completed his reconnaissance, or had been forced to abort the mission, he would be back. The only explanation for his continued absence was capture or death.

Maelon fought the urge to abandon his position immediately. Veteranus had been clear about what to do if things went wrong, head back toward Ordovices territory and don't look back. It was sound advice, the kind that kept people alive in dangerous situations. But something held him in place, perhaps loyalty to the man who had trusted him enough to accept his guidance, perhaps simple curiosity about what had happened during the night.

The decision was made for him as the sun climbed higher and the camp below began to stir with unusual activity. Even from his distant vantage point, Maelon could see that this was not the normal routine of a military encampment beginning its day. Men moved with urgent purpose, gathering in groups around what appeared to be leaders giving instructions. Weapons were being distributed, supplies prepared, horses readied. They were organizing search parties.

Maelon's blood turned to ice as the implications crashed home. The Shadow Walkers knew about Veteranus, which meant they probably knew about him as well. Whether the Roman was alive or dead, whether he had talked under torture or simply been discovered during his infiltration, the result was the same. Every warrior in the camp would soon be scouring the surrounding forest for additional intruders.

Without hesitation, he began gathering his meagre possessions, and within moments, he was moving away from his observation point, heading northeast toward what he hoped was safety.

The terrain that had provided such excellent concealment during their approach now became a treacherous maze of obstacles. Fallen logs that had offered cover now blocked his path, forcing him to climb over or around them with precious time lost at each barrier. Dense thickets that had hidden their position now caught at his clothes and exposed skin, every snag a potential delay that might cost him his life.

Behind him, the sounds of organized pursuit grew steadily clearer. Voices called back and forth through the trees, coordinating search patterns, maintaining the disciplined communications of experienced hunters. Maelon recognized the efficiency in their methods and knew he was being hunted by men who understood this forest far better than he did.

He pushed himself harder, abandoning stealth for speed as the distance between him and his pursuers steadily decreased. His breath came in ragged gasps as he forced his way through undergrowth that seemed determined to entangle him, his legs burning with the effort of maintaining pace over increasingly difficult terrain.

The first baying of hounds reached his ears when he was perhaps two miles from the camp. Dogs could follow scent trails that would be invisible to human trackers and could maintain pursuit long after human hunters had exhausted themselves, running their quarry to ground.

Maelon's pace increased to a desperate run, all thoughts of concealment abandoned in favour of distance. Branches whipped at his face, leaving stinging cuts across his cheeks and forehead. His feet seemed to find every root and stone, sending jolts of pain up his legs, but he forced himself to maintain the punishing speed that represented his only hope of survival.

The baying grew louder, closer, accompanied now by the crash of large bodies moving through the undergrowth. Desperation drove Maelon toward the sound of running water he could hear somewhere ahead through the trees. Water offered the only possibility of breaking his scent trail, confusing the dogs enough to buy precious time. He crashed through a final screen of bushes and found himself at the edge of a substantial stream, perhaps twenty paces wide and running fast over a bed of smooth stones.

Without hesitation, he plunged into the freezing water, gasping as the cold shocked his system. The current was stronger than it had appeared from the bank, tugging at his legs and threatening to sweep him downstream.

The baying of the hounds reached a frenzied pitch as they reached the water's edge, becoming confused and agitated as they lost the clear scent trail they had been following. Maelon could hear their handlers calling out, trying to direct them to places that might relocate the trail on the opposite bank.

He moved downstream quickly, using the noise of the rushing water to mask any sounds he might make. The cold was already numbing his legs, but he forced himself to continue, knowing that every yard he travelled in the water increased his chances of escaping the immediate pursuit.

But even as he moved, Maelon knew this was only a temporary reprieve. The moment he left the water, he would begin laying down a fresh scent trail that the dogs could follow. And the longer he stayed in the stream, the weaker he would become from cold and exhaustion.

The sound of the dogs grew louder again. Time was running out, and Maelon had to make a decision about where and how to leave the water.

Ahead, an ancient oak leaned out over the stream, its massive trunk scarred by decades of spring floods. One of its lower branches hung directly above the water, perhaps six feet above the surface, while several larger limbs extended back toward the main trunk like the rungs of a natural ladder.

Maelon looked back toward the sounds of pursuit, calculating distances and time. The dogs were perhaps half a mile behind him. They would soon be upon him if he remained in the water, but if he could reach that overhanging branch without leaving any scent trail on the banks...

The plan that formed in his mind was desperate, but it was the only chance he could see. Moving to the side of the stream where the water had carved a deeper pool beneath the overhanging roots, he began stripping off his clothes with numb fingers. Each garment was thoroughly soaked in the cold water before being placed carefully in the pool, weighted down with stones so they would remain submerged.

Every muscle in his body contracted involuntarily as the cold penetrated to his core, but he forced himself to duck completely beneath the surface, allowing the current to wash away any traces of sweat or human scent that might cling to his skin.

When he could hold his breath no longer, he surfaced gasping and immediately reached up toward the overhanging branch. His numbed fingers could barely feel the rough bark, but desperation gave him strength as he pulled himself upward, using the branch to reach the larger limb above.

The climb to the main trunk was agony, his frozen muscles responding sluggishly to commands from his increasingly clouded mind. But somehow he managed it, pulling himself higher into the spreading canopy until he found a natural hollow where the trunk divided into several major branches.

The hiding place was perfect, a depression in the living wood that could conceal a man from observation below while providing solid support. Maelon wedged himself into the hollow, drawing his knees up to his chest in an attempt to conserve what little warmth remained in his naked body.

Below, the sounds of pursuit grew steadily louder. Human voices called back and forth, as the first hound reached the water's edge directly below, its nose working frantically as it tried to locate the scent trail it had been following. The dog cast back and forth along the bank, whining with frustration as it failed to find any indication of where its quarry had left the water.

More dogs arrived, their handlers following close behind. Maelon could see them clearly through the screen of leaves, dangerous-looking men with the lean build and alert eyes of professional hunters. They wore the blue woad patterns of the Silures, and their weapons were close at hand as they worked to solve the puzzle of the vanished trail.

For long minutes, they searched the area with systematic thoroughness. Maelon remained absolutely motionless, controlling his breathing to the point where it was barely perceptible.

The cold was becoming a serious problem. His naked body had no protection against the morning air, and the water that still dripped from his skin carried away what little warmth he had left. He could feel his thinking becoming sluggish, his reactions slowing as hypothermia began to take hold.

Below, the search continued with professional persistence. The handlers knew their quarry was somewhere nearby, that a man couldn't simply vanish from a scent trail in open forest, and they expanded their search pattern, casting wider circles as they looked for any sign of where the trail might resume.

Maelon's heart nearly stopped as he realized they were looking for his clothes. If they found the bundle he had weighted down in the side pool, they would know exactly what had happened and would begin searching the overhanging trees systematically.

But the pool was well-concealed beneath the oak's spreading roots, and the searchers were looking for a body, not discarded clothing. After several minutes of searching the more obvious locations, they moved on downstream, their voices gradually fading as they expanded their search pattern.

Silence gradually returned to the stream, broken only by the gurgle of running water and the whisper of wind through leaves. Maelon remained motionless in his hollow, knowing that premature movement could still mean death if any of the searchers doubled back or if additional parties were working the area.

The cold was now his greatest enemy. His body heat

was leaching away steadily, and he could feel his muscles becoming increasingly unresponsive. If he waited too long to move, he might find himself too weak to climb down from his perch, freezing to death in the very hiding place that had saved his life.

But the alternative was worse. Moving too soon would expose him to capture by searchers who might still be within hearing distance. All he could do was wait, pray to whatever gods might be listening, and hope that when the time came to move, he would still have the strength to do so.

Chapter Twenty-Eight

The Settlement

For three days and nights, the Occultum had maintained their watch over the larger Silures settlement from the concealed observation post on the western ridge. They worked in shifts, two men at a time spending long hours studying the patterns of life in the valley below, absorbing every detail that might provide intelligence about their target.

Marcus and Decimus had taken the first rotation, noting the apparent hierarchy among the settlement's inhabitants and identifying what appeared to be the most important structures. Falco and Talorcan followed, the Belgic scout proving particularly adept at reading the subtle signs of a community's daily rhythms. Finally, Sica and Seneca maintained the watch through the darkest hours, when movement was minimal but when any unusual activity would be most significant. The results had been frustratingly inconclusive.

'Nothing,' Marcus reported during their evening briefing in the ravine hideout. 'No sign of druids, no ceremonies, no indication that anyone of Mordred's stature is present in the settlement.'

'The people go about their business like any tribal community,' Decimus added. 'Farming, cooking, training their warriors. But I've seen no evidence of the kind of reverence or special activity you'd expect around a powerful druid.'

Seneca absorbed this information while weighing their options. Intelligence gathering was often a process of elimination, ruling out possibilities until the truth emerged by default. But in hostile territory, with limited supplies and growing risk of discovery, patience had its own costs.

'There's been no religious activity at all?' he asked.

'Daily offerings at what appears to be a shrine near the centre of the settlement,' replied Decimus, 'but routine. Nothing suggesting a druid of importance. The large roundhouse built into the hillside belongs to their war chief and he was probably the man we saw take charge when that woman was brought in. But again, no signs of divided authority or deference to religious leadership.'

Seneca stared into the small, carefully concealed fire that provided their only light in the hidden camp. The flame had been built in a deep pit and shielded with stones to prevent any glow from escaping, but it still felt dangerously exposed in enemy territory.

'We need better intelligence,' he decided finally. 'Observation from distance has its limits. Tonight, Sica and I will conduct a close reconnaissance of the settlement itself.'

The others absorbed this decision without comment, though Seneca could see the concern in their expressions. Infiltrating an enemy settlement was one of the most dangerous operations the Occultum performed, requiring perfect coordination and leaving no margin for error.

'If we're not back by dawn,' Seneca continued, 'wait one full day for our return. If we don't appear by the following sunset, continue the mission without us. Mordred is the objective, not our individual survival.'

Falco shifted uncomfortably at this stark reminder of their priorities.

'And if you find him?'

'Then we complete the mission,' Seneca replied simply. 'By whatever means necessary.'

The descent began at midnight, when the settlement's

activities had reached their lowest ebb. Seneca and Sica moved with the patient precision of predators stalking prey, each step calculated to avoid the slightest sound that might alert sentries to their presence.

Like Veteranus to the north, the technique was one they had perfected through years of similar operations. Rather than moving continuously toward their target, they advanced in stages, spending long minutes motionless between each movement while they assessed the changing tactical situation. Every shadow was evaluated for concealment potential, every guard position noted, and his pattern of observation predicted.

Sica led the way, his smaller frame and uncanny ability to read terrain making him ideally suited for this kind of work. Behind him, Seneca followed in his exact footsteps, trusting his teammate's judgment about the safest route through the increasingly dangerous ground ahead.

They reached the settlement's perimeter without incident, finding themselves at the edge of cultivated fields that surrounded the main cluster of buildings. Here, the real challenge began. The open ground between the fields and the settlement proper offered little concealment, and any movement would be visible to alert sentries.

But Seneca had noted during their days of observation that the guard posts were positioned to watch the main approaches to the valley, not to observe the settlement itself. The assumption, reasonable enough, was that any threat would come from outside rather than from enemies already within the defensive perimeter.

It was an assumption the Occultum had exploited many times before.

They waited until a guard's attention was focused away from their intended route, then moved swiftly across the exposed ground to the shelter of the nearest building. Once there, they pressed themselves against the structure's wall, listening for any sound that might indicate their movement had been detected.

Silence.

The settlement's buildings were arranged in concentric circles around a central gathering place, with the most important structures occupying the inner ring. Seneca had identified their primary target during the daylight observations: the large structure built partially into the hillside, which showed all the signs of being both a residence and a meeting place for the settlement's leadership.

If Mordred was present in this community, that building was the most likely location for him to be housed or to conduct whatever business had brought him here.

Moving between the buildings required even greater care. Unlike the approach through the valley, here they risked encountering inhabitants moving about on nighttime business, guards conducting internal patrols, or simply someone stepping outside to relieve themselves. Any unexpected encounter would likely mean discovery and death.

They used every technique in their extensive repertoire. When dogs began to stir at their approach, they froze until the animals settled again, when voices sounded from within buildings, they timed their movements to coincide with the loudest conversation and when a warrior emerged from his dwelling to check on something, they melted into shadows so complete they seemed to become part of the architecture itself. But finally, they reached the base of the target building, pressing themselves against the side wall where the structure was built into the natural slope of the hillside.

The construction was more substantial than most of the

settlement's other buildings, and through gaps in the wall construction, they could see the faint glow of a fire burning within, suggesting the building was currently occupied.

Both men pressed their ears to the wooden walls, straining to hear any conversation that might reveal the identity or activities of the occupants.

For long minutes, they detected nothing but the normal sounds of a building at rest: the settling of timber, the whisper of air through gaps in the construction, the soft crackle of a banked fire. Then, faintly, voices became audible from within.

The conversation was too muffled for Seneca to make out individual words, but the cadences were clear enough. Two men, speaking in what sounded like the formal tones of a serious discussion.

Seneca felt his pulse quicken. That second voice could belong to Mordred, though he couldn't be certain without hearing more. He shifted position slightly, trying to find a gap in the wall construction that might allow clearer hearing.

But despite Seneca's best efforts, he couldn't make out enough individual words to determine the subject of their discussion or to confirm the identity of either speaker. The building's construction was too solid, the voices too carefully modulated for eavesdropping from outside.

The Syrian assassin caught Seneca's eye and shook his head slightly, indicating he too was unable to gather useful intelligence from their current position.

As the night wore on, the conversation within gradually died away and eventually, even the faint glow of firelight disappeared, suggesting the building's occupants had retired for the night.

The return proved even more challenging than the infiltration. Guards were more alert as dawn approached, and early risers were beginning to stir within some of the buildings. Twice, they were forced to freeze for extended periods as people moved through the settlement on early morning business, but their training and experience carried them through.

By the time the sun cleared the eastern horizon, they were climbing back up the ridge toward their hidden camp, having successfully penetrated enemy territory and returned with at least some intelligence, however incomplete.

'Negative identification,' Seneca reported to the assembled Occultum once they had reached the security of their ravine hideout. 'Two men in conversation, one likely the settlement's leader. The other could have been Mordred, but I can't confirm it.'

'Could you determine the subject of their discussion?' Marcus asked.

'No, and we need more definitive proof before committing to action. I believe this settlement is not the location of our target at all.'

Falco expressed what they were all thinking.

'So we move on?'

'We move on,' Seneca confirmed. 'If Mordred was here, his presence would have been more obvious by now. The intelligence reports suggested multiple Silures communities in this region. We'll continue southwest, deeper into their territory.'

The decision made, they spent the remainder of the day preparing for departure. The second cache would be buried here, providing emergency supplies if they needed to retreat through this area during the final extraction. Like the first cache, it was carefully concealed and marked with signs only they would recognize.

As evening approached, they conducted their final preparations for movement deeper into hostile territory. Each man checked his equipment and redistributed supplies to ensure balanced loads, for the challenges ahead.

Their mission continued, but they were now venturing into the true heart of Silures lands, where discovery would mean not just failure, but almost certain death. Behind them lay their established escape route and hidden supplies. Ahead lay the unknown, and somewhere in that unknown, the man that Emperor Claudius wanted dead.

As darkness fell, the six members of the Occultum slipped out of their ravine hideout and melted into the forest, moving deeper into enemy territory with the methodical patience of hunters pursuing the most dangerous prey of all.

Chapter Twenty-Nine

The Camp of the Shadow Walkers

Veteranus awoke in slightly better circumstances than the previous day. He was upright, his back pressed against a wooden post driven deep into the earth, his arms pulled back and secured behind him.

As his vision cleared, he found himself in a dim roundhouse lit only by a small fire burning in a central pit. The smoke rose lazily toward a hole in the thatched roof, creating shifting patterns of light and shadow that danced across the curved walls.

Across from him, perhaps six feet away, sat Mordred.

The druid had seemingly aged since their last encounter on Isla Mona. His hair, once merely streaked with grey, now had more white strands, pulled back and bound with a leather cord that gave his angular features a severe, ascetic appearance. His beard, too, seemed longer and whiter, reaching nearly to his chest but his eyes remained unchanged, dark and intelligent, holding the same penetrating intensity that had marked him as dangerous from their first meeting.

He was eating dried berries and nuts methodically from a wooden bowl, though his gaze never left Veteranus's face, studying the Roman with detached interest.

The silence stretched between them, heavy with unspoken history and mutual recognition. Veteranus tested his bonds without making obvious movements, feeling for any weakness in the ropes or the post that held him but there was none. Whoever had secured him understood the art of imprisonment.

Finally, Mordred spoke, his voice carrying the same

cultured tones that had once attempted to seduce Veteranus to the Celtic cause.

'You look older, my friend. The intervening months have not been kind to you.'

Veteranus met his gaze steadily, refusing to show the fear that gnawed at his stomach.

'Captivity has that effect on men.'

'Indeed.' Mordred selected another piece of dried fruit, holding it up to examine it in the firelight before popping it into his mouth. 'Though I recall offering you something rather different than captivity when last we met. Freedom, purpose, a chance to serve something greater than Rome's insatiable appetite for conquest.'

'I made my choice.'

'You did.' Mordred's tone carried no anger, only the mild disappointment of a teacher whose student had failed to grasp an important lesson. 'And yet here you are, bound and helpless in the heart of Silures territory. Perhaps it would have been wiser to accept my offer when it was made in friendship rather than find yourself here as my prisoner.'

Veteranus said nothing, watching as Mordred set his bowl aside and reached for a leather flask that sat beside it. The druid uncorked it and took a measured drink before placing it just beyond Veteranus's reach.

'But enough reminiscence,' Mordred continued, settling back into a more comfortable position. 'We have more pressing matters to discuss. Beginning with why you are here.'

'I told you on Mona,' Veteranus replied carefully. 'I have no interest in your war against Rome.'

'And yet you participated in the rescue operation that saved Emperor Claudius. That hardly suggests neutrality in our conflict.'

'I was a prisoner escaping captivity,' replied Veteranus. 'Nothing more. The fact that my escape coincided with your attack was simply fortune.'

'Fortune.' Mordred repeated the word as if tasting something bitter. 'An interesting choice of words. Do you truly expect me to believe that your presence here, now, in the depths of Silures territory, is merely another coincidence?'

'I came with a trading mission to the Ordovices,' Veteranus replied, sticking to the story that had served him so far. 'When they demanded someone search for a kidnapped woman, I volunteered.'

'Ah yes, the missing princess.' Mordred's expression showed he was aware of the situation. 'Rhiannon, daughter of Cartimandua. A valuable prize, certainly. But hardly the sort of mission that would require the skills of the Occultum.'

The casual mention of his unit's name hit Veteranus like a physical blow, though he fought to keep his reaction from showing on his face. Mordred knew exactly who he was, what he represented, and probably why he was here.

'I know all about your comrades, Veteranus,' Mordred continued, apparently reading his thoughts. 'The question that interests me is what impossible task brought you all to these particular forests.'

Veteranus maintained his silence, knowing that any response would only provide Mordred with more information to work with.

'Come now,' the druid said, his tone becoming almost conversational. 'We both know you didn't come alone. The Occultum never operates with single agents on missions of importance. Your companions are out there somewhere, probably quite close, possibly watching this very settlement. What I cannot determine is whether their mission is the same as yours, or whether you were sent to accomplish different objectives.'

When Veteranus still didn't respond, Mordred rose to his feet and began pacing slowly around the fire, his movements casual but predatory.

'You see, this creates a tactical problem for me,' continued Mordred. 'If I simply eliminate you now, your companions will eventually realize you've been captured and will likely abort their mission, whatever it might be. But if I keep you alive, they may attempt a rescue operation that could endanger my work here.' He paused in his pacing, fixing Veteranus with a direct stare. 'Unless, of course, they're here for me specifically, in which case, keeping you alive serves as excellent bait to draw them into a trap.'

The pieces of Mordred's reasoning were falling into place with terrifying clarity. The druid had identified not just Veteranus's presence, but the likely presence of his fellow operatives. Now he was calculating how best to use that knowledge to his advantage.

'So tell me, old friend,' Mordred continued, settling back into his original position. 'Are you here to kill me? Is that why the Occultum has ventured so far into hostile territory? Have I become such a threat to Roman interests that Claudius has dispatched his finest killers to eliminate me?'

Veteranus forced himself to maintain steady eye contact.

'I told you why I'm here. Nothing more, nothing less.'

'Still lying, I see.' Mordred shook his head with what appeared to be genuine sadness. 'You could have had such power, Veteranus. Such purpose. My offer on Mona was sincere, you know. A man of your skills, fighting for the freedom of these lands rather than their subjugation, could have achieved greatness that would be remembered for generations.'

'Serving your vision of greatness,' Veteranus replied. 'Not mine.'

'And what is your vision?' Mordred asked. 'Endless conquest? The transformation of every free people into Roman slaves? The destruction of cultures that have existed since before Rome was even founded?'

'I serve Rome,' said Veteranus simply. 'Whatever Rome requires.'

'Even unto death?' Mordred asked softly.

'If necessary.'

The druid studied him for a long moment, then reached inside his robes and withdrew a knife. The blade was curved, its edge honed to gleaming sharpness, its handle carved with symbols that seemed to writhe in the firelight.

'You know,' Mordred said conversationally, testing the blade's edge with his thumb, 'the Silures have elevated torture to an art form. They can keep a man alive and screaming for days, peeling away layers of flesh and consciousness until the victim begs to reveal everything he has ever known, just for the mercy of death.' He looked up at Veteranus, his expression mild, as if discussing the weather. 'But perhaps such elaborate methods are unnecessary. Perhaps I should simply handle this matter myself, quietly, efficiently. Save us both the unpleasantness of extended interrogation.'

Mordred rose and walked slowly toward the bound Roman, the knife held casually at his side. His movements were unhurried, almost ceremonial, as if he were performing a ritual he had conducted many times before.

'Last chance, Veteranus. Tell me why you're really here, who sent you, and what your mission entails. Make this easy for both of us.'

Veteranus met his approach with steady silence, though his mind was racing through rapidly diminishing options. Bound as he was, there was no possibility of physical resistance.

Mordred stopped directly in front of him, close enough that Veteranus could smell the dried herbs that permeated the druid's robes, close enough to see the fine lines that age and responsibility had etched around his eyes.

'So be it,' Mordred said quietly, and placed the flat of the blade against Veteranus's throat.

The metal was cold against his skin, a line of chill that seemed to burn despite its temperature. Veteranus could feel his pulse beating against the steel, each heartbeat a reminder of how quickly life could be severed.

'You realize,' Mordred continued, his voice now barely above a whisper, 'that your death accomplishes nothing? Your mission, whatever it truly is, will fail. Your companions will die in these forests, hunted down like animals by warriors who know every tree, every path, every hiding place. And I will continue my work, rallying the free tribes against Roman tyranny.'

The blade turned slowly, its keen edge now resting against the great vein that carried blood from Veteranus's brain to his heart. One quick motion, one decisive cut, and everything would end.

For the first time in longer than he could remember, Veteranus found himself reaching out to the gods he had long ignored. Not to Jupiter or Mars, the official deities of Rome's military machine, but to the older powers his childhood had known, the household gods who protected families, the spirits of ancestors who watched over their descendants.

'If I am to die,' he thought, 'it will be with whatever honour remains to me.'

Mordred's grip on the knife tightened, his muscles tensing for the killing stroke that would end the interrogation permanently but as he relished the moment, footsteps crashed through the entrance, accompanied by urgent voices that shattered the ritual solemnity of the moment.

'Lord Mordred!' a warrior called, his voice tight with excitement and apprehension. 'Forgive the interruption, but…'

Mordred spun away from his prisoner, the knife still in his hand, his face showing the cold fury of a man whose concentration had been broken at a critical moment.

'This had better be worth your life,' he snarled, his cultured composure vanishing to reveal the dangerous predator beneath.

The warrior, dropped to one knee in a gesture of desperate respect.

'My lord, someone has arrived. Someone important. We need you.'

'Who?' Mordred demanded. 'Who would dare interrupt me at such a time?'

The messenger raised his head, his eyes wide with a mixture of awe and fear.

'Caratacus, my lord. The great war leader. He's here, but… but something is wrong. He's sick, very sick. His followers say he needs healing that only you can provide.'

The words hit Mordred like a thunderbolt and Veteranus saw his entire posture change.

Mordred looked back at his prisoner, calculation warring with duty in his dark eyes.

'This is not finished,' he said finally. 'When I return, we

will complete our conversation. And I promise you will tell me everything I wish to know.'

With that, he turned and strode from the roundhouse, leaving Veteranus alone with his bonds, his fears, and the knowledge that he had been granted a reprieve he had neither expected nor earned. But for how long, and to what end, only the gods could say.

Chapter Thirty

The Camp of the Shadow Walkers

From his precarious perch high in the ancient oak, Maelon waited another hour before deciding to move. The hypothermia that had threatened to claim him was now his greatest enemy, his muscles cramped and unresponsive, his thinking sluggish from the prolonged exposure.

Finally, when he was certain the immediate danger had passed, he began the careful descent from his hiding place. His numbed fingers could barely grip the rough bark, and twice he nearly lost his hold as frozen muscles refused to respond properly. But desperation drove him downward, branch by branch, until he could drop the final distance to the forest floor.

His clothes bundle was exactly as he had left it, still submerged beneath the overhanging roots. He plunged his arms into the freezing water, gasping as the cold shocked his already hypothermic system, and retrieved the sodden garments.

Dressing in wet clothes while suffering from exposure was an exercise in misery that tested the limits of his endurance. The fabric clung to his skin like ice, providing no warmth and seeming to leach away what little heat his body still generated, but clothing, even freezing clothing, was better than nakedness in the wilderness.

As he forced his stiff limbs to move, generating the friction that would gradually restore warmth to his core, Maelon began the long journey back toward the Shadow Walker camp. He knew it was dangerous to retrace his route, but he had no choice. Veteranus was somewhere in that camp, and Maelon's survival now depended on determining whether his companion was alive or dead.

The return journey was a nightmare of cold and exhaustion. His wet clothes chafed against skin that was already raw from exposure, and every step sent jolts of pain through feet that had been numbed beyond feeling. But movement generated heat, and gradually, agonizingly, life began to return to his extremities.

By midday, he had regained enough function to move with something approaching his normal stealth. The search parties had not returned to this area, apparently convinced that their quarry had either drowned or escaped far downstream and Maelon used their absence to make better time, pushing himself toward a confrontation he knew might well be his last.

As darkness fell, he found himself back at his original observation point overlooking the Shadow Walker camp.

In a roundhouse larger and more substantial than the others, Mordred knelt beside a crude wooden cot where a man lay burning with fever. Even in the dim light cast by oil lamps arranged around the interior, Caratacus was immediately recognizable, his legendary presence diminished but not erased by illness.

The great war leader's face was flushed with fever, his breathing shallow and rapid. A wound in his side, partially hidden by bloodstained bandages, was the obvious source of his distress, the flesh around the injury swollen and discoloured, speaking of infection that had spread beyond the original cut.

Mordred worked with the focused intensity of a man fighting death itself. His hands moved surely among an array of healing supplies arranged on a low table beside the cot: clay pots containing various powders and liquids, bundles of dried herbs, bone needles, and strips of clean linen.

'Hold him steady,' Mordred commanded the two warriors who flanked the cot. Caratacus had begun to thrash weakly as delirium took hold, his fevered mind fighting battles that existed only in his burning unconsciousness.

The druid selected a clay pot containing a thick, greenish paste made from ground willow bark, meadowsweet, and honey, ingredients known to reduce fever and fight infection. With careful movements, he spread the mixture directly onto the infected wound, pressing it deep into the suppurating flesh despite Caratacus's unconscious moans of pain.

Next came a poultice of comfrey and plantain leaves, herbs that promoted healing and drew corruption from infected tissue. Mordred had prepared them by grinding the fresh leaves with a mortar and pestle, creating a pulpy mass that would draw poison from the wound while providing nutrients to damaged flesh.

'Lift his head,' Mordred instructed, reaching for a wooden cup containing a steaming liquid. The brew was complex, containing willow bark to break the fever, yarrow to strengthen the body's natural defences, and a carefully measured amount of poppy extract to ease pain without inducing an even deeper and more dangerous unconsciousness.

Caratacus's lips were cracked and dry, his body dehydrated from days of fever. Mordred poured the healing draught slowly into his mouth, massaging his throat to encourage swallowing. Much of the liquid ran down the war leader's chin, but enough entered his system to begin its work.

The druid then turned to the brazier that dominated one corner of the roundhouse. Into its glowing coals, he cast a mixture of sacred herbs: juniper for purification, sage for wisdom and healing, and frankincense to carry prayers to the gods. The smoke that rose was thick and aromatic, filling the enclosed space with fumes that made the oil lamps flicker and dance.

As the sacred smoke swirled around them, Mordred began to chant in the old tongue, his voice rising and falling in rhythms that seemed to echo the laboured breathing of his patient. The words were ancient, calling upon Lugus the healer, Brigantia the protector, and Dian Cécht the physician of the gods. He beseeched them to drive the corruption from Caratacus's body, to restore the strength that Britannia needed in its darkest hour.

Outside the healing hut, the camp had transformed into something resembling a military gathering. Throughout the day, more of Caratacus's followers had arrived, warriors whose loyalty to their leader had brought them deep into Silures territory despite the risks. They came in small groups, travel-worn and watchful, their weapons never far from hand.

The Silures received them with cautious respect. These were fellow enemies of Rome, men who had fought and bled in the same cause that drove the Shadow Walkers to their raids and ambushes. Food was shared, water provided, horses tended, but always with the wary courtesy of allies who remained fundamentally strangers.

Around the healing hut, a crowd had gathered, warriors from both tribes standing in silent vigil. Some prayed to their own gods, others simply waited with the patience of men accustomed to the arbitrary nature of life and death. All understood that more than one man's life hung in the balance within those walls.

If Caratacus died, the unified resistance he was building might die with him. If he lived, the war against Rome would continue with renewed vigour. The fate of entire tribes, perhaps the entire island, might depend on Mordred's skill as a healer.

Back in his prison hut, Veteranus had spent the hours since Mordred's departure testing his bonds with systematic thoroughness. The ropes were expertly tied, the post solid and deep-set. Every attempt to loosen his restraints only succeeded in tightening them further, the hemp cutting deeper into his already raw wrists.

Exhaustion and the aftermath of fear had finally claimed him, his head dropping forward as he dozed fitfully despite his uncomfortable position. Dreams came and went, confused images of past missions, faces of dead comrades, the cold certainty that he would soon join them.

He was jerked awake by a soft scratching sound from behind him, as if something small were clawing at the wall of the hut. A rat, perhaps, or one of the camp dogs seeking scraps. He tried to ignore it, focusing instead on listening for any sounds that might indicate Mordred's return.

The scratching continued, growing more deliberate, more purposeful. Then, impossible though it seemed, he heard Maelon's voice, barely audible, whispering urgently in his ear.

'Veteranus. Don't move. Don't speak.'

Maelon, having cut his way through the roundhouse wall, now turned his attention onto Veteranus's binds.

'Hurry,' he hissed.

Finally, blood rushed back into his hands as the restraints fell away, bringing with it a painful tingling that made his fingers clumsy. But there was no time for recovery. At any moment, a guard might notice the damage to the hut, or Mordred might return to continue his interrupted interrogation.

Veteranus forced his stiff limbs to move, following

Maelon through the hole and out into the night beyond. They had escaped, but their situation remained desperate. They were deep in enemy territory, without supplies or clear knowledge of how to reach safety. The night had only begun, and already it promised to test every skill they possessed simply to see the dawn.

Chapter Thirty-One

Camulodunum

The autumn rain drummed steadily against the leather roof of the crude shelter that housed the off-duty Exploratores, creating a monotonous rhythm that had persisted for three days without respite. Inside the cramped quarters, six men tried to find ways to pass the time while their equipment dried, and their horses rested in the fort's stables.

Maxima sat on his sleeping roll, methodically cleaning his sword for the third time that day, not because it needed attention but because idle hands led to restless thoughts. The blade was his father's, inherited when the old man had finally succumbed to wounds taken in the Germanic campaigns, and its familiar weight provided comfort during uncertain times.

Around him, his fellow scouts engaged in the usual diversions of soldiers with too much time and too little to do. Lucius and Gaius played knucklebones with a set carved from deer antler, their quiet conversation punctuated by the occasional curse when fortune turned against them. Quintus worked on a letter to his wife back in Gaul, his stylus moving slowly across the wax tablet as he struggled to find words that would convey reassurance without revealing the true dangers of their work.

But Maxima's mind was elsewhere, ranging westward across the hills and forests where he had deposited Seneca and his men over a month ago. The mission had been straightforward enough in its execution: escort the Occultum to the edge of Silures territory, ensure their safe insertion, and return to Camulodunum to await further orders. He had accomplished those objectives with professional efficiency, bringing his men back intact and ready for their next assignment.

Yet something nagged at him, a persistent unease that had grown stronger with each passing day. It was nothing he could quantify or explain in any formal report, merely the instinct of a man who had spent years operating in hostile territory and learned to trust his intuition about when situations were developing badly.

The Occultum were skilled, certainly among the best operatives Rome had ever produced. But they were also operating in some of the most dangerous territory in Britannia, among people who had elevated guerrilla warfare to an art form. Even the most capable men could find themselves overwhelmed by circumstances beyond their control.

'Still thinking about those men we dropped off?' asked Quintus, looking up from his letter.

Maxima nodded, not bothering to deny what had apparently become obvious to his men.

'They've been out there for over a month now. No word, no contact, no indication they're even still alive.'

'That's how they work, isn't it?' Lucius pointed out, rattling the knucklebones in his cupped hands before casting them onto the leather groundsheet. 'Silent operations, no communication until the mission's complete.'

'Maybe,' Maxima conceded. 'But they're operating far beyond any possible support. If something's gone wrong...'

He left the sentence unfinished, but his men understood the implications. The western territories were weeks of hard travel from the nearest Roman outpost. If the Occultum had been compromised, captured, or simply encountered more opposition than anticipated, there would be no rescue, no reinforcement, no extraction.

Gaius collected the knucklebones, studying the patterns with disappointment.

'Bad cast,' he muttered. 'The bones say trouble's coming.'

'The bones say whatever you want them to say,' Quintus replied dismissively, but Maxima noticed he made a small gesture to ward off ill luck.

The rain continued its relentless assault on their shelter, and Maxima found himself unable to concentrate. Instead, his mind kept returning to that night at the river crossing, watching six men disappear into hostile territory with no guarantee they would ever emerge. Finally, he made his decision.

'I'm going to see Lepidus,' he announced, setting his sword aside and reaching for his cloak.

'In this weather?' Lucius asked, glancing toward the shelter's entrance where rain could be seen falling in sheets.

'The weather isn't going to improve,' Maxima replied, pulling the oiled leather around his shoulders. 'And neither is my mood if we sit here much longer doing nothing.'

Senator Lepidus maintained his temporary quarters in one of the more substantial buildings within Camulodunum's expanding fortifications, a wooden structure that served as both residence and administrative centre for intelligence operations in the region. Despite the hour and the weather, lamps burned behind oiled parchment windows, suggesting the senator was still conducting business.

Maxima announced himself to the guard stationed outside and was admitted without delay. Inside, he found Lepidus hunched over a desk covered with scrolls and tablets, the tools of a man whose wars were fought with information rather than steel.

'Maxima,' Lepidus greeted him, looking up from a report written in the cramped handwriting of a field agent. 'I wasn't expecting you. Is there a problem?'

'No, Dominus. They're all in good health and ready for duty.' Maxima remained standing, water still dripping from his cloak despite his attempt to shake it off outside. 'I wanted to speak with you about a potential mission.'

Lepidus set down the scroll he had been reading, his expression shifting to one of professional interest.

'I'm listening.'

'My men and I are currently standing down, awaiting new orders. It seems a waste of our capabilities to have us sitting idle when we could be conducting useful reconnaissance.'

'What did you have in mind?'

Maxima had rehearsed this conversation during his walk through the rain, knowing he would need to present his proposal in terms that appealed to Lepidus's strategic thinking rather than his own personal concerns.

'The Occultum have been operating in hostile territory for over a month with no communication. While I understand that operational security requires their silence, I believe it would be prudent to establish a forward observation post near their insertion point.'

Lepidus leaned back in his chair, his fingers steepled as he considered the suggestion.

'You're concerned about their welfare.'

'I'm concerned about the intelligence they're gathering,' Maxima corrected carefully. 'If they've discovered something significant about enemy dispositions or intentions, we have no way of receiving that information until they complete their mission and return. Meanwhile, tactical situations can change rapidly.'

It was a reasonable argument, though both men understood it wasn't the complete truth.

'And what would this observation post accomplish, practically speaking?'

'Several things,' Maxima replied, warming to his prepared arguments. 'First, it would provide a secure location for supply caches that could extend the Occultum's operational endurance. Second, it would serve as a communications relay point if they need to send information back to Camulodunum. Third, it would give us early warning if any enemy forces were moving in that area.'

'And fourth,' Lepidus added quietly, 'it would provide extraction support if the mission has encountered difficulties.'

Maxima nodded, accepting that his underlying motivations were transparent to the experienced intelligence officer.

'It is a good idea,' continued Lepidus, 'but we should have thought about it before they went. What good is a forward support base if Seneca does not even know it is there?'

'A fair point,' said Maxima. 'But if they do manage to get out, there is a strong chance they will go back to where they hid the first cache, if only to get more food. In that event, they will no doubt be exhausted from their expedition, and we can help bring them safely back to the fort.'

Lepidus stared at the Exploratores officer, considering his argument.

'My Exploratores are ideally suited for this type of operation,' continued Maxima. 'We know the terrain, we've established the insertion route, and we can operate independently for extended periods without support.'

Lepidus rose from his chair and moved to a large map

mounted on the wall, its surface marked with known enemy positions and Roman outposts. The western territories where the Occultum were operating appeared as a vast blank space, marked only with weak intelligence and estimates.

'It's a considerable risk,' he observed, studying the distances involved. 'You'd be operating almost as far from support as the Occultum themselves. If something goes wrong...'

'We're prepared for that contingency,' Maxima replied. 'We've operated in hostile territory before. We know how to remain undetected and how to withdraw if necessary.'

'And your men? Are they willing to undertake such a mission?'

'They're Exploratores, Dominus. They'll go where they're ordered. But yes, I believe they share my concerns about our comrades' welfare.'

Lepidus continued studying the map, his mind clearly working through the strategic implications of the proposal. Finally, he turned back to face Maxima.

'I'll need to clear this with the Vespasian. Officially, I can't authorize independent operations without his approval, but unofficially, I think you're right to be concerned. The Occultum are valuable assets, and although we can't do much while they are behind enemy lines, we can't afford to lose them to preventable circumstances.' He moved back to his desk, already reaching for writing materials. 'How soon could you be ready to depart?'

'My men and equipment are ready now. We'd need additional supplies for extended operations, extra horses to carry provisions, but we could be mounted and moving within hours of receiving orders.'

'Good.' Lepidus began writing rapidly, his stylus

scratching across a wax tablet. 'I'll speak with Vespasian tonight. Assuming he approves the operation, you'll depart at dawn tomorrow.'

Relief flooded through Maxima, though he kept his expression professionally neutral.

'Thank you, Dominus. I believe this is the right decision.'

'I hope you're right,' Lepidus replied without looking up from his writing. 'Because if you're wrong, I'll have risked two of our most effective units for no good reason.'

Dawn came grey and misty, the rain having finally stopped during the night but leaving the world sodden and dripping. In the Exploratores' quarters, the men prepared for the dangerous assignment, checking equipment, distributing supplies, ensuring that every detail was attended to before departure.

Maxima had briefed them the night before, explaining the mission's objectives while carefully avoiding any mention of his personal motivations. They understood duty and accepted risks as part of their profession, but he could see in their faces that they shared his concerns about their missing comrades.

The additional supplies Lepidus had authorized were substantial: extra rations for extended operations, medical supplies, and weapons that could be cached for the Occultum's use if needed. Six additional horses carried these provisions, their loads carefully balanced and secured for the difficult journey ahead.

As the fort's gates creaked open in the pre-dawn darkness, Maxima led his column out into the countryside beyond Camulodunum's walls. Behind them, the settlement still slept, its inhabitants unaware that another group of Romans was heading west into the dangerous territories where civilization gave way to ancient enemies and deadly feuds.

The road stretched ahead, leading toward hills that grew progressively more hostile with each mile travelled. But Maxima felt the familiar satisfaction of action replacing uncertainty, purpose replacing idle worry. Whatever had happened to the Occultum, whatever dangers awaited in the western forests, he and his men would face them with the professional competence that had kept them alive through years of similar missions.

This time, they were searching for fellow Romans who might desperately need the support only brotherhood-in-arms could provide, and as the morning mist began to lift, the Exploratores settled into the steady pace that would carry them back to the edge of the world they knew, and perhaps beyond.

Chapter Thirty-Two

The Western Forests

The ancient forest pressed around them like a living cathedral, its canopy so dense that even at midday only scattered beams of sunlight penetrated to the forest floor. Seneca led his men in single file along what might charitably be called a deer path, though even the local wildlife seemed to have abandoned this particular route in favour of easier passages through the undergrowth.

For three days they had been traveling deeper into Silures territory, the landscape growing increasingly wild and primeval with each mile. The trees here were giants, oaks and yews that had stood since before Rome was founded, their massive trunks creating natural pillars that supported a roof of interwoven branches far above their heads.

The density of the forest had forced them to abandon night movement entirely. Unlike the more open terrain they had traversed earlier, these ancient woodlands were virtually impassable in darkness, filled with hidden roots, sudden drops, and deadfall that could break a man's leg or alert every enemy within miles. Daylight travel meant greater risk of detection, but at least they could see where they were going.

'No sign of local activity,' Talorcan murmured over his shoulder, his voice barely audible even in the forest's oppressive silence.'

Seneca nodded, though he remained alert. The absence of human presence could be as telling as its detection. The Silures were said to melt into their forests like ghosts, appearing and disappearing at will and the very quietness might simply mean they were being skilfully avoided rather than going unnoticed.

The afternoon wore on with agonizing slowness, each step calculated to avoid the dry branches and loose stones that might betray their presence, every sense straining for signs of danger.

Behind them, Falco shifted his massive frame with practiced silence, his hand never far from his weapon. The former gladiator had grown increasingly restless as they penetrated deeper into hostile territory, his instincts crying out for direct action rather than the patient stealth their mission demanded.

'How much further do you estimate to the next settlement?' Marcus whispered during one of their brief halts.

'Unknown,' Seneca replied. 'The intelligence was vague about locations beyond the first site we observed. We'll continue until we find something.'

As evening approached and the already dim light began to fade further, Sica suddenly held up his hand. The scent reached the others a moment later, wood smoke, faint but unmistakable, drifting through the still air between the trees.

Seneca moved forward to join his point man, studying the terrain ahead with practiced eyes. The forest opened slightly here, the massive trees giving way to a more varied landscape of smaller growth and natural clearings. Somewhere ahead, hidden among the shadows, someone had lit a fire.

'How far?' he whispered.

'Perhaps two hundred paces,' Sica replied, his nose working like a hunting hound's. 'Small fire, well-concealed.'

Seneca considered the implications. Whether it were hunters, local woodsmen, or simply travellers seeking shelter for the night, in Silures territory, any human presence was potentially hostile, and potentially valuable for intelligence gathering.

Seneca turned to his men who were already down on one knee.

'Sica and I will take a look,' he said. 'The rest of you maintain position here and watch our backs.'

The rest of the Occultum spread out, each facing a different direction as Seneca and Sica continued.

The clearing, when they finally reached it, was almost perfectly circular, as if carved from the forest by design rather than chance. Ancient stones marked its perimeter at regular intervals, weathered monoliths that had stood here since before memory, their surfaces carved with spiral patterns that seemed to shift and writhe in the firelight.

Eight men sat around a small, expertly banked fire that produced minimal smoke and light and from their concealed position behind a massive fallen oak at the clearing's edge, Seneca could observe them with perfect clarity while remaining completely hidden.

These were warriors of exceptional quality, that much was immediately obvious. They were large men, powerfully built, with the relaxed confidence that came only from years of surviving deadly encounters. Each wore the distinctive spiral tattoos of the Silures that transformed them into something more than human, more primal and dangerous.

The warrior nearest to Seneca's position was perhaps thirty summers old, his thick black hair rolling down over his shoulders and past his substantial beard. Scars crisscrossed his bare arms, evidence of countless battles survived, and a long sword lay across his knees, its blade catching the firelight as he absently checked its edge with his thumb. His eyes constantly scanned the forest perimeter, never settling in one place for long, the automatic behaviour of a man who expected trouble.

Beside him sat a younger warrior, perhaps twenty-five summers, but already marked with the ritual scars that indicated multiple kills. His beard was braided with small bones, human trophies taken from fallen enemies and a war spear rested against his shoulder, its iron point gleaming wickedly in the firelight.

The third warrior was older, grizzled, his hair shot through with grey and as Seneca watched, the man carved strips of venison from the freshly killed deer that lay beside their fire, its carcass already expertly skinned and gutted. He examined each piece carefully before placing it on a flat stone near the fire to cook. His weapons were fewer but of exceptional quality, a single sword that showed the care of decades of maintenance, and a knife with a handle worn smooth by countless hands.

But it was the fourth man who commanded Seneca's attention, and for reasons that made his blood run cold. This one was the largest of the group, perhaps forty summers old, his massive frame draped in a cloak of wolf fur that gave him an almost bestial appearance. His face was heavily marked with woad patterns that extended down his neck, creating a map of spiral designs that spoke of high rank among the Silures hierarchy. But it wasn't his appearance that froze Seneca's attention, it was what he held in his hands.

The warrior was methodically sharpening a knife, drawing a whetstone along its curved edge with slow, practiced strokes. Each pass of the stone sent tiny sparks into the firelight, and the blade's distinctive profile was clearly visible in the dancing flames.

Seneca's heart hammered against his ribs as he studied the weapon with growing certainty. The curve of the blade was unique, not the straight edge favoured by most warriors but a subtle arc that made it ideal for both cutting and thrusting. The crossguard bore the telltale marks of the master smith who had forged it, three small notches that served no functional purpose but marked the craftsman's work as surely as any signature.

Most distinctive of all was the handle. Bone and bronze fittings wrapped in leather that had darkened with years of use, its surface worn smooth in the exact places where a man's grip would naturally fall. Seneca had seen that handle a thousand times, watched its owner clean and maintain the blade through countless campaigns across the Empire.

It belonged to Veteranus.

The warrior holding it seemed to take particular satisfaction in the sharpening process, testing the edge against his thumb before returning to the rhythmic strokes of stone against steel. He spoke occasionally to his companions, his voice a low rumble that carried the authority of leadership, but Seneca was too far away to make out individual words.

As Seneca watched in growing alarm, the warrior finished his sharpening and slid the blade into a leather sheath at his belt, but not before holding it up to examine it in the firelight, turning it slightly so that the flames caught the metal and revealed every detail of its construction.

There could be no mistake. That was Veteranus's personal weapon, as distinctive as a man's face to anyone who knew what to look for. For it to be in the hands of Silures warriors meant only one thing, something had gone catastrophically wrong with Veteranus's mission among the Ordovices.

The conversation around the fire continued in low tones, the warriors clearly discussing matters of importance. Occasionally one would gesture toward the south, as if referring to locations or events in that direction. Another pointed east, toward what Seneca assumed were the territories they had recently left. But the distance and the crackling of the fire made eavesdropping impossible.

After perhaps twenty minutes of observation, Seneca touched Sica's shoulder and gestured for withdrawal. They had learned what they could from visual reconnaissance, and lingering longer only increased the risk of detection. These were clearly experienced warriors, men who would notice any disturbance in their environment.

The retreat required the same careful precision as their approach, each step planned and executed with methodical patience. They moved like shadows, using every available cover to mask their withdrawal from the sacred clearing and its ominous occupants.

When they finally rejoined the others, Seneca's expression was grim enough to immediately alert his men that something significant had occurred.

'Gather close,' he ordered quietly. 'We need to talk.'

The Occultum formed a tight circle in the gathering darkness, their faces barely visible but their attention focused completely on their leader.

'Our mission parameters may have just changed,' Seneca began. 'I've just seen something that suggests one of our own is in serious trouble.'

'Who?' asked Marcus with concern.

'Veteranus,' Seneca replied simply. 'One of those warriors was sharpening his knife.'

Falco frowned in confusion.

'Veteranus's knife?' he asked. 'How can you be sure?'

Instead of responding verbally, Seneca reached down and drew his own knife from its sheath. Even in the dim light, the others could see its distinctive design, the curved blade, the unique crossguard with its three small notches, the carefully crafted handle of bone and bronze wrapped in darkened leather. It was clearly the mate to the weapon he had just described.

'Only two were ever made,' Seneca explained quietly, holding the blade so the others could examine it more closely. 'Years ago, by a blacksmith named Gaius Fabius who did special work for the Occultum. He was an old legionary who understood what we needed, weapons that were distinctive enough to identify their owners, but not so ornate as to attract unwanted attention.'

He turned the knife slightly, letting what little light remained catch the metal and reveal the craftsmanship in every detail.

'Fabius spent a month forging these blades. The curve isn't decorative, it makes them more effective for the close work we sometimes have to do. The bronze fittings are from metal taken from a temple in Syria, blessed by priests before it was melted down. The bone comes from the femur of a lion killed in the arena at Rome.' Seneca's voice grew quieter, more personal as he continued. 'When Veteranus joined us many years ago, Fabius presented him with one of these knives. It was the old man's way of welcoming him into our brotherhood. I received the other, as team leader.' He met each man's eyes in turn. 'They're identical in every detail and there's no possibility of mistake about what I saw tonight.'

The weight of this revelation settled heavily over the group. Each man understood what it meant to see a comrade's personal weapon in enemy hands and the implications were dark and immediate.

'But how?' Talorcan asked, his Belgic pragmatism cutting to the heart of the matter. 'I thought he was on a separate mission far to the north.'

'I don't know,' Seneca admitted, his voice heavy with concern. 'Veteranus was supposed to be amongst the Ordovices. I wasn't briefed on his specific objectives but for him to end up here, in Silures territory, something must have gone catastrophically wrong.'

He stared down at his own knife, its familiar weight suddenly feeling heavier in his hand.

'The only intelligence I received placed him with a trading caravan, operating under diplomatic cover. That was over a month ago.'

'He could be dead,' said Falco bluntly, voicing what they were all thinking. 'Those bastards could have taken his knife as a trophy after killing him.'

'It's possible,' Seneca acknowledged, though his tone suggested he wasn't entirely convinced. 'But he could also still be alive, being used for information or leverage.'

The former gladiator's scarred face showed scepticism.

'After what he did? After he helped ruin their attack on Claudius? They'd skin him alive given the chance.'

'Maybe they would,' Seneca replied evenly. 'But despite everything that happened on Mona, despite the complications with Mordred and the druids, Veteranus is still one of us. He's Occultum and we don't abandon our own.'

Marcus leaned forward, his centurion's training making him focus on practical considerations.

'What are you saying, Seneca? That we postpone the hunt for Mordred to search for Veteranus?'

'I'm saying we find him first,' Seneca stated firmly. 'Or at least confirm he's dead. We can't complete our primary mission knowing one of our brothers might be suffering in enemy hands. It goes against everything we stand for.'

Decimus nodded slowly, understanding the burden of command that weighed on their leader's shoulders.

'The mission comes first, that's always been our way. But so has loyalty to each other.'

'Exactly,' Seneca confirmed. 'And right now, those two obligations align. Those warriors I observed weren't casual raiders or hunters passing through. They were too disciplined, too professional. They might be connected to wherever Mordred is hiding, which means finding their base could serve both purposes.'

'How do we find them?' Marcus asked practically. 'They could disappear into these forests, and we'd never see them again.'

Seneca looked back toward the direction of the clearing, his mind already working through the tactical possibilities.

'Those men couldn't be far from their main camp. I saw them preparing food, they'd killed a deer recently, probably today. Fresh meat like that doesn't keep long, especially in this climate. They'll want to get it back to their people while it's still good.' He gestured toward the darkening forest around them. 'They're not going to travel at night through terrain like this, not with a deer carcass to carry. They'll camp tonight and move out at first light. All we have to do is follow them.'

Sica's dark eyes glinted with understanding.

'Back to their base. Where they might be holding Veteranus.'

'And where Mordred might also be hiding,' Seneca added. 'Two objectives, one operation.'

Talorcan shifted his weight, his Belgic instincts for direct action clearly approving of the plan.

'When do we move?'

'Before dawn,' Seneca decided. 'We position ourselves

to observe their departure, then follow at a safe distance. These are their forests, they'll know every path and hiding place. But they won't be expecting pursuit, and we know how to remain unseen.'

Falco cracked his knuckles, a sound that seemed unnaturally loud in the forest quiet.

'Finally, some action. I was getting tired of all this skulking about.'

'This will require more skulking, not less,' Marcus warned. 'Following them undetected through their home territory will be one of the most challenging operations we've ever attempted.'

'But necessary,' Seneca concluded. 'Veteranus would do the same for any of us. The mission continues, but now it has two phases. First, we find our missing brother. Then, we complete our original objective.'

The men absorbed this in thoughtful silence, each contemplating the challenges ahead. Following enemy warriors through hostile territory was dangerous enough. Doing so while maintaining operational security and preparing for potential combat at the end made it even more complex.

'Rest now,' Seneca ordered quietly. 'We move before dawn, and tomorrow could be a very long day.'

Chapter Thirty-Three

The Silurian Forests

Veteranus and Maelon crashed through the undergrowth, abandoning all attempts at stealth in favour of raw speed. Behind them, the Shadow Walker camp still remained blissfully unaware of the escape, its inhabitants focused on the drama unfolding in the healing hut where Mordred fought to save Caratacus's life.

Veteranus's legs burned from the sustained effort of running through terrain that seemed designed to trip and ensnare the unwary. Roots caught at his feet, low branches whipped at his face, and fallen logs forced him to leap or scramble over obstacles that cost precious energy with each encounter. But the knowledge that discovery meant certain death drove him forward with desperate determination.

Maelon followed behind. The boy seemed to flow around obstacles that challenged Veteranus, finding paths through the dense undergrowth that a casual observer might miss entirely. His breathing remained steady despite their punishing pace, a testament to the harsh conditioning of his slave years.

For over an hour they maintained their headlong flight, putting as much distance as possible between themselves and the camp while their absence remained unnoticed. The darkness that had made their escape possible now worked against them, forcing them to slow their pace as the risk of serious injury from unseen obstacles grew too great to ignore.

Finally, when Veteranus felt his lungs might burst from the sustained effort, Maelon led them to a shallow depression between two massive oak trees. The natural hollow was partially concealed by fallen branches and thick undergrowth, providing some shelter from both the elements and potential pursuit.

They collapsed to the damp earth, gasping for breath while their hearts hammered against their ribs. For several minutes, neither could speak, their bodies focused entirely on recovering from the punishing run through hostile territory.

'How far?' Veteranus finally managed between ragged breaths.

'Perhaps three miles,' Maelon replied, his own voice strained but controlled. 'Far enough that casual sounds won't carry back to the camp, but not far enough if they bring dogs.'

The reminder of pursuit sent a chill through Veteranus that had nothing to do with the cool night air. He had seen the quality of the Shadow Walker camp's security and the professional competence of its inhabitants. When his escape was discovered, the response would be swift and deadly.

'We need to keep moving,' he said, forcing himself to his feet despite the protests from his exhausted muscles. 'We still need to find the woman.'

Maelon stared at him in disbelief.

'You can barely stand,' he replied, 'and we have no food, no water, no weapons beyond my knife and sling. And you still want to continue searching for the woman?'

'Too much rests on the outcome,' Veteranus replied grimly. 'If Rhiannon isn't returned to her people, the political alliance between the Brigantes and Ordovices collapses. That forces the Ordovices into an alliance with Caratacus and the Silures against Rome.' He met the boy's sceptical gaze with steady determination. 'I've seen what Caratacus can accomplish when he unites the tribes against a common enemy. If he gains the support of the Silures and Ordovices while he recovers his strength...' Veteranus shook his head. 'Rome could lose this entire province.'

'And you believe we can still find her? Just the two of us, alone, in the heart of Silures territory, probably hunted by the best trackers in the whole of Britannia?'

'I believe we have to try,' Veteranus replied, studying the sky through breaks in the canopy to orient himself by the stars. 'The alternative is unacceptable. We'll continue through the night but by morning, we'll need food and water. Do you still have that sling?'

'Yes,' said Maelon. 'I should be able to get some birds, squirrels if I'm fortunate but nothing large enough to sustain us for long.'

'It will have to do. Once we've eaten, we decide our next move.'

As they prepared to resume their journey, Maelon shook his head in what might have been admiration or disbelief.

'You Romans are either very brave or very stupid. I haven't decided which.'

'Sometimes there's little difference between the two,' Veteranus replied with grim humour. 'Come. Dawn won't wait for us.'

The first grey light of morning was beginning to filter through the forest canopy when one of the guards approached Veteranus's prison hut.

He pushed aside the leather door covering and stepped into the dim interior, a wooden bowl of thin gruel balanced in one hand. The words of mockery he had prepared died in his throat as he stared at the empty hut, the severed ropes that had bound the prisoner, and the gaping hole cut through the rear wall.

For a moment, shock held him motionless. Then training took over, and he spun toward the entrance, his voice rising in urgent alarm.

'Alarm! The prisoner has escaped!'

The cry echoed through the camp like a stone thrown into still water, creating ripples of activity that spread outward from the prison hut. Warriors emerged from their shelters, weapons in hand, while others rushed toward the source of the disturbance to assess the situation.

Within minutes, Cadoc arrived at the scene, his massive frame filling the hut's entrance as he surveyed the evidence of the night's work. His scarred face showed no emotion, but those who knew him well could see the cold fury building behind his eyes.

'How long?' he demanded of the guard, who stood rigid with fear, knowing he had failed in his duties.

'I don't know, lord. I last checked at midnight, as ordered. The prisoner was secure then.'

Cadoc knelt beside the severed ropes, examining the cuts. The work was clean, efficient, done with a sharp blade.

'He had help,' he concluded, rising to inspect the hole cut through the wall. 'This wasn't the work of one man.'

Mordred appeared at the entrance, his white robes stained with blood from his work in the healing hut. His face was drawn with exhaustion from the night's struggle to save Caratacus, but his eyes blazed with fury at this new complication.

'How is this possible?' he demanded. 'Your men were supposed to be watching him.'

'My men did watch him,' Cadoc replied evenly, though his tone carried warning. 'But someone came from outside to free him. Someone who knew where he was being held and how to reach him undetected.'

The druid's expression darkened further as the implications became clear.

'The other members of the Occultum. Which means they're closer than we thought, and more dangerous than we anticipated.'

Around them, the camp buzzed with activity as warriors prepared for pursuit. Weapons were checked, supplies gathered, dogs prepared for tracking.

Cadoc turned to his second-in-command, a lean warrior whose face was marked with the ritual scars of many kills.

'Gather the hunting party. Our best trackers, our fastest runners. Take the dogs and whatever supplies you need for extended pursuit.'

As the warrior moved away to organize the pursuit, Mordred stepped closer to the war leader.

'I should come with you. I know this Veteranus, his capabilities, his weaknesses.'

Cadoc shook his head firmly.

'Your place is with Caratacus. If he dies because you abandoned your healing work to chase escaped prisoners, his followers will blame us for his death.

The druid's face showed his frustration, but he recognized the wisdom in Cadoc's reasoning.

'Then kill them both quickly. Don't try to take them alive.'

'I had no intention of doing otherwise,' Cadoc replied grimly. 'The Roman has caused enough trouble. This time, when I find him, there will be no cage, no interrogation, no second chances.'

The hunting party assembled with impressive speed,

Cadoc's finest warriors mounted on the hardy ponies that could navigate the forest terrain at speed. Each man carried weapons suitable for pursuit and combat, along with supplies for several days in the wilderness if necessary.

Cadoc mounted his own horse, a black stallion that had carried him through countless raids against tribal enemies. Around him, his warriors waited for the command that would begin their pursuit of the escaped prisoners.

'Remember,' he called out, his voice carrying clearly across the assembled hunters. 'The Roman is dangerous, trained in arts of war most of us have never encountered. Don't underestimate him, don't take unnecessary risks. Kill him from distance if possible, but don't let him escape again.'

With that, he spurred his horse toward the forest edge, the hunting party streaming behind him in disciplined formation. The dogs bounded ahead, their noses already working the scent trail that would lead them to their quarry.

Behind them, the camp returned to its normal routines, though with an undercurrent of tension that spoke to the seriousness of the situation. In the healing hut, Mordred resumed his desperate fight to save Caratacus's life, knowing that the war leader's survival might depend as much on eliminating the Roman threat as on any medicine he could provide. The hunt had begun, and in the forests of the Silures, few prey ever escaped the Shadow Walkers once they took up the chase.

Chapter Thirty-Four

The Forests of Siluria

Dawn broke grey and misty over the forest as Seneca led his men followed the faint trail left by the eight Silures warriors they had observed the previous evening. The tracking was challenging work in the dim light, requiring all of Talorcan's Belgic woodcraft to maintain contact without losing the trail or alerting their quarry to pursuit.

The warriors had moved out at first light as Seneca had predicted, carrying the butchered deer carcass between them on improvised poles. Their route led steadily southwest, following ancient paths that wound through the densest parts of the forest.

'They know where they're going,' Marcus observed during one of their brief halts, studying the clear trail the warriors had left. 'This isn't random movement.'

'Back to their main camp,' Seneca agreed. 'Probably where they're holding Veteranus, if he's still alive.'

For most of the day they maintained their pursuit, the Occultum using every technique in their considerable repertoire to remain undetected while keeping their targets in sight.

The eight warriors were clearly visible now, perhaps half a mile ahead. Seneca studied the looming terrain carefully.

'We'll continue along that ridge,' he decided, nodding to the feature ahead, but as they were about to move, the lead warrior below suddenly raised his hand in a silent signal and the entire group dropped immediately to the ground, disappearing into the tall grass as if they had never existed.

Seneca and his men followed suit instinctively, pressing

themselves flat against the earth while scanning the valley below for whatever had triggered the warriors' alert response.

Movement caught Seneca's eye, two figures moving across the valley floor, perhaps a mile distant. Even at that range, their flight was obviously laboured, the stumbling gait of exhausted men pushing themselves beyond their limits.

'Fugitives,' Decimus observed quietly, his veteran's eye reading the tactical situation immediately. 'Running from something.'

Below them, the Silures warriors had risen from concealment and were quickly shedding their packs and the deer carcass, keeping only their weapons and essential equipment. Their body language spoke of sudden urgency, the focused alertness of hunters who had spotted unexpected prey.

'They're going after them,' Marcus noted, watching as the warriors began descending into the valley.

Seneca studied the fleeing figures more carefully, something about their movement pattern nagging at his tactical instincts. One was smaller, lighter, moving with the desperate efficiency of youth. The other was larger, more powerful, but clearly exhausted from sustained effort.

'We'll follow,' Seneca decided, and started moving carefully down the hillside, using the terrain to mask their approach while keeping the hunting party in sight.

Within the hour, the chase had moved into more open ground where the individual figures were clearly visible across a harvested field. The two fugitives stumbled across the stubbled earth, their exhaustion now obvious even from distance. Behind them, the hunting party closed the gap with methodical precision.

It was then that Seneca saw the larger fugitive's face clearly for the first time.

'*Jupiter's balls,*' he gasped, recognition hitting him like a physical blow, '*it's Veteranus.*'

The silence that followed was heavy with implication. Each member of the Occultum stared down at the unfolding chase, watching one of their own brotherhood being hunted like an animal across the Silures countryside.

The tactical situation was clear and dangerous. Intervention would mean revealing their presence to the enemy, compromising their mission and potentially alerting every Silures settlement in the region to the presence of Roman operatives. Their orders were specific, locate and eliminate Mordred, maintaining operational security at all costs, but the man being hunted below was their brother, a member of the Occultum, and bonds forged in shared danger transcended written orders.

Seneca turned to face his men, studying each face in turn. In their expressions, he saw his own conflict reflected, duty warring with loyalty, mission requirements clashing with brotherhood.

'This wasn't part of the plan,' he said quicky. 'Intervention means compromising everything we've worked for but that's Veteranus down there. One of us.'

'In my homeland,' said Sica, 'we have a saying. A man who abandons his brothers to save himself has lost his soul. Better to die with honour than live with shame.'

Seneca felt the weight of command settle on his shoulders. Every instinct screamed that intervention was tactically unsound, strategically dangerous, and potentially catastrophic for their primary mission. But those same instincts also told him that some bonds transcended orders, some loyalties ran deeper than duty.

'Packs off,' he ordered sharply. 'We're going to be

running hard and fighting harder.'

They shed their heavy packs with practiced efficiency, retaining only what they would need for immediate combat and as they prepared to descend into the valley, Seneca took one last look at the chase below. Veteranus and his companion were clearly at the end of their endurance, stumbling across the open ground while their pursuers closed for the kill.

'Move,' he commanded, and the Occultum erupted into motion, racing down the hillside toward a confrontation that would determine whether they saved their brother or died beside him in the fields of enemy territory. The hunt was about to become a battle.

Chapter Thirty-Five

The Forests of Siluria

The cliff face rose like a grey wall before them, its weathered stone offering no escape route and precious little cover. Veteranus turned and pressed his back against the cold rock, his chest heaving from the desperate run that had brought them to this final refuge. Beside him, Maelon clutched his sling with white-knuckled intensity, his young face set in grim determination despite the hopelessness of their situation.

The eight Silures hunters emerged from the treeline, spreading into a loose semicircle that blocked any possibility of retreat.

Their leader stepped forward slightly. His eyes held no malice, only the cold professionalism of a man completing necessary work.

Veteranus said nothing, conserving his breath while his eyes catalogued every detail of their attackers. Eight men, all experienced warriors bearing a variety of well used weapons.

Maelon's hand trembled slightly as he reached for the knife at his belt, his only weapon besides the sling. Without hesitation, he pressed the bone handle into Veteranus's palm.

'Take it,' the boy whispered urgently. 'You'll make better use of it than I will.'

The blade was small, little more than an eating knife, but its edge was sharp. It wouldn't save them, but it might allow them to die with some measure of dignity.

'We could surrender,' Maelon suggested quietly.

Veteranus shook his head grimly.

'They'll kill us anyway, probably slowly. Better to die fighting.'

The hunters had completed their encirclement now, eight points of steel reflecting the late afternoon sun. They stood perhaps twenty paces away, close enough to rush forward in seconds, far enough to avoid any desperate last gambit their prey might attempt.

One of the warriors raised his spear slightly, and Veteranus tensed for the final charge. This was how it would end then, cornered like a beast in the forests of Britannia, his mission incomplete, his brothers unaware of his fate, but before the warrior could launch his spear, the boy's sling whipped through the air in a tight circle, the leather cord singing as it built momentum.

The stone flew like a thunderbolt, striking the warrior squarely in the temple with a crack that echoed off the cliff face. The warrior dropped instantly, his spear clattering harmlessly to the ground as he collapsed in a boneless heap.

For a heartbeat, shock held the remaining hunters motionless, then fury replaced surprise, and they surged forward with savage war cries that split the evening air.

Veteranus met the first attacker at the base of the cliff, ducking under a spear thrust that would have pinned him to the stone. His knife found the gap beneath the man's ribs, sliding between bone and muscle to pierce the heart with surgical precision. Hot blood sprayed across his hands as the warrior stumbled backward, already dying but still dangerous.

Maelon scrambled away, using the scattered boulders as cover while he loaded another stone into his sling. A sword blade rang against stone where his head had been a moment before, and a spray of sparks flew from the impact.

Two more hunters converged on Veteranus from opposite sides, and he twisted away from a sword thrust, feeling the blade part the air beside his ear, but the movement put him directly into the path of a spear point that grazed his shoulder and opened a line of pain across his back.

The remaining hunters pressed forward, driving their prey back against the unyielding stone. Veteranus felt his back touch the cliff face, they were trapped now, cornered with nowhere left to retreat. Blood ran warm down his arm from the spear cut, and his breath came in ragged gasps. Beside him, Maelon pressed against the stone, his sling useless in the close quarters.

The hunters paused, their circle tightening but not quite closing. They could see their prey was finished, and there was no rush now. Better to savour the moment, to let fear do its work before the final kill.

The scarred leader stepped forward, his spear point aimed at Veteranus's chest. His smile was cold and satisfied, the expression of a killer completing difficult work.

Veteranus straightened despite his wounds, meeting the warrior's gaze with steady defiance. If he was to die here, he would do so with whatever dignity remained to him.

The spear drew back for the killing thrust but before it came, an almighty roar shattered the air, a sound of pure rage and bloodlust that seemed to come from the very depths of Hades itself as Falco erupted from the treeline, his massive frame moving with impossible speed for something so large. The blood-rage was in his eyes, the berserker fury that had made him legendary in the arena and feared on a dozen battlefields. His sword was already moving as he struck the nearest hunter, the blade sheering through neck and spine in a single devastating cut that sent the man's head spinning through the air in a fountain of gore.

Before the remaining Silures could react to this impossible development, the rest of the Occultum poured into the clearing behind their maddened comrade. Marcus came from the left, his gladius finding kidney and liver with the precision of a trained killer. Talorcan attacked from the right, his Belgic war-cry mixing with the clash of steel as he engaged two warriors simultaneously.

But these were no ordinary tribal fighters, these were Shadow Walkers, veterans of countless raids and ambushes. Their shock lasted only seconds before their own fury reasserted itself and they turned to face this new threat with fierce pride and anger.

The fight that followed was brutal beyond description, the five remaining Silures warriors against six of Rome's deadliest operatives in a confined space that turned every movement into potential death. Steel rang against steel with bell-like clarity, sparks flew from parried blows, and men grunted with effort as they sought openings in their opponents' defences.

Sica moved like a shadow among the combatants, his curved blade finding gaps with surgical precision, a Silures warrior grimacing as the Syrian's steel slid between his ribs from behind, puncturing lung and heart with clinical efficiency.

Decimus fought with the steady competence of a veteran, his sword work economical and deadly. He caught a spear thrust on his blade, turned it aside, and drove his pommel into his attacker's face with enough force to shatter bone and scatter teeth across the rocky ground.

The confined space worked against the hunters now, and the Occultum pressed their assault with relentless fury, each man protecting his brothers' flanks while seeking to end the fight as quickly as possible.

Falco's massive frame dominated the centre of the combat, his sword rising and falling like a butcher's cleaver.

Blood soaked his arms to the elbows, some his own from minor cuts, most belonging to enemies who had learned too late that the former gladiator's reputation was built on mountains of corpses, and one by one, the Shadow Walkers fell. Their skill was considerable, their courage unquestionable, but they faced men whose brotherhood had been forged in the crucibles of the Empire's bloodiest campaigns.

The last hunter died with Talorcan's spear in his chest, his final breath a curse in the old tongue that echoed off the cliff face before fading into silence.

The sudden quiet was almost shocking after the cacophony of combat. The Occultum stood among the carnage, bloodied but victorious, their breath coming in harsh gasps as combat fury slowly faded.

One of the fallen warriors staggered to his feet and started running towards the treeline. Blood streamed from a chest wound, but he was still moving fast, and they knew that if he reached the safety of the treeline, they would probably never find him. Sica cursed and started to run after him but seconds later, the crack of Maelon's sling split the air again, and the fleeing man fell to the ground, his head spilt wide open

Sica reached the groaning warrior, and his curved blade whispered across his throat, sending arterial blood spraying across the rocky ground.

Silence returned to the clearing, broken only by the sound of blood dripping onto stone and the harsh breathing of exhausted men. The Shadow Walkers were dead, all eight of them, but their deaths had come at a cost that went far beyond the minor wounds the Occultum had sustained. Their presence in Silures territory would no longer be a secret.

Chapter Thirty-Six

The Forests of Siluria

The ancient hunting shack huddled beside the stream like a forgotten relic of better times, its timber walls green with moss and its thatched roof collapsed in several places where years of neglect had taken their toll. Vines and brambles had claimed most of the structure, creating a natural camouflage that rendered it nearly invisible unless one knew exactly where to look.

Inside the cramped confines, the Occultum tended their wounds. Marcus bound a deep cut on Decimus's forearm while Talorcan cleaned a gash across his own shoulder, grimacing as he worked antiseptic herbs into the wound. The injuries were minor but needed attention, infection could kill as surely as any blade in these hostile lands.

Veteranus sat against the far wall, allowing Maelon to clean the spear cut that ran across his back. The boy's hands were steady despite everything they had endured, his experience as a slave having taught him the basics of wound care. The cut was shallow but painful, a reminder of how close death had come in that final desperate fight.

A hundred paces away, Sica crouched motionless in the dense undergrowth beside the stream, his dark eyes scanning both approaches to their refuge. From his position, he could observe anyone approaching along the water or through the forest without being seen himself. His presence was their early warning system, their guarantee that conversation could proceed without fear of surprise.

'Tell me what happened,' said Seneca quietly, settling beside Veteranus once Maelon had finished his work. 'From the beginning. How did you end up in Silures territory?'

Veteranus leaned back against the rotting timber, organizing his thoughts before beginning the tale. His voice was low, pitched to carry no further than the confines of their shelter, but clear enough for all to hear.

'The trading mission to the Ordovices proceeded as planned initially. Bodvoc received us with proper courtesy, and the negotiations seemed to be progressing well. But then...' He paused, remembering the moment when everything had gone wrong. 'A messenger arrived with news that changed everything. I'd been recognized by an Ordovices warrior who had seen me with the druids on Mona.'

'Compromised,' Marcus observed grimly.

'Completely. They knew exactly who I was and what I represented. But rather than simply execute me as a spy, Bodvoc offered an alternative.' Veteranus met Seneca's eyes directly. 'Rhiannon, daughter of Cartimandua, had been kidnapped by Silures raiders. If I could find her and bring her back, both the trader Adgennus and I would be allowed to live.'

'And you accepted?'

'The alternative was death for the entire caravan. More importantly, the political implications were severe. Rhiannon had been traveling to her betrothal ceremony with Einion, Bodvoc's son. The raiders killed him and his entire escort before taking her.'

Falco whistled softly, understanding immediately what this meant.

'Without the marriage, any alliance between the Brigantes and Ordovices would collapse.'

'And the Ordovices would be forced into a new alliance with Caratacus and the Silures,' Veteranus confirmed. 'The united opposition that would create could drive Rome out of

Britannia entirely.'

Seneca absorbed this information while considering its implications for their own mission. The political ramifications were staggering, but they also created opportunities that hadn't existed before.

'So you came south, searching for the woman,' he prompted.

'With Maelon as my guide. He'd been a slave among the Shadow Walkers for three years before escaping. He knew their territory, their methods, their main camp locations.' Veteranus glanced at the boy, who was listening intently to the conversation. 'We managed to infiltrate one of their camps, but I was captured during the reconnaissance. Mordred was also there.'

'*Mordred?*' gasped Seneca.

'Yes. He questioned me about why I was there and who else accompanied me, but his patience was wearing thin. He was about to revert to more, shall we say, traditional methods of interrogation before he found out that Caratacus himself had also arrived and was badly wounded. Luckily for me Mordred had to leave to try and save his life.'

'But you escaped before he could complete his interrogation.'

'Maelon freed me during the night. We've been running ever since.'

Seneca turned to the boy, who had remained silent throughout the exchange.

'This war camp, is it far?'

'Perhaps ten miles west of here,' Maelon replied without hesitation. 'Hidden in a valley that's almost impossible to find unless you know the way.'

The silence that followed was heavy with calculation.

Each man understood what they had stumbled upon, not just Mordred, their original target, but Caratacus himself, wounded and vulnerable in a location they could potentially reach easily.

'What about your mission?' Veteranus asked eventually.

'We'd eliminated several possibilities,' Seneca replied. 'Observed settlements, gathered intelligence, but nothing definitive until now.' He looked around the circle of faces. 'It seems we've each discovered the other's objective by accident.'

'The gods' work,' Decimus murmured, making a gesture to ward off ill luck.

'Perhaps,' Seneca agreed. 'The question is, what we do with this information?'

'The situation has changed dramatically,' Marcus pointed out with his centurion's practicality. 'Our presence is now known and every Silures warrior in these hills will be hunting us within hours.'

'But the opportunity for success is huge,' said Talorcan. 'Caratacus and Mordred together, both vulnerable. When will we have such a chance again?'

'Never,' Falco growled. 'This is the sort of opportunity that comes once in a lifetime. We'd be fools not to take it.'

'But we would probably end up as dead men,' Decimus countered grimly. 'An army of Shadow Walkers defending their most important leaders, on ground they know better than we ever will. It's suicide.'

'All our missions are potentially suicide,' Falco replied with a shrug. 'That's what makes them worthwhile.'

The debate continued in whispered tones, each man weighing the incredible opportunity against the almost certain death that pursuing it would entail. The elimination of both Caratacus and Mordred would cripple British resistance for years, possibly ending the war entirely. But the camp Maelon described was well defended and they were only seven men, eight including Maelon, against hundreds.

Throughout the discussion, Veteranus remained silent, his expression thoughtful as he listened to the arguments. Finally, as the debate reached its natural conclusion and the decision crystallized, he spoke.

'You're all correct,' he said quietly. 'The death of both Caratacus and Mordred would send a message that would echo across all of Britannia. Every tribe would understand that Rome's reach extends into the deepest forests, that no leader is safe from imperial justice.' He paused, meeting each man's eyes in turn. 'It would also demonstrate that the Empire's enemies can run, but they cannot hide. That resistance is futile, that accommodation with Rome is the only path to survival.'

'But?' Seneca prompted, sensing there was more.

'But we have to consider the alternative,' Veteranus continued, his voice carrying the weight of harsh experience. 'We also have a chance to rescue Rhiannon. And whilst that may not seem like the obvious choice when weighed against killing Caratacus and Mordred, we have to consider the ensuing consequences of each decision.'

He looked around the circle of faces, ensuring he had their complete attention.

'If Rhiannon dies in Silures captivity, what happens next? The treaty between the Ordovices and Brigantes will collapse and Cartimandua will demand blood vengeance for her daughter's death, but the Silures will come to the Ordovices' aid, seeing it as an opportunity to strike at Cartimandua's Roman alliance.'

The implications began to dawn on the others as Veteranus continued his grim analysis.

'Once that happens, other western tribes will probably

join the new alliance. The Deceangli, the Dobunni, even perhaps the Cantiaci. Together, they would create a problem probably too big for Rome to overcome.' He met Seneca's eyes directly. 'Hundreds of romans would die, perhaps thousands, and we might be forced to retreat back to Gaul entirely. Abandon Britannia to save what legions we could.'

Falco's face showed shock at this assessment.

'But Mordred and Caratacus! You're talking about the two most dangerous enemies Rome faces. If we could eliminate both of them...'

'I understand the importance,' Veteranus replied calmly. 'But consider the options. If we fail in the attempt, which is likely given the odds, and both leaders survive, we've accomplished nothing except getting ourselves killed. But if Rhiannon dies, the tribal alliance I described becomes inevitable.'

Seneca felt the weight of command settle heavily on his shoulders again as he processed this analysis. His frustration was evident in his expression, but so was his recognition of the brutal logic in Veteranus's assessment.

'You're right,' he said finally, the words seeming to cost him physical effort. 'When I weigh up which option would mean the least Roman soldiers dying, it's obvious.'

He looked around at his men, seeing his own reluctance reflected in their faces.

'We cannot risk that alliance forming. The political ramifications outweigh even the military opportunity.'

This time, he didn't offer them a vote. The decision was too important, the consequences too far-reaching, to be decided by democratic process. As their leader, he would bear the responsibility for what came next.

'We rescue the girl,' he declared firmly. 'No matter the

odds, no matter the cost.'

The silence that followed was heavy with disappointment and resignation. Each man understood the strategic necessity of the decision, but that didn't make it easier to accept.

'Rest now,' Seneca continued. 'Eat what food we have. Tonight we return to the camp where we saw her, and we attempt an extraction.' He paused, meeting each man's eyes in turn. 'If any of us survive the attempt, we get back to the legions as quickly as we can. The intelligence we've gathered about Caratacus and Mordred's location is valuable, even if we can't act on it ourselves.'

As his men settled back to rest and consume their sparse rations, Seneca stared out through a gap in the ruined wall at the darkening forest beyond. Somewhere out there lay the most dangerous mission of their careers, infiltrating a heavily defended enemy settlement to rescue a single woman whose political value could save a province.

The irony wasn't lost on him. They had found the greatest military targets in Britannia, only to walk away from them in favour of a diplomatic rescue that might well prove impossible. The die was cast. All that remained was to see how it would fall.

Chapter Thirty-Seven

The Silurian Settlement

The evening fire cast dancing shadows across the faces of the women gathered in its warm circle, their voices a soft murmur against the backdrop of the camp's settling nighttime sounds. Rhiannon sat cross-legged on a woven mat, her fine wool dress replaced with simpler garments more suited to life in a warrior's camp, though even these humble clothes could not disguise her noble bearing.

The fire pit was situated in a sheltered area between several roundhouses, partially screened from the main camp by carefully placed wooden screens that provided both privacy and protection from the evening breeze. Clay pots bubbled gently at the fire's edge, filling the air with the rich aroma of stewed vegetables and herbs, while the women worked at various tasks, mending clothes, preparing food, or simply enjoying the rare luxury of conversation without the presence of their menfolk.

Beside Rhiannon sat Nerys, a woman of perhaps twenty-five summers with intelligent dark eyes and auburn hair that caught the firelight. Unlike many of the other women, whose faces bore the hard lines of constant struggle, Nerys possessed a gentle beauty that spoke of inner strength rather than mere survival. She was the wife of one of Belenos's senior warriors, a man whose status afforded her slightly better treatment than many others in the camp.

'Your hands,' Nerys observed quietly, gesturing toward Rhiannon's slender fingers. 'They are so soft, so unmarked. Do Brigantes women not work?'

Rhiannon looked down at her hands, suddenly conscious of how different they must appear to these women whose palms were calloused from grinding grain and whose fingers were stained from dyeing cloth and preparing hides.

'We work,' she replied with a slight smile, 'but not as you do. My work was learning languages, understanding the movements of traders and diplomats, managing the household accounts of my mother's court.'

'Languages?' Another woman, older and weathered, leaned forward with interest. 'You speak more tongues than our own?'

'I speak the Roman tongue. Some of the Gallic dialects from traders who visited our lands. Even a little Greek, though I confess I'm not fluent.' Rhiannon shifted on her mat, drawing her borrowed cloak closer against the night air. 'My mother believed that to rule effectively, one must understand all the peoples under your influence.'

Nerys's eyes widened at this revelation.

'You can speak with Romans? In their own language?'

'I can. My mother's alliance with them required frequent negotiations, treaty discussions, trade agreements. Someone had to serve as translator when their representatives couldn't speak our tongue well enough for complex talks.'

The women exchanged glances, clearly fascinated by this glimpse into a world so different from their own. Here was someone who had not only seen Romans but had spoken with them as equals, negotiated with them as representatives of royal power.

'Tell us about them,' urged Gwenith, a middle-aged woman whose husband was one of Belenos's lieutenants. 'The Romans. Are they truly the monsters our warriors claim? Do they really eat the flesh of their enemies and sacrifice children to their gods?'

Rhiannon couldn't suppress a laugh at these questions,

though she quickly controlled it when she saw the serious expressions around the fire.

'No, nothing like that. They're men, much like your own warriors in many ways. They fight fiercely when they must, show loyalty to their comrades, care for their families.' She paused, choosing her words carefully. 'But they're also very different from us in how they think about the world.'

'How so?' asked Nerys, her voice carrying genuine curiosity rather than suspicion.

'They build things to last forever. Not just for this generation, or the next, but for centuries. Their roads, their buildings, their laws, everything is planned as if they expect their empire to endure until the end of time.' Rhiannon stirred the fire with a long stick, sending sparks spiralling up into the night sky. 'And perhaps most importantly, they believe that their way of life is better than all others, that everyone should live as they do.'

'Is it?' The question came from Cerys, a young woman barely past her first childbirth, her infant son sleeping peacefully in her arms. 'Is their way better?'

Rhiannon considered this carefully, aware that her answer might influence how these women viewed the world beyond their hidden valleys.

'In some ways, yes. Roman women can own property, can inherit wealth from their fathers, can even divorce their husbands if they're badly treated. They have physicians who understand the workings of the body, who can heal injuries and illnesses that would mean death among our people.'

She gestured around the fire circle, noting the obvious signs of hardship in the women's faces and clothing.

'I have never been there, but it is said that in their homeland, their houses have heated floors in winter, and glass windows that let in light but keep out cold and rain. Their markets offer goods from across the known world, silk from distant lands, spices that can make even simple food taste wonderful, and wines aged in special caves until they're smoother than honey.'

The women listened with rapt attention, their eyes reflecting not just the firelight but a hunger for knowledge about possibilities they had never imagined.

'But surely they demand a terrible price for such luxuries?' Gwenith asked. 'Our men say Romans are slavers who would chain us all.'

'Some Romans are slavers,' Rhiannon admitted honestly. 'But so are some of our own people. Even the Silures have slaves. The difference is that Roman slavery often leads to freedom. Many slaves earn their liberty through service, and their children are born free.'

Nerys leaned forward, her voice dropping to barely above a whisper.

'What of Roman women? Do they truly rule in their own households as we've heard?'

'The wealthy ones do.' Replied Rhiannon. 'A Roman matron controls the household finances, manages the education of her children, receives guests, even influences her husband's political decisions.' Rhiannon's voice carried a note of wistfulness. 'They can read and write, can study philosophy and poetry, can travel to distant cities to see wonders we can barely imagine.'

'Your mother allies with them,' said Nerys, 'but other tribes resist. Why?'

It was a perceptive question that cut to the heart of the political complexities Rhiannon had lived with all her life.

'Because alliance means change, and change is

frightening. It means our children might grow up speaking Latin instead of our tongue, worshipping Roman gods instead of our own, thinking Roman thoughts instead of the wisdom passed down by our ancestors.'

She stirred the fire again, watching the flames dance higher.

'My mother chose alliance because she believed it would protect our people, give them opportunities for prosperity and growth. But others see it as surrender, as betrayal of everything that makes us who we are.'

The silence that followed was heavy with contemplation. Each woman was processing this information through the lens of her own experience, weighing the promises of Roman civilization against the costs of abandoning traditional ways.

'Do you think...' Nerys began hesitantly, then stopped herself.

'Speak freely,' Rhiannon encouraged. 'Whatever you're thinking, I won't judge you for it.'

'Do you think there could be a middle path? A way to gain some of these benefits without losing ourselves entirely?'

Before Rhiannon could answer, Gwenith spoke up, her voice carrying the practical wisdom of a woman who had raised children in a world of constant uncertainty.

'Perhaps that's what your mother was trying to achieve. Not surrender, but... adaptation. Taking the best of what Romans offer while keeping the best of what we are.'

'It's possible,' Rhiannon replied thoughtfully. 'Though it requires leaders wise enough to choose carefully, and people brave enough to embrace change when it serves them well.'

Around the fire, the women fell into contemplative silence, each lost in thoughts of possibilities and consequences.

The conversation had opened windows into worlds they had never imagined, challenging assumptions they had held since childhood about what life could be.

In the distance, the sounds of the camp continued, warriors discussing the day's patrol reports, children being settled for sleep, the occasional call of a sentry. But here, in this small circle of firelight, a different kind of conversation was taking place, one that might prove as significant as any battle or raid in shaping the future of their peoples.

In the treeline above the Silures camp, Seneca pressed himself flat against the damp earth, his eyes fixed on the settlement through a gap in the undergrowth. Beside him, Veteranus and Maelon maintained the same motionless vigilance, each man focused on the scene unfolding in the firelight far beneath them.

They had been observing all day, taking turns to watch the camp's routines while the others rested in a concealed position deeper in the forest. The settlement's patterns were becoming clear, guard changes, mealtimes, the movement of people between different areas of the camp. But until now, they had not been able to confirm their primary objective.

The women's fire circle was clearly visible from their elevated position, the dancing flames illuminating the faces gathered around it. Seneca could see perhaps eight or ten women, their forms distinct against the orange glow, but identifying individuals at this distance required patience and careful observation.

'There,' Maelon whispered, so quietly the sound was barely more than an exhaled breath. His finger pointed toward the fire circle with minute precision. 'The one sitting on the far side. That's her.'

Seneca followed the boy's indication, focusing on a figure whose posture and bearing stood out even among the other women. Where the others sat with the casual familiarity of people in their own territory, this one maintained a subtle dignity, a way of holding herself that spoke of noble birth and formal training.

'You're certain?' asked Veteranus.

'Absolutely,' Maelon confirmed. 'I have seen her many times.'

Seneca studied the woman more carefully, noting details that confirmed Maelon's identification.

'Rhiannon,' he murmured, committing every detail of her appearance and position to memory. 'Daughter of Cartimandua, bride-to-be of Bodvoc's son.'

'Was bride-to-be,' Veteranus corrected grimly. 'Einion is dead, killed by the same raiders who took her. That marriage alliance died with him.'

Seneca continued his observation, noting the guards visible around the camp's perimeter, the placement of weapons near the fire circles, the locations of the various roundhouses that might serve as escape routes or obstacles. Every detail would be crucial when they made their attempt. Finally they saw Rhiannon and one other woman leave the fire and enter one of the smaller huts, unwittingly identifying the Occultum's target.

'We have little time,' said Seneca. 'As soon as word reaches here about the men we killed, this place will be impossible to enter.'

He took one final look at the scene below, memorizing the exact position of their target relative to the various landmarks and structures. In the darkness of their planned infiltration, such reference points would be essential for navigation.

'We've seen enough,' he said. 'Time to rejoin the others and finalize our plans.'

Once they had put sufficient distance between themselves and the camp, they moved quickly through the darkness, following paths that Maelon had identified during their reconnaissance. The boy's knowledge of the local terrain was proving invaluable, and without his guidance, they might have wandered these forests for weeks without finding their objective.

They found the rest of the Occultum where they had left them, concealed in a natural depression that was invisible from more than a few paces away. Marcus looked up as they approached, his expression questioning.

'She's there,' said Seneca simply, settling onto the ground beside his men, 'in the women's area near the central fires. Maelon's identification confirmed it.'

The relief in the group was palpable, though tempered by the knowledge that finding their target was only the beginning of their challenges.

'We make our move tonight,' said Seneca. 'We extract her quietly if possible, but fight our way out if necessary. But the objective is extraction, not body count.'

He looked around the circle of faces, noting the mixture of determination and concern in his men's expressions. They had undertaken impossible missions before, but this one carried political implications that went far beyond their usual objectives.

'Rest while you can,' he ordered. 'We move when their guard routines are at their lowest ebb. Once we commit to this, there's no turning back.'

As his men settled back to conserve their strength for

the trial ahead, Seneca found himself staring up at the stars visible through breaks in the forest canopy. Tonight would determine whether Rome's hold on Britannia survived, or whether the Empire's greatest conquest became its most spectacular failure.

Chapter Thirty-Eight

The Silures Settlement

The night air was thick with mist as the Occultum moved into their final positions around the Silures camp. Each man had been briefed, and knew his specific responsibility in the complex choreography that would either see them victorious or dead before dawn. The darkness was their ally now, but it was also their enemy, one misplaced step, one carelessly kicked stone, could alert the entire settlement to their presence.

From his concealed position overlooking the camp's eastern approach, Veteranus studied the settlement with professional interest. Unlike the Shadow Walker camp where he had been held captive, this place had a more permanent feel to it. The structures were better built, the defensive positions less militaristic, the overall atmosphere suggesting a community rather than a military outpost.

'Different,' he murmured to Marcus, who crouched beside him in the undergrowth. 'This doesn't feel like the same kind of threat.'

'How so?' replied Marcus, his centurion's eyes cataloguing the same details but reaching different conclusions.

Before Veteranus could respond, Maelon's voice reached them from their communication point, barely audible even in the forest quiet.

'This is a regular settlement,' the boy explained, his knowledge of Silures organization proving invaluable once again. 'The Shadow Walkers are different, they're like a spearpoint on the end of an arrow. The most feared warriors among all the Silures, men who live only for war and raiding.

This place...' He gestured toward the sleeping camp below. 'These are families, craftsmen, the people who support the warriors but don't live as they do.'

The distinction was important, and it explained the different security arrangements they had observed. A Shadow Walker camp of this size would have been virtually impregnable to infiltration, manned by warriors who slept with one eye open and woke at the slightest disturbance. This settlement, while still dangerous, was inhabited by people who expected to sleep safely in their beds.

As the communal fires began to die down and the camp settled into its nighttime routines, Seneca gave the signal for the final phase to begin. Most of the settlement's inhabitants had retired to their roundhouses, leaving only the perimeter guards and the occasional late wanderer still moving about.

Sica, Maelon and Seneca began their descent into the camp itself. Each step was calculated, each pause timed to coincide with the movement patterns of the guards they had observed during their surveillance. They were no longer merely infiltrating enemy territory, they were entering the heart of a sleeping community, where discovery would mean not just their own deaths but potentially the deaths of innocents caught in the resulting chaos.

The camp's layout had been memorized during their reconnaissance, but moving through it in darkness while avoiding detection required absolute concentration. The roundhouse where Rhiannon was being held stood near the centre of the settlement, close enough to the main fires to benefit from their warmth and light, but positioned to provide privacy for its high-status occupant. A single guard stood at its entrance, his spear held in relaxed readiness, his attention focused outward toward the camp's perimeter rather than on the building behind him. The man never saw death approaching.

Sica materialized smoothly from the shadows, his curved blade sliding across the guard's throat with surgical precision. The cut was deep and decisive, severing both the carotid arteries and the windpipe in a single motion that prevented any possibility of an outcry.

With practiced efficiency, he caught the falling body and dragged it back into the deeper shadows beside the roundhouse, positioning it where it wouldn't be immediately visible to casual observation. He cleaned his blade on the dead man's clothing before taking up position at the entrance, his eyes scanning the surrounding area for any sign that the killing had been detected.

Nothing. The camp continued its peaceful slumber, unaware that death had walked among them.

Seneca and Maelon slipped through the leather door covering into the roundhouse's dim interior. The structure was more spacious than most they had seen, with sleeping platforms arranged around the central hearth where the last embers of the evening's fire cast a faint red glow. Two figures lay on the platforms, wrapped in warm furs against the night's chill.

They approached with infinite care, each footstep placed with deliberate precision on the rushes that covered the earthen floor. The wrong movement could wake either woman, and if they cried out in alarm, the entire settlement would be roused within moments.

Seneca positioned himself beside the nearer figure while Maelon moved to what they hoped was Rhiannon's sleeping form. In the dim light, it was difficult to be certain of identities, but the quality of the sleeping furs and the woman's positioning suggested this was indeed their target.

At Seneca's silent signal, both men moved simultaneously. Seneca's hand clamped down over the nearer woman's mouth while his blade pressed against her throat, the steel cold against her skin. Her eyes flew open in terror, but his grip prevented any sound from escaping.

Maelon gently shook Rhiannon's shoulder, his touch light but insistent. She stirred slowly, the deep sleep of exhaustion giving way gradually to wakefulness. When her eyes opened and focused on the stranger leaning over her, Seneca saw them widen with fear and the beginning of what might become a scream.

'Pray be quiet, noble one,' Maelon whispered urgently, 'we're here to rescue you, not harm you.'

He could see the disbelief in her eyes, the natural assumption that this was simply another abduction by different captors. Moving slowly, he gestured toward Seneca and the terrified woman he held captive.

'We are not Silures,' he continued, his words carefully chosen. 'We have been sent by Bodvoc to bring you home safely.'

Recognition flickered in Rhiannon's eyes as she processed this information. The mention of Bodvoc's name seemed to penetrate her fear, suggesting these might indeed be rescuers rather than new captors.

'Nerys,' she whispered, looking toward her friend who remained frozen under Seneca's restraining hand.

'Your friend will not be harmed,' Maelon assured her, 'but we need her silence. We need you both to be silent. Any sound will bring the entire camp down upon us.'

Seneca watched this exchange with growing impatience, acutely aware that every second they spent in the roundhouse increased their risk of discovery. But he also understood the delicate nature of the situation, if Rhiannon didn't trust them, if she believed this was simply another kidnapping, she might resist in ways that would doom them all.

Rhiannon nodded slowly, indicating her understanding and cooperation. But her eyes remained fixed on Nerys, and when she spoke, her voice carried the unmistakable authority of royal blood.

'I will come with you,' she said quietly, 'but only if you release my friend unharmed. She has shown me nothing but kindness during my captivity.'

Seneca felt frustration rise in his chest. The tactical situation was precarious enough without adding complications, but the woman's demand created a serious problem. Leaving witnesses alive violated every principle of clandestine operations.

'We cannot risk her raising the alarm,' he replied in a harsh whisper. 'The moment we leave, she could cry out and bring every warrior in the camp after us.'

Rhiannon's expression hardened, and Seneca could see the steel beneath her noble bearing. This was not a woman who could be easily intimidated or coerced.

'Then you have a choice,' she said with quiet determination. 'Release her and trust in her discretion, or I will raise the alarm myself right now. I will not be party to the murder of an innocent woman who has been kind to me.'

The standoff stretched between them, each party recognizing the resolve in the other. Seneca's blade remained at Nerys's throat, but he could see in Rhiannon's eyes that she meant exactly what she said. If he killed the Silures woman, their target would fight them with every fibre of her being, making extraction impossible.

Slowly, reluctantly, Seneca withdrew his blade and

released his grip on Nerys's mouth. The woman immediately rolled away from him, her breathing coming in frightened gasps, but she made no sound that would alert the camp.

Rhiannon moved immediately to her friend's side, embracing her with obvious affection.

'I'm sorry,' she whispered into Nerys's ear. 'I'm so sorry this had to happen.'

The two women clung to each other in the dim light of the dying fire, one facing freedom and the other left behind to face the consequences of her friend's escape. It was a moment of human connection that transcended the political and military considerations that had brought them all to this point.

Seneca found himself caught in an impossible tactical situation. They couldn't take both women, the additional burden would slow their escape and double their risk of detection. But killing Nerys would likely turn Rhiannon against them completely, making extraction by force a nightmare that would almost certainly fail.

He was weighing these impossible options when Nerys suddenly turned to face him directly. Her eyes were still wide with fear, but there was something else there now, a desperate kind of determination. She spoke rapidly in the Silures tongue, her words urgent and insistent.

Maelon listened intently, then translated in a shocked whisper.

'She says you have to hit her hard and then tie her up. Make it look like she was attacked and couldn't stop you.'

'No!' Rhiannon protested immediately, her voice rising before she caught herself and dropped back to a whisper. 'I won't let you hurt her.'

But Nerys gripped her friend's hands, speaking again with quiet intensity. Maelon continued translating.

'She says it's the only way. If they find her unharmed, if she admits she let you take you willingly, they'll kill her as a traitor. But if she's been beaten, tied up, left unconscious... then she's a victim, not a collaborator.'

The logic was brutal but undeniable. Seneca could see the truth of it in the way Nerys looked at him, not with hatred, but with the desperate hope of someone who had found the only path to survival in an impossible situation.

Rhiannon's face showed her anguish, but slowly, reluctantly, she began to nod.

'She's right,' she whispered, tears beginning to form in her eyes. 'It's the only way to protect her.'

The two women disentangled themselves slowly, their final embrace carrying the weight of farewell. Nerys positioned herself facing Seneca, her back straight despite her obvious terror. She closed her eyes tightly and clenched her fists at her sides, her whole body tensing in preparation for what was to come.

Seneca took a deep breath, centering himself for what had to be done. He had killed men in battle, eliminated targets in darkness, done whatever violence his missions required. But striking an innocent woman who was trying to help them felt fundamentally wrong.

Moments later, his fist connected with the side of Nerys's head with precisely calculated force, hard enough to cause obvious injury and temporary unconsciousness, but carefully aimed to avoid her jaw where the bones might shatter. She crashed to the earthen floor with a muffled cry of pain, her body going limp as consciousness fled.

Moving quickly, Seneca retrieved rope from his equipment and bound her hands behind her back, then stuffed a piece of cloth into her mouth as a gag. When he rolled her onto her side, he could see that her face was already beginning to swell and bruise, a trickle of blood running down her cheek from where his knuckles had split the skin.

Nerys stirred slightly, her eyes opening to meet his for just a moment. Despite the pain and the blood, despite the tears that ran freely down her face, there was no accusation in her gaze, only a desperate gratitude that they had found a way to spare her life in a difficult situation.

'I'm sorry,' Seneca whispered, the words inadequate but genuine. 'I'm truly sorry.'

He turned away from the injured woman, unable to look any longer at the results of his necessary brutality. The sight of her would haunt him, he knew, regardless of how essential it had been to their mission's success.

Nodding to Maelon and Rhiannon, he indicated that it was time to leave. They had spent too much time in the roundhouse already, and dawn was still hours away. If they were going to escape with their prize, they needed to move now, while darkness still offered them protection. Outside, Sica waited with deadly patience, and beyond him, the rest of the Occultum prepared for the next phase of their desperate gamble against impossible odds.

Chapter Thirty-Nine

The Silures Settlement

Seneca led the way from the roundhouse. Behind him, Rhiannon and Maelon followed while Sica brought up the rear, his eyes constantly scanning their surroundings for any sign of detection.

They didn't head back toward the hill from which they had observed the camp, instead, Seneca guided them along the very edge of the settlement, using the deep shadows cast by the roundhouses to mask their movement. They moved from shadow to shadow, timing each advance to coincide with the movements of the perimeter guards, freezing motionless when anyone passed nearby.

A hundred paces or so beyond the camp's edge, Seneca raised his hand in a silent signal, bringing their small party to a halt. He tilted his head back slightly and produced a soft, haunting call, the hoot of a hunting owl that carried clearly through the night air but would sound perfectly natural to anyone who heard it.

Rhiannon watched in confusion. To her, it seemed like unnecessary noise in a situation that demanded absolute silence but moments later, her confusion turned to amazement as three figures materialized from the darkness leading a pair of horses.

Marcus, Talorcan and Decimus approached. The horses they led were sturdy mountain ponies, stolen from the corral at the end of the camp.

Behind them, invisible in the deeper shadows, lay the bodies of the guards who had been silently eliminated to secure their escape route.

'Mount up,' Seneca whispered to Maelon and

Rhiannon, gesturing toward the horses. 'Quickly now.'

Maelon moved immediately to help Rhiannon onto one of the ponies, adjusting the stirrups to accommodate her shorter legs while she settled into the unfamiliar saddle. Despite her noble upbringing, she was clearly an accomplished rider, her seat natural and confident even in these unusual circumstances.

'Are you not coming with us?' she asked quietly, noting that only two horses had been provided.

'We'll create a diversion and head back a different way,' replied Seneca. 'You just make sure you reach your people and prevent the war that your death would certainly cause.' He turned to Maelon, studying the boy's face in the dim light.

'You're certain you can make it?'

'Absolutely,' Maelon replied without hesitation. 'As soon as we're out of hearing distance from the camp, we'll head north at full gallop. The horses are rested and strong, we'll be at the border just past dawn.'

Seneca nodded, satisfied with the boy's confidence. Maelon had proven himself repeatedly during their brief time together, demonstrating both courage and competence far beyond his years. If anyone could guide Rhiannon to safety through hostile territory, it was him.

Maelon gathered his reins, his young face set with determination. He had come so far from the terrified slave who had first guided Veteranus into Silures territory. Now he carried the responsibility for a princess's life and a kingdom's future on his shoulders.

'For what it's worth,' he said quietly to Seneca, 'you Romans aren't quite the monsters I was taught to believe. Some of you, at least.'

'Some of us,' Seneca agreed with a slight smile. 'Now go. And ride hard for dawn brings discovery.'

The two horses moved away into the darkness, their riders bent low over their necks to present smaller silhouettes against the night sky. Maelon led the way, following routes he had memorized during his years of captivity, paths that would take them away from the settlement and toward the distant safety of allied territory.

Despite their success so far, Seneca knew the operation was far from over and for the remaining members of the Occultum, the night's work was far from over.

As Marcus and Decimus melted back into the shadows to rejoin Falco and Veteranus at a predetermined rally point deeper in the forest, Seneca turned to the one man who still had a major part to play.

'Are you ready?' he asked Talorcan.

'I am,' said Talorcan. 'You get back to the others. I'll see you again back at Camulodunum.

Seneca took his wrist in respect. The next part of the plan was dangerous, but the Belgic scout was the perfect man to carry it out.

'May your Gods go with you,' he said and without another word, slipped into the darkness to join the others.'

Chapter Forty

The Silures Settlement

Dawn crept across the Silures valley like a grey tide, its pale light gradually revealing the details of a settlement still blissfully unaware of the night's intrusions. Most of the Occultum were already miles away, following carefully planned escape routes that would take them through the deepest parts of the forest where pursuit would be most difficult.

But one man remained conspicuously absent from their withdrawal.

Talorcan lay motionless in a shallow depression beside the horse paddock, his hunter's patience serving him well as he waited for the right moment to act. Around him, the settlement began to stir with the lazy rhythms of a community awakening to another day. Smoke rose from cooking fires, children's voices carried on the morning air, and the guards began their routine shift changes.

It would not be long now before someone discovered the missing guards at the paddock, or noticed that the sentry at Rhiannon's roundhouse had vanished during the night. Once that happened, the entire camp would erupt into frantic activity as the scope of the infiltration became clear.

Talorcan knew he had already given the escapees as much time as possible but one final distraction was needed, something dramatic enough to focus every warrior's attention on the immediate threat rather than organizing a pursuit.

Slowly, he rose from his concealment and began moving through the horse paddock with practiced stealth. The animals sensed his presence, some lifting their heads to study this strange intruder, but none showed alarm. He had always possessed an affinity for horses, a gift inherited from his tribal ancestors who had lived and died on horseback across the Germanic plains.

Moving from animal to animal, he cut their tethering ropes with quick, precise strokes of his knife. The horses milled about in growing confusion as their restraints fell away, some wandering toward the paddock gate while others simply stood in bewildered groups, unsure what this newfound freedom meant.

Once the last rope was severed, Talorcan made his way toward the large haystack that dominated one corner of the paddock area. The covered dried grass was perfect fuel, seasoned by months of storage and positioned where any fire would be immediately visible from across the settlement.

Taking a deep breath to steady himself, he reached for his flint and tinder. The familiar ritual of fire-making calmed his nerves even as his mind calculated the rapidly diminishing time before discovery. Spark struck stone, tinder caught, and a small flame began to grow in his cupped hands.

He fed the fire carefully, adding progressively larger pieces of dried grass until it was strong enough to survive on its own. Then, with deliberate purpose, he touched the flame to the base of the haystack and watched as the fire spread with hungry eagerness through the accumulated fuel.

The hay caught with a whoosh of displaced air, flames leaping upward with startling speed as the dry material provided perfect conditions for combustion. Within moments, the entire stack was ablaze, sending a column of black smoke into the morning sky that would be visible for miles.

Talorcan knew he probably had only moments before the alarm was raised, but instead of running toward the hills and the safety of the forest, he moved quickly in the opposite direction. His escape route led not upward to the obvious refuge of the treeline, but down toward the stream that ran along the settlement's eastern edge.

The water was icy cold, fed by mountain springs that never warmed even in summer's heat. But more importantly, the stream's banks were lined with a drainage ditch that had been excavated to prevent flooding during the spring melt. The ditch was filled with thick, clinging mud and overgrown with reeds and marsh grass, perfect concealment for someone desperate enough to use it.

Talorcan lowered himself into the cold morass, gasping involuntarily as the temperature shocked his system. The mud was deeper than he had anticipated, reaching nearly to his chest as he forced himself deeper into the concealment of the reeds. Every instinct screamed at him to escape this freezing trap, but discipline held him in place.

A voice called out in alarm from the direction of the paddock, someone had discovered the fire and within seconds, other voices joined the first, creating a chorus of urgent shouts that echoed across the settlement. Talorcan smiled grimly as he heard the panic in their tones. The diversion was working exactly as planned.

The horses, already nervous from the fire and the shouting, began to panic in earnest. Their milling confusion transformed into outright terror as flames and smoke filled their world with unfamiliar dangers. As one, the herd bolted toward the paddock gate, streaming through the opening in a thunder of hooves that would trample anything in their path, including the bodies of the guards that he had killed during the night.

Talorcan could hear the chaos even from his position in the drainage ditch, men shouting orders, others crying out in shock as they discovered the corpses and the continued drumming of hoofbeats as panicked horses raced through the settlement.

As the commotion reached its peak, Talorcan smeared handfuls of the clinging mud across his face and neck, obliterating any trace of skin that might catch a searcher's eye. Then he pushed himself even deeper into the reeds, working his body down until only his nose and eyes remained above the surface of the frigid mud. He was cold, uncomfortable, and in considerable danger, but he was also invisible, hidden literally under the noses of every warrior who would soon be searching for the infiltrators who had struck their settlement. The diversion had succeeded beyond his wildest hopes. All he had to do now was survive long enough to escape.

Chapter Forty-One

The Forests of Siluria

The ancient forest seemed to press in around them as Seneca led his remaining men through the early morning light, their footsteps muffled by centuries of accumulated leaves and forest debris. They had been pushing hard throughout the night, abandoning all pretence of stealth in favour of raw speed and distance from the settlement they had violated.

All unnecessary equipment had been discarded hours ago, and now they carried only the essentials: weapons, water skins, and strips of dried meat that would sustain them through the immediate crisis.

Each man bore the signs of their desperate flight, sweat-stained clothing, scratched faces from low-hanging branches, the hollow-eyed exhaustion that came from sustained effort without rest. But their pace never slackened, their formation never wavered. Years of training and shared hardship had forged them into a machine that could function even when individual strength began to fail.

Seneca eventually called a halt beside a small clearing where a fallen oak had created a natural barrier against observation. The men collapsed gratefully onto the moss-covered ground, their chests heaving as they gulped the cool morning air.

Falco wiped sweat from his massive brow, his gladiator's conditioning evident in how quickly he recovered from even extreme exertion.

'Do you think Talorcan made it?' he asked, voicing the question that weighed on all their minds. 'That fire was visible for miles, if he was caught in the open when it started...'

'He's fine,' Sica interrupted with quiet certainty. 'Talorcan is a man of the woods. He knows how to use them to his advantage, and how to become invisible when necessary. If anyone can disappear into hostile territory and emerge safely, it's him.'

Seneca looked up at the rising sun, calculating their position by its angle and the lay of the land around them. Navigation in dense forest was always challenging, but years of operating in hostile territory had taught him to read the subtle signs that revealed direction and distance.

'We're making good progress,' he announced, accepting a piece of dried beef from Marcus. 'Perhaps eight miles from the settlement, moving roughly northeast toward what should be safer territory.'

The meat was tough and salty, requiring considerable chewing to break down, but it provided essential sustenance for bodies pushed to their limits.

'How much further to anything resembling safety?' Marcus asked between bites.

'Unknown,' Seneca admitted. 'The intelligence was vague about territorial boundaries in this region, but the further we get from Silures heartland, the better our chances of avoiding organized pursuit.'

'And if we can't avoid it?' asked Falco.

'Then we make them pay dearly for catching us,' Seneca replied grimly. 'But our objective is escape, not engagement. Dead heroes accomplish nothing.'

They finished their hasty meal and prepared to resume their flight. The brief rest had helped, but Seneca could see the accumulated fatigue in his men's movements. They couldn't maintain this pace indefinitely for the preceding weeks had taken their toll, but they had to push as far as possible before their pursuers could organize an effective response.

'Formation as before,' he ordered, rising to his feet. 'Marcus takes point. And remember, always assume we're being tracked. Make the trail as difficult as possible without sacrificing speed.'

They set out again, their pace somewhat reduced by exhaustion but still covering ground at a rate that would challenge any pursuit. The Occultum had learned their woodcraft from some of the finest scouts in the Empire, men who understood that survival often depended on making yourself as difficult to follow as possible.

They crossed streams at angles that would confuse trackers, doubled back on their own trail before branching off in new directions, and used rocky ground to obscure footprints whenever possible. Each technique cost time and energy, but potentially bought them precious hours if their pursuers had to puzzle out the route.

As the day progressed and the sun climbed higher, they found themselves ascending a substantial hill that offered the first clear view they had enjoyed since beginning their flight. At its crest, Seneca called another brief halt while they caught their breath and assessed their situation.

'Up here,' he called quietly, gesturing toward a gap in the trees that provided a clear view back toward the territory they had crossed.

The men gathered at the observation point, their eyes scanning the forest they had traversed during their escape. For a moment, there was nothing visible but endless green canopy stretching to the horizon. Then Marcus pointed toward a distant hill.

'There,' he said simply.

Even at this distance, the pursuit was visible, a line of

riders moving through the forest with considerable speed. The distinctive patterns of their movement marked them as experienced trackers, men who knew how to follow a trail through difficult terrain.

'How many?' Falco asked, though the distance made accurate counting impossible.

'Enough,' Seneca replied grimly. 'More than we want to fight unless we have no other choice. keep moving.'

They descended the hill's opposite face with renewed urgency, the knowledge of pursuit adding fresh energy to legs that had begun to falter. The terrain here was more broken, cut by ravines that offered both obstacles and opportunities for someone fleeing pursuit.

Near the bottom of the slope, they encountered a substantial stream, perhaps twenty feet across and running fast over a bed of smooth stones. The water was clear and cold, obviously fed by mountain springs, and deep enough in places to reach a man's waist.

'Perfect,' said Seneca, studying the watercourse with satisfaction. 'We follow it downstream, staying in the water as much as possible. No tracks or scent trail for dogs.'

The water was shockingly cold, but they waded in without hesitation. Moving downstream required careful footing on the slippery stones, but it was far preferable to leaving an obvious trail for their pursuers to follow.

They moved in single file, each man placing his feet carefully to avoid the falls that could injure or create noise that might carry to hostile ears. The cold water leached heat from their bodies, but it also provided something more valuable than warmth, it gave them invisibility.

Behind them, somewhere in the forest they had left, experienced trackers followed a trail that would soon disappear into running water. How long it would take them to find the point where their quarry had entered the stream, and whether they would guess correctly about which direction had been taken, remained to be seen.

For now, the Occultum had bought themselves time. Whether it would be enough to secure their escape depended on factors beyond their control, the skill of their pursuers, the terrain ahead, and the simple luck that determined the outcome of so many desperate flights, but for the moment, in the waters of a mountain stream, the Occultum had found temporary sanctuary from the forces gathering to destroy them.

Chapter Forty-Two

The Silures Settlement

Talorcan knew he could wait no longer. The cold had penetrated so deeply into his bones that his muscles barely responded to his commands. The mud-filled ditch that had concealed him from searchers was now threatening to become his tomb.

He emerged from the freezing morass like some primordial creature rising from the depths, mud sliding from his body as he forced himself upright on legs that shook with cold and exhaustion. The camp around him had grown quiet, most of its warriors having departed in pursuit of the men responsible for the night's chaos. Only a few guards remained, and they were focused outward, watching for external threats rather than enemies that might already be within their perimeter.

Talorcan had known he would be cold after his ordeal in the marsh, but this was beyond anything he had anticipated. The wet mud had leeched away his body heat with merciless efficiency, leaving him in a state where continued exposure meant certain death. Despite the daylight and the obvious risks, he had no choice but to seek warmth and dry clothing.

Moving with the careful stealth that had kept him alive through countless dangerous situations, he made his way through the settlement toward the longhouse that served as quarters for the unmarried warriors. The structure was larger than the family roundhouses, built to accommodate perhaps thirty men in communal sleeping arrangements.

The entrance was unguarded, its occupants having joined the search parties or been assigned to other duties in the aftermath of the night's disasters. Talorcan slipped inside, his bare feet making no sound on the packed earth floor as he surveyed the interior.

The longhouse was dimly lit by a few oil lamps, their flickering flames casting dancing shadows across the walls. Along the far wall, he could see piles of clothing and personal belongings arranged near the sleeping areas, tunics, cloaks, boots, and other garments that represented warmth and salvation to his hypothermic body.

He moved quickly but quietly toward the clothes, his need for warmth overriding the tactical caution that normally governed his actions. At the pile nearest the wall, he began stripping off his sodden, mud-caked garments, his numb fingers struggling with simple tasks like undoing ties and pulling fabric over his head.

The relief of removing the freezing, wet clothes was immediate and profound. Air that had seemed cold before now felt warm against his skin, and he could feel circulation beginning to return to his extremities as he hastily pulled on dry garments from the pile before him.

A woollen tunic, rough but warm, came first. Then leather breeches that fit reasonably well, followed by a thick cloak that wrapped around his shoulders like salvation itself. Boots came last, sturdy leather footwear that his feet welcomed after their ordeal in the freezing marsh.

As he fastened the cloak's bronze clasp, Talorcan heard a sound behind him, the soft scrape of a foot against the earth floor. He spun around, his hand instinctively reaching for the knife that should have been at his belt, but his fingers found nothing but empty space. The blade lay somewhere among the discarded pile of his muddy clothes, forgotten in his desperate need for warmth.

Before him stood Belenos, the settlement's chief, his massive frame filling the longhouse entrance. The Silures leader held a long spear levelled directly at Talorcan's chest, its iron point gleaming in the lamplight.

'So,' Belenos said, his voice shaking with barely controlled rage. 'You were stupid enough to hide among us rather than flee with the others.'

Talorcan didn't understand the words, but his mind was rapidly calculating distances and angles as his body prepared for the fight that was now inevitable. The chieftain was larger, stronger and armed with a weapon that gave him considerable reach advantage. But Talorcan was desperate, and desperation could sometimes overcome superior force.

The chieftain lunged forward with surprising speed, the spear point driving toward Talorcan's heart, but the Belgic scout had been expecting the attack, and he moved with the reflexes honed by years of experience.

Talorcan threw himself sideways, the spear point passing close enough to part the fabric of his stolen tunic. His roll carried him away from the weapon's reach, but also brought him perilously close to the longhouse wall where manoeuvring room was limited.

Belenos recovered quickly, spinning to face his opponent while drawing the spear back for another thrust. But Talorcan was already moving, launching himself forward in a tackle that caught the larger man around the waist and drove them both crashing to the ground.

The impact knocked the breath from both men, but Belenos's superior size and strength quickly began to tell. He wrapped his massive hands around Talorcan's throat, his fingers closing like iron bands around the smaller man's windpipe.

Talorcan struggled desperately, his hands clawing at the chieftain's wrists while his vision began to darken around the edges. Belenos's grip was like a vice, inexorably tightening as he poured all his considerable strength into ending the fight quickly and decisively.

But in his focus on strangling his opponent, the war chief had forgotten about the discarded clothing that lay scattered nearby and among the muddy garments, Talorcan's knife still rested where he had dropped it during his frantic change into dry clothes.

Talorcan's right hand abandoned its futile attempt to break Belenos's grip and instead stretched toward his fallen possessions. His fingers brushed through the sodden fabric, searching desperately until they found the familiar weight of his blade's handle.

Belenos realized the danger an instant too late. His eyes widened in shock as he saw Talorcan's hand close around the knife, but his choking grip prevented him from pulling away quickly enough to avoid what came next and Talorcan drove the iron point upward with all the strength remaining in his oxygen-starved body. The blade punched through Belenos's ribs just below the heart, sliding between bone and muscle to pierce the vital organ.

The chieftain gasped in shock and sudden agony, and as his hands released Talorcan's throat, he fell sideways, gasping at the excruciating pain.

Talorcan rolled away from the dying war chief, gasping for air as feeling returned to his abused throat. Belenos lay motionless now, his lifeblood spreading across the packed earth floor in a growing pool that reflected the flickering lamplight.

For a moment, Talorcan simply lay there, recovering from both the cold and the violence. Then survival instinct reasserted itself, and he began to consider his next moves. He had killed the settlement's leader, but that would only buy him a brief respite before the body was discovered.

He had warm, dry clothes now, and a weapon. But he was still deep in enemy territory, surrounded by a settlement full of people who would kill him without hesitation if they discovered what he had done.

The escape from the longhouse would be only the beginning of what promised to be the most challenging test of his considerable survival skills.

Chapter Forty-Three

The Northern Border

The rhythm of hoofbeats carried Maelon and Rhiannon through the darkness and into the pale light of dawn, two riders pushing their mounts hard across terrain that seemed determined to exhaust both horse and rider.

They had made excellent time initially, the horses responding well to the urgent need for speed and distance from the Silures settlement. The animals were hardy mountain ponies, bred for endurance rather than speed, and they had covered impressive ground during the first hours of flight.

But even the finest horses had their limits and as the sun climbed higher, Rhiannon's mount began to show signs of distress, its gait becoming increasingly uneven.

'Something's wrong,' she called, pulling gently on the reins to slow her increasingly erratic mount. 'He's favouring his left foreleg.'

Maelon wheeled his own horse around, studying Rhiannon's animal with concern. The pony's head was up, its ears pricked with pain, and its left front hoof barely touched the ground with each step.

'Lame,' he confirmed grimly, dismounting to examine the injured limb more closely. 'The hoof's not split, but there's definite swelling above the fetlock.'

Rhiannon dismounted as well, running her hands along the horse's neck.

'Can he continue?'

'Not at speed,' Maelon replied honestly. 'And not for long at any pace. We'll have to double up on my horse.'

They turned the lame horse loose to fend for itself

before transferring quickly to Maelon's mount, The additional weight immediately made the remaining pony's task more difficult, but the animal responded gamely to the challenge, maintaining a steady pace despite its increased burden.

For another hour they continued their flight, the single horse carrying them both with admirable determination. But the inevitable strain of endurance was working against them, and one animal carrying two riders simply couldn't maintain the pace.

The horse began to falter as the morning progressed, its breathing becoming laboured and its gait increasingly unsteady. Maelon could feel the animal's strength ebbing beneath them.

'We're going to have to dismount,' he said over his shoulder to Rhiannon. 'He can't carry us both much further.'

Even as he spoke, the sound they had been dreading reached their ears, the distant thunder of hoofbeats behind them, growing steadily louder as their pursuers closed in.

They slid from the horse's back and immediately broke into a run, leaving the exhausted animal behind as they pushed their own bodies has hard as they could. The terrain here was more open, rolling hills covered with grass and scattered copses that offered little concealment but allowed for faster movement on foot.

Ahead, perhaps half a mile distant, Maelon could see the river that marked the boundary between Silures territory and the lands of the Ordovices. Safety lay beyond that water, if they only could reach it before their pursuers ran them down.

'*The border,*' he called to Rhiannon, pointing toward the river. 'Once we cross, we're in Ordovices territory.'

They increased their pace despite the burning in their lungs and the protests from muscles pushed beyond normal limits. Behind them, the sound of pursuit grew louder and more distinct, individual riders could now be distinguished, along with the occasional shout of the men coordinating their hunt.

The river, when they reached it, was broader than Maelon had remembered from his years of captivity, creating a substantial barrier that would challenge even strong swimmers. But there was no choice, the alternative was capture and almost certain death.

They plunged into the cold water without hesitation, wading across the swift current while fighting to maintain their footing on the slippery rocks beneath. The water reached their waists at the deepest point, the current tugging at their legs with surprising strength, but they pressed forward with desperate determination.

Gasping and sodden, they emerged on the far bank, officially in Ordovices territory and under the protection of Bodvoc's rule. For a moment, hope flared in both their hearts as they realized they had achieved what had seemed impossible hours earlier. But their relief proved premature as the pursuers kept on coming, and they turned to continue their desperate flight.

The Silures patrol reached the river's edge moments later, their horses snorting and pawing as the riders surveyed the water barrier. Without hesitation, the lead rider spurred his mount into the current, followed immediately by his companions. Political boundaries meant nothing to men whose blood was up and whose pride had been wounded by the night's humiliation.

'They're still coming,' gasped Rhiannon, without turning.

Maelon looked around desperately for some defensible position, some terrain feature that might allow them to make a stand. But the ground here was open, offering no cover and no advantage to fugitives on foot facing mounted warriors.

'Keep running,' he replied, though his voice carried little hope. 'Until we can't run anymore.'

They stumbled forward across the grassland, their waterlogged clothes weighing them down, their exhausted bodies protesting every step. Behind them, the Silures patrol completed their river crossing and spurred their horses into a gallop, the gap closing rapidly as their mounted pursuit closed in on their fleeing prey.

Finally, with the sound of hoofbeats almost upon them, Maelon and Rhiannon could run no more. Their legs simply refused to carry them further, and they collapsed to their knees on the open hillside, turning to face their fate with whatever dignity remained to them.

The Silures riders thundered closer, their weapons ready, their faces showing the grim satisfaction of hunters who had run their quarry to ground. Victory was moments away, and with it the recovery of the valuable prisoner whose escape had cost them so much. But then, inexplicably, the pursuit halted.

The lead rider pulled his horse to a stop perhaps two hundred paces away, his arm raised to signal the others. The entire patrol sat motionless on their mounts, no longer advancing but not retreating either, as if frozen by some invisible barrier.

Maelon and Rhiannon stared in confusion at their pursuers, unable to understand why the final charge had been aborted when success was so close at hand. Then the thunder of new hoofbeats reached their ears, coming from behind them, from deeper in Ordovices territory.

They turned to see a sight that filled their hearts with desperate hope, hundreds of Ordovices riders descending from the hill behind them, their war cries echoing across the grassland as they galloped toward the confrontation. At their head rode a figure whose presence transformed the entire situation, Bodvoc himself, the great chieftain whose territory had been violated by the Silures patrol.

The Ordovices cavalry swept past Maelon and Rhiannon like a tide of vengeance, their ponies sure-footed on the familiar ground, their weapons gleaming in the morning sun. The Silures patrol, suddenly outnumbered ten to one and caught in enemy territory, wheeled their horses and fled back toward the river with all the speed they could muster.

The chase was brief but decisive. The Silures reached the water ahead of their pursuers, but several riders were overtaken in the shallows, their screams cut short by Ordovices spears. The few survivors who reached their own territory did so with the knowledge that their violation of the border had been answered with swift and deadly force.

As the sounds of combat faded and the Ordovices warriors began returning from their successful pursuit, Bodvoc himself rode toward the two exhausted fugitives who knelt on his grassland. His expression was unreadable as he studied the bedraggled pair who had caused such upheaval in the borderlands.

'Rhiannon, daughter of Cartimandua,' he said formally, his voice carrying across the quiet hillside. 'Welcome back to the protection of the Ordovices. Your journey has been long and difficult, but it is over now.'

Rhiannon raised her head, meeting the chieftain's gaze with the dignity that had sustained her through captivity and flight.

'Great Bodvoc,' she replied, her voice hoarse but steady. 'I am grateful for your protection, and for the brave souls who freed me from captivity. My mother will want to hear of their courage.'

The political ramifications of her rescue would unfold in the days and weeks ahead, but for now, the immediate crisis was over. She was safe, the alliance that her survival made possible was preserved, and the Silures had learned that their territory was not inviolate.

The flight was over, but the real work of preventing a war was just beginning.

Chapter Forty-Four

The Forests of Siluria

The mountain stream carried them westward for more than a mile, its icy waters numbing their legs while providing the invisible highway they desperately needed. Seneca led the way, testing each step carefully on the slippery stones while his men followed in single file, their movements creating minimal disturbance in the swift-flowing current.

The cold was brutal, but it was also their salvation. No tracker, however skilled, could follow a trail that flowed away downstream at the speed of running water and no dog could detect a scent that had been washed clean by mountain springs.

Finally, when Seneca judged they had put sufficient distance between themselves and any pursuers, he led them out of the water onto a rocky outcrop that would leave no footprints. They emerged like half-drowned spirits, water streaming from their clothing, their skin pale and mottled from prolonged exposure to the cold.

'Keep going east,' Seneca commanded through chattering teeth, 'we need distance, and we need warmth. Keep moving.'

They struck out across country with the relentless pace that had characterized their entire flight, but now the accumulated effects of their ordeal were beginning to show. The brief rest by the stream had been their first real halt since beginning their escape, and their bodies were starting to rebel against the demands being placed upon them.

Exhaustion weighed on them like a physical burden and the lack of food was becoming a serious problem. They had consumed the last of their meagre rations and their bodies were now burning through reserves that had already been depleted by weeks of careful rationing in hostile territory. Hunger gnawed at their bellies with increasing insistence, sapping strength they could ill afford to lose.

'We can't maintain this pace much longer,' said Marcus grimly, hauling himself back to his feet after a fall.

Seneca nodded, though he knew they had little choice but to continue. Somewhere behind them, their pursuers were following whatever trail they could find, closing the distance whenever the fugitives were forced to rest or slow their pace.

It was Decimus who spotted the birds first, dark shapes wheeling in the sky perhaps half a mile ahead, their circling flight patterns unmistakable to anyone familiar with the behaviour of scavengers.

'Carrion,' he said simply, pointing toward the aerial activity. 'Something dead, probably recent.'

The prospect of food, even spoiled meat, was enough to inject fresh energy into their flagging steps. They altered course toward the birds, hoping desperately that whatever had attracted the scavengers might provide sustenance for humans as well.

The scene they discovered was less promising than they had hoped but better than nothing. A deer carcass lay in a small clearing, already well-picked by the various creatures that had found it before them. The animal had been dead for at least two days, its flesh beginning to turn but not yet completely putrid.

A large wolf stood over the carcass as they approached, its head raised alertly as it caught their scent. For a moment, predator and humans stared at each other across the clearing. Then the wolf decided that discretion was the better part of valour and loped away into the forest, leaving its meal to these strange two-legged scavengers.

'Not much left,' Falco observed, studying the remains, 'but something is better than nothing.'

They fell upon the carcass with knives and desperate efficiency, carving away any tiny strips of meat remaining on the bones. The flesh was tough and gamy, already beginning to acquire the distinctive taste of decomposition, but it was protein, and their bodies craved it desperately.

They ate the meat raw, tearing at it with their teeth like the wild animals they were becoming. There was no time or safety for the luxury of cooking, no opportunity to properly clean or prepare what they consumed. Survival had reduced them to the most basic level of existence, finding food, eating it, and moving on.

'Better,' Marcus admitted, wiping congealed deer blood from his chin with the back of his hand. 'Not good, but better.'

They resumed their eastward journey, but the brief halt had allowed the full weight of their exhaustion to settle upon them. The adrenaline that had sustained them through the night and morning was finally wearing off, leaving behind the accumulated fatigue of days spent in hostile territory under constant stress.

A few hours later, it became clear that they could not continue much longer without rest. Their pace had slowed to little more than a stagger, and men who normally moved with cat-like grace were stumbling over obstacles that should have presented no challenge.

'We need shelter,' Seneca admitted finally. 'Somewhere defensible where we can rest without being surprised.'

Sica, despite his own exhaustion, still possessed enough woodcraft to locate what they needed, a dense thicket of brambles and fallen timber that had grown up around the base of a massive oak tree. The natural barrier would provide both concealment and some protection from the elements.

They crawled into the undergrowth like wounded animals seeking a den, forcing their way through thorns and branches that caught at their clothing and scratched their exposed skin. The space they found was cramped and uncomfortable, but it was hidden and defensible.

Seneca began to organize the watch schedule that would ensure their security during the rest period, but his words trailed off as he looked around at his men. One by one, they were already succumbing to sleep, their bodies finally claiming the rest that had been denied too long.

Marcus lay curled against the base of the oak, his breathing deep and regular. Decimus had propped himself against a fallen log, his head tilted back and his mouth slightly open and even Falco, whose gladiator's conditioning usually kept him alert longer than the others, had found a relatively comfortable position and fallen into exhausted slumber.

Seneca tried to maintain his vigilance, knowing that someone needed to keep watch, but his eyelids grew increasingly heavy despite his efforts to stay alert. The accumulated strain of command, of making life-and-death decisions while exhausted and hungry, finally overwhelmed even his considerable reserves of willpower and within moments, he too had joined his men in the deep, dreamless sleep of total exhaustion. Their bodies, pushed beyond normal limits for too long, had simply shut down, demanding the rest necessary for survival.

Chapter Forty-Five

The Cache

The sun's rays filtering through the canopy brought the Occultum slowly back to consciousness, their bodies protesting every movement as they emerged from the deep sleep of total exhaustion. Seneca was the first to fully wake, and the sight of bright daylight streaming through their shelter sent a cold shock of realization through him.

'Jupiter's balls,' he cursed quietly, checking the sun's position through gaps in the brambles. 'We've slept the entire night.'

The others stirred at his voice, groaning as stiff muscles and cramped limbs reminded them of their ordeal. What should have been a brief rest of a few hours had turned into a full night's sleep, precious time lost while their enemies might have been closing the distance between them.

'How long?' Marcus asked, working his shoulders to ease the knots that had formed during their uncomfortable rest. His veteran's body showed the strain of sleeping on uneven ground, and he grimaced as he tried to work feeling back into his left arm.

'Too long,' Seneca replied grimly, studying the angle of sunlight with practiced eyes. 'Dawn passed hours ago. The sun's already climbing toward midday. We've let our own standards slip.'

It was a harsh assessment, but an accurate one. In their years of working together, the Occultum had prided themselves on maintaining alertness even under the most challenging conditions. Sleeping through an entire night without posting watches was exactly the kind of mistake that got elite units killed in hostile territory.

Despite the self-recrimination, they all felt markedly better for the rest. The bone-deep weariness that had plagued them the previous day had lifted somewhat, replaced by the kind of manageable fatigue that came from hard work rather than the complete depletion that had threatened to end their flight entirely. Their movements, while still stiff from sleeping rough, had regained some of their usual coordination.

'Sica,' Seneca ordered as they prepared to leave their shelter, 'scout ahead. Get the lay of the land, see if you can determine our exact position and the best route forward. We need to know if our pursuers are still behind us, and how much of a lead we might have gained.'

The Syrian nodded and slipped away through the undergrowth with his characteristic silence, becoming invisible within moments of leaving their concealed position.

His absence stretched long enough for concern to grow among those who waited. In their current situation, any delay could prove fatal, and the longer Sica remained away, the more worried his companions became about what he might have encountered.

Marcus positioned himself at the edge of their shelter, his eyes scanning the forest in the direction Sica had taken. His weathered face showed the concern they all felt, in hostile territory, separated team members had a disturbing tendency to disappear permanently.

'He should have been back by now,' Decimus muttered, checking his weapons for perhaps the tenth time that morning. 'Either he's found something that requires extensive observation, or...'

He didn't finish the sentence, but they all understood the alternatives. Sica might have been captured, killed, or simply lost in terrain that looked deceptively similar in all directions. Any of those possibilities would leave them blind in enemy territory, deprived of their finest scout when they needed his skills most desperately.

When Sica finally did return, however, his expression carried the first genuine hope they had seen in days. He materialized from the undergrowth as silently as he had departed, but now his usually impassive features showed something approaching satisfaction.

'Good news,' he reported quietly, settling into the centre of their small circle. 'I recognize those hills.' He pointed toward distant peaks visible through breaks in the forest canopy, their blue-grey silhouettes standing out against the morning sky. 'Our first cache is on the far side of the furthest one. We're closer than I thought, perhaps six or seven miles if we take the most direct route.'

The effect on the group's morale was immediate and profound. After days of uncertainty, of not knowing exactly where they were or how far they had to travel, the prospect of reaching their supply cache felt like salvation itself. Food, proper equipment, weapons, medical supplies, everything they needed to transform themselves from desperate fugitives back into effective operatives.

'You're certain?' Seneca asked, though Sica's reputation for navigation made the question almost unnecessary.

'I am,' Sica confirmed with quiet confidence. 'We should reach the site by mid-afternoon if we maintain good pace.'

Falco cracked his knuckles with anticipation, the sound somehow managing to convey his satisfaction.

'Real food,' he said with obvious longing. 'Proper rations, instead of rotting flesh from wolf kills.'

With renewed spirits and a definite objective, they set out through the forest with something approaching their normal efficiency. The prospect of resupply had transformed their movement from desperate flight to purposeful advance toward a known goal. Their steps carried new energy, their formation tightened into proper tactical spacing, and for the first time in days, they moved with the confident precision that marked them as elite operatives rather than exhausted fugitives.

The terrain cooperated with their improved fortunes, offering easier going than they had encountered during the previous day's ordeal. Well-established game trails provided clear paths through the undergrowth, carved by generations of deer and other forest creatures seeking the most efficient routes through the wilderness. The forest itself seemed less dense here, its canopy broken by clearings that allowed for better visibility and faster movement.

They made excellent time, covering ground with the knowledge that they were moving toward relief rather than simply away from pursuit gave new purpose to their efforts.

By early afternoon, they had covered the distance Sica had estimated and found themselves approaching the stream where they had concealed their emergency supplies weeks earlier. The landscape was exactly as they remembered, the distinctive bend in the water where it curved around a small hill, the cluster of ancient yew trees that had provided such perfect camouflage, the rocky outcrop that had served as their primary landmark.

'There,' said Falco with deep satisfaction, pointing toward the stone they had used to mark their cache location. 'Just as we left it.'

They approached the site with the mixture of hope and caution that characterized men who had learned not to trust good fortune too readily. Years of experience had taught them that the moment when success seemed certain was often when disaster struck with devastating effect.

But everything appeared undisturbed. The stone marker was in its correct position, carefully placed to look natural while indicating the exact burial location to those who knew what to look for. The surrounding ground showed no signs of interference, no footprints or disturbance that might indicate unwelcome visitors. The concealment they had so carefully arranged remained intact, appearing to casual observation as nothing more than an unremarkable section of forest floor.

Veteranus studied the area with professional interest, noting the skill with which the cache had been concealed. Even knowing approximately where to look, it took him several moments to identify the exact location of the buried supplies.

Falco knelt beside the marked stone and began the excavation, using his knife to dig frantically through the earth that covered their buried supplies. The work was harder than he had expected, the soil had settled and compacted during the weeks since burial, and what had seemed like loose earth when they had covered the cache now required considerable effort to penetrate.

'Here,' said Marcus, producing his own knife. 'Let me help. Two can work faster than one.'

They worked in shifts, one digging while the other cleared away loose soil, maximizing their efforts while minimizing the time required.

Finally, Falco's knife struck something that wasn't earth, the distinctive sound of steel against oiled leather. With a cry of triumph, he cleared away the remaining soil and hauled the precious sarcina from its hiding place, holding it aloft like a trophy won in hard-fought battle.

The pack was exactly as they had left it, wrapped in oiled leather that had kept moisture at bay during its burial. It felt reassuringly heavy in Falco's hands, promising relief from the hunger and deprivation that had plagued them for days.

'We'll eat well tonight,' he declared, his face split by the first genuine smile any of them had worn in days. 'Fresh water, proper rations. By Jupiter's beard, I'll feel human again instead of like some sort of forest savage.'

His enthusiasm was infectious, and even Seneca allowed himself a moment of satisfaction as he contemplated their good fortune, but as the rest of the Occultum started to feel a modicum of relief, Falco's words died in his throat, the smile fading from his features as his eyes focused on something behind his companions. The others spun around, following his horrified gaze toward the forest they had just traversed, their weapons already appearing in their hands.

A line of horsemen was emerging from the treeline perhaps three hundred paces away, moving at an unhurried walk that spoke of absolute confidence in their quarry's capture, predators who knew their prey was trapped.

These were clearly not the same as those they had observed at the settlement where Rhiannon had been held. Everything about them radiated a different and far more dangerous quality, their equipment was uniformly excellent, their horses were superior animals that moved with perfect discipline, and their bearing carried the unmistakable confidence of elite warriors who had never known defeat.

Their weapons were varied but of high quality, long cavalry spears with wicked iron points, swords that showed the careful maintenance of professional warriors, bows that looked capable of accurate shooting at considerable distance. But it was their faces that marked them as truly dangerous, cold, impassive expressions that suggested men who killed without emotion or hesitation.

Veteranus recognized them immediately from his time in captivity. The distinctive spiral tattoos that covered their faces and visible skin, the wolf pelts draped across their shoulders, the bone ornaments woven into their hair, all marked them as members of the Silures' most elite fighting force.

'Shadow Walkers,' he said quietly, the words carrying like a death sentence across the small clearing. 'These aren't ordinary Silures warriors, they're the spearpoint of their army, the most dangerous fighters in all Britannia.'

The identification sent a chill through the group that had nothing to do with the cool forest air. They had heard stories of the Shadow Walkers from Maelon who regarded them as almost supernatural warriors who could appear and disappear at will, who killed without sound or warning, who had never been defeated in open combat.

Now, faced with the reality of their presence, the Occultum understood that those stories had not been exaggerated. These men moved with a fluid grace that spoke of perfect conditioning and absolute confidence. Their horses responded to subtle signals that suggested years of training and partnership and everything about them radiated lethal competence.

Their formation was perfect, a line of over thirty riders that could shift instantly into attack formation or pursuit pattern depending on their quarry's response. Each rider maintained exact spacing from his companions, ensuring that no gap existed that might be exploited by desperate fugitives. Their weapons remained ready but not obviously threatening, the casual preparedness of professionals who knew that violence was only moments away.

The Occultum found themselves caught in the worst possible tactical situation, trapped in the open with their precious cache finally within reach but useless now that discovery had robbed them of the time needed to organize and resupply. Behind them lay a stream that would slow any retreat, before them advanced death on horseback, and around them stretched forest that offered concealment but no real escape from mounted pursuit.

After all their struggles, all their sacrifices, all their desperate efforts to complete their mission and escape with their lives, they had been run to ground by the finest warriors their enemies could field. The irony was bitter, salvation had literally been in their hands when death had finally caught up with them. The final confrontation was at hand, and the odds had never been worse.

Chapter Forty-Six

The Cache Site

The Shadow Walkers dismounted with fluid precision, each man sliding from his horse in perfect synchronization with his companions. They spread out in a loose semicircle, their formation designed to prevent escape while maintaining clear fields of fire for their bows.

In the centre of their line stood their leader, and Veteranus felt his blood turn cold as he recognized the massive figure. Cadoc, the war chief who had held him captive. The Silures warrior looked exactly as Veteranus remembered him: enormous, scarred, radiating the kind of quiet menace that came only from years of surviving deadly encounters.

The war chief stepped forward, his eyes fixed directly on Veteranus with unmistakable intent. When he spoke, his voice carried clearly across the clearing, the words shaped with deliberate precision despite the foreign tongue.

'What's he saying?' Seneca asked quietly, not taking his eyes off the surrounding warriors who had positioned themselves for optimal tactical advantage.

Veteranus listened carefully, his time in captivity having given him a rudimentary understanding of the Silures dialect. The words came slowly, but their meaning was clear enough.

'He wants to fight me,' Veteranus translated, his voice tight with apprehension. 'Single combat. He says... he says I made him look weak when I escaped from his camp. His warriors question his strength because he couldn't hold one Roman prisoner.'

'Why?' demanded Seneca. 'What does he gain from personal combat?'

'Honour,' Veteranus replied grimly. 'He has been humiliated so his leadership becomes questionable. This isn't about tactics or strategy, it's about personal pride.'

Before anyone could respond, Falco stepped forward into Cadoc's direct line of sight, removing his cloak.

'If there's fighting to be done,' he said, 'then I'll be the one to do it.'

The others stared at him in shock as he stripped off his tunic to reveal the network of scars that covered his torso, evidence of countless arena battles fought before crowds that screamed for blood. His body was a map of violence survived, each mark telling the story of an opponent who had tried and failed to kill him.

'Falco, what are you doing?' demanded Marcus.

'What I was trained for,' replied Falco, reaching for his sword and knife. 'This is what I do, single combat against skilled opponents while others watch. I've done it a thousand times before in front of crowds that wanted me dead.'

He selected his weapons with the care of a craftsman choosing tools, testing the balance of his sword before sliding a knife into his other hand, perfectly weighted for both cutting and throwing.

Cadoc watched this display with obvious interest, his warrior's eye immediately recognizing the quality of his unexpected opponent. Where Veteranus moved like a scout or spy, quick and clever, but not primarily a close-combat fighter, this new challenger carried himself like a born killer. The scars, the weapon selection, the confident way he tested his balance, everything marked him as a man who lived for personal combat.

After a long moment of consideration, Cadoc nodded slowly and began his own preparations. He stripped off his wolf-fur cloak and leather jerkin, revealing a torso that rivalled Falco's for size and scars. His skin was decorated with ritual tattoos that spiralled across his chest and arms, blue patterns that seemed to writhe in the dappled forest light.

For weapons, he selected a single-bladed war axe with a long handle that would give him reach advantage, and a curved knife similar to the one Veteranus carried. The axe was clearly his preferred weapon, its handle showed the wear patterns of long use.

The two warriors approached each other, stopping perhaps ten paces apart, each taking the measure of his opponent.

Falco shook the tiredness from his body, his gladiator training asserting itself as muscle memory took over from conscious thought. His breathing was controlled, his stance balanced, his weapons held in the classical position that arena masters had drilled into him through years of brutal practice.

Cadoc moved differently, more like a hunting cat than a trained fighter. His stance was looser, more fluid, adapted for the chaos of battlefield combat rather than the formal duelling of the arena. But his eyes never left Falco's face, reading intentions in micro-expressions that would give warnings of any attacks before they began.

The fight erupted without warning as both men moved simultaneously, their weapons meeting in a shower of sparks that rang across the clearing like a bell. Falco's sword slid along the axe handle, seeking the hands that gripped it, while Cadoc's knife darted toward the Roman's exposed ribs.

Both men twisted away from the other's attack, circling each other with predatory grace as they tested defences and looked for openings. The preliminary exchange had told each warrior what he needed to know, his opponent was skilled, experienced, and completely committed to victory.

Cadoc attacked again, his axe sweeping in a horizontal arc that would have taken Falco's head from his shoulders if it had connected. But the gladiator ducked under the blow and lunged forward, his sword point seeking the gap between the Silures warrior's ribs. Cadoc twisted desperately away, the blade drawing a line of blood across his side before he could escape its reach.

The sight of blood seemed to ignite something primal in both men. They came together again with renewed fury, weapons clashing in a deadly symphony of steel against steel. Falco's training showed in the precision of his attacks, each cut calculated to disable or kill, each movement flowing naturally into the next in combinations practiced thousands of times.

But Cadoc fought with the raw cunning of a man who had survived countless battles where formal technique meant nothing. He used his axe not just as a cutting weapon but as a tool for controlling distance, its long handle allowing him to keep Falco's shorter sword at bay while he looked for opportunities to close with his knife.

Blood began to flow more freely as both warriors found their range. Falco's knife opened a gash along Cadoc's forearm, while the war chief's axe bit deep into the Roman's shoulder, sending blood streaming down his sword arm. Neither man showed any sign of slowing despite their wounds.

The pace of combat intensified as both fighters realized that endurance would determine the outcome as much as skill. They traded blow for blow, neither able to gain a decisive advantage over the other. Falco's arena experience served him well in reading his opponent's patterns, but Cadoc's battlefield cunning allowed him to vary his attacks in ways that kept the Roman from settling into a comfortable rhythm.

A particularly vicious exchange left both men bloodied and breathing hard. Cadoc's axe had opened a deep cut along Falco's side, while the gladiator's sword had carved a furrow across the war chief's chest that wept blood with each heartbeat. They circled each other more cautiously now, each recognizing that the next mistake might be fatal.

Cadoc feinted with his axe, then rushed forward with his knife leading the attack. Falco tried to sidestep but his wounded leg betrayed him, slowing his movement just enough for the blade to find flesh. The knife sliced deep into his thigh, severing muscle and sending him stumbling backward as his leg nearly collapsed beneath him.

The Silures war chief pressed his advantage, raining blows with both weapons as Falco struggled to maintain his defence with a wounded leg. The gladiator's responses grew slower, his movements less precise as blood loss began to take its toll. For the first time since the fight began, it appeared that he might actually lose.

But Falco had not survived years in the arena by yielding to adversity and even as Cadoc's axe opened another wound on his sword arm, the Roman's blade found its mark, sliding through the flesh to shatter a Celtic rib. Cadoc staggered backward in pain, desperately trying to catch his breath.

Both warriors were now severely wounded, their movements growing sluggish as blood loss and exhaustion took their toll. They came together one final time in a flurry of desperate strikes, each seeking to end the fight before his strength failed completely. Steel rang against steel in a final exchange that left both men kneeling on the blood-soaked ground, staring at each other across the small space that separated them.

They were both covered in blood, their own and each

other's, and breathing in ragged gasps that spoke of bodies pushed beyond normal limits. Neither had the strength for another attack, yet neither would yield to his opponent. It was a stalemate born of mutual destruction, two warriors who had fought each other to exhaustion without achieving victory.

Across the clearing, one of the other Silures warriors had grown impatient with the prolonged combat and drawing his bow with smooth precision, took careful aim at Falco's exposed back. The shot was clear, the range unmissable, one arrow would end the fight and eliminate the Roman who had wounded their chief so severely.

Cadoc noticed the movement from the corner of his eye and realising it was treachery of the worst kind, roared out a command in the Silures tongue, but it was too late, the shot that had already been committed.

The arrow flew across the clearing with deadly accuracy, but Falco's gladiator instincts served him even in his exhausted state. He twisted away at the last instant, the point that should have pierced his heart instead driving deep into his upper arm. The impact sent him sprawling to the ground, where he lay gasping in pain and shock.

Sica roared at the archer's treachery and responded with lethal efficiency. His throwing knife spun across the clearing in a perfect arc, the blade turning end over end before sinking deep into the bowman's chest. The Silures warrior dropped his bow and staggered backward, his hands clutching futilely at the steel that had pierced his heart before collapsing without a sound, dead before his body hit the ground.

The death of their comrade shattered whatever restraint had kept the other Shadow Walkers in check and with savage war cries, they drew their weapons and charged toward the Romans, abandoning any pretence of honouring single combat in favour of the massacre they had originally intended.

The Occultum responded instantly and formed a defensive circle around their wounded comrade. The brief respite of watching the duel was over, now came the real fight, outnumbered and caught in the open by some of the finest warriors in Britannia.

Chapter Forty-Seven

The Cache Site

The forest clearing erupted into chaos as the Shadow Walkers charged. Their war cries split the air, not the undisciplined screaming of barbarian raiders, but the controlled battle calls of professional warriors who used sound as another weapon to unnerve their enemies.

The Occultum met their charge with the disciplined precision that had kept them alive through countless impossible situations. Marcus took the first attacker, his gladius sliding between the man's ribs with surgical precision and the Silures warrior died silently, his body already falling as Marcus turned to engage the next threat.

Decimus fought with the brutality of a veteran who had learned that wasted motion meant death. His sword work was unremarkable but devastatingly effective, each cut calculated to disable or kill without exposing him to counterattack. A Shadow Walker's axe rang off his blade, the parry flowing seamlessly into a thrust that punched through leather armour to find the heart beneath.

Sica moved like liquid death among the attackers, his curved blade finding gaps in defences that shouldn't have existed. He killed two men in as many heartbeats, then melted away from a spear thrust that would have skewered a slower fighter. His style was pure assassination, silent, efficient, leaving his opponents dead before they realized they were in danger.

But the Shadow Walkers were not ordinary tribal fighters. These were men who had survived countless battles through skill, courage, and an absolute refusal to yield ground once committed to combat. They absorbed the Romans' initial counter and pressed forward with implacable determination, their own weapons finding flesh despite the defensive skills arrayed against them.

A Silures warrior with intricate facial tattoos drove his spear toward Veteranus's chest, the iron point aimed with deadly precision. Veteranus twisted aside at the last instant, the blade parting the air where his heart had been, but the movement put him directly into the path of another attacker's sword and only Seneca's intervention saved him, his gladius taking the swordsman's arm off at the elbow in a spray of arterial blood.

The battle raged with savage intensity, neither side giving ground despite mounting casualties. The Shadow Walkers fought with the fearless aggression of men who knew that death in battle was preferable to the shame of retreat. They pressed their attacks despite wounds that would have felled lesser warriors, their eyes blazing with the cold fire of professional killers who had never known defeat.

But numbers began to tell, and fresh Shadow Walkers stepped over the bodies of their fallen comrades to continue the assault. Small wounds accumulated into serious injuries, and serious injuries began to slow their responses to levels that invited fatal mistakes.

Marcus grunted in pain as a war axe opened his shoulder to the bone, the impact staggering him backward into Decimus. Blood streamed down his sword arm, weakening his grip and slowing his defensive movements. A Silures warrior noticed the injury and pressed his attack with renewed vigour, sensing weakness that could be exploited.

Veteranus found himself facing two opponents simultaneously, their coordinated assault forcing him to give ground steadily as he struggled to parry attacks coming from multiple angles. His knife work was skilful but defensive, lacking the power to drive back attackers who showed no fear of death.

The defensive circle began to contract as the Occultum were forced backward by the relentless pressure. They fought with desperate courage, but the reality was clear, six wounded men could not indefinitely hold off the onslaught of so many fresh and experienced warriors.

As they retreated, Seneca's foot caught in the hole they had excavated to retrieve their cache. His ankle twisted painfully as he fell backward, his sword flying from his grip to land several paces away. He hit the ground hard, the impact driving the breath from his lungs and leaving him momentarily helpless.

A Shadow Walker immediately seized the opportunity, raising his war axe high above his head for the killing blow. The weapon's edge gleamed wickedly in the dappled forest light and as it reached the apex of its arc, poised to split Seneca's skull like ripe fruit, the Roman leader stared up at his approaching death, too winded and disoriented to roll away from the descending blade.

But before the axe could complete its lethal arc, an arrow appeared as if by magic in the warrior's throat. The iron point punching through flesh and cartilage to emerge from the back of his neck in a spray of blood. The shadow walker's eyes widened in shock and pain before he toppled backward, the axe falling harmlessly beside Seneca's prone form.

A familiar voice roared across the clearing, cutting through the clash of weapons and cries of wounded men, and with a silent gasp of relief to the gods, Seneca watched as Maxima appeared out of nowhere, leading his freshly arrived men into the battle, their horses' hooves churning the forest floor as they drove straight into the melee. The riders struck the

Shadow Walkers' flank like a cavalry hammer, scattering the Silures formation and transforming an organized assault into confused individual combats.

Maxima himself led the charge, his spear taking one Shadow Walker through the chest while his horse trampled another beneath iron-shod hooves. The Exploratores followed their commander's example, their lances and swords reaping a bloody harvest among enemies caught between mounted attackers and the recovering Occultum.

The Shadow Walkers' formation disintegrated under the impact of the cavalry charge and men who had been pressing forward in coordinated assault only moments earlier, suddenly found themselves isolated, fighting desperately against mounted opponents who struck from above with devastating effect.

But these were Shadow Walkers, not ordinary tribal fighters. Even caught off-guard and outnumbered, they fought with the savage skill that had made them legendary throughout Britannia. Several Exploratores paid for their victories with blood, crying out as Silures weapons found gaps in their defences.

The battle that followed was brief but savage. The Shadow Walkers, recognizing that the tactical situation had shifted irrevocably against them, began fighting their way toward the forest edge where their superior knowledge of the terrain might allow escape. They withdrew in good order, covering each other's retreat with professional competence even in the face of overwhelming odds.

A few never made it to the treeline, and their bodies joined those of their comrades who had fallen during the initial assault. But most of the survivors melted into the forest with the fluid grace that had given them their name, disappearing among the trees as if they had never existed.

The Exploratores regrouped in the centre of the clearing, their horses snorting and stamping as the excitement of combat began to fade. Several bore wounds from the encounter, but none were seriously injured. Maxima dismounted and strode toward where Seneca was picking himself up from the ground, his expression mixing relief with professional concern.

'Are you hurt?' he asked, extending a hand to help his fellow commander to his feet.

'Bruised and embarrassed,' Seneca replied, accepting the assistance gratefully. 'But alive, thanks to your intervention. Another few moments and you would have arrived to bury us rather than rescue us.'

All of Seneca's men showed signs of the brutal combat they had just survived. Marcus held his left arm close to his body, blood still seeping from the axe wound that had laid his shoulder open. Decimus sported a gash across his forehead that had filled his left eye with blood while Veteranus moved stiffly, favouring his right side where a spear point had found its mark between his ribs. Even Sica, despite his supernatural grace in combat, bore cuts on both arms where enemy blades had penetrated his defences.

But it was the scene at the centre of the clearing that drew everyone's attention. Cadoc and Falco still knelt facing each other, both too weak from blood loss and exhaustion to stand. They stared into each other's eyes with the mutual respect of warriors who had tested their skills against an equal and found no clear victor.

Maxima approached the Silures war chief with drawn sword, his intention obvious. Here was an enemy leader, wounded and helpless, eliminating him would strike a significant blow against Silures capabilities and remove a dangerous opponent from future battles.

'No,' said Falco quietly, his voice carrying despite his weakness. 'Leave him be.'

Maxima paused, confusion evident in his weathered features.

'He's their war chief. Killing him could end their resistance in this region.'

'He's a warrior,' Falco replied simply, his eyes never leaving Cadoc's face. 'A worthy opponent who fought with honour. Tend his wounds, feed him, and let him go.'

'That's not tactically sound,' Maxima protested, looking to Seneca for support. 'He'll return to his people and continue fighting against Rome.'

'You heard the man,' said Seneca finally, recognizing something in his subordinate's tone that transcended military considerations. 'Do as he says.'

For the next several hours, the clearing became an improvised field hospital as the Exploratores tended to the wounded.

Cadoc accepted treatment with stoic dignity, saying nothing as his wounds were cleaned and bandaged. His eyes tracked the movements of his captors, but showed no fear, only the patient alertness of a predator temporarily restrained. The Romans treated him with professional courtesy, recognizing in him a fellow soldier despite their opposing allegiances.

As preparations began for departure, Falco rose unsteadily to his feet and walked toward the treeline where Cadoc waited under guard. The Silures war chief had been given food and water and his wounds properly dressed. With his strength partially restored, he would be released to make his way back to his people.

No words were spoken between the two warriors as Falco approached. The gladiator carried Cadoc's weapons, the war axe and curved knife that had come so close to ending his own life during their brutal combat. Without ceremony, he extended the weapons toward their original owner.

Cadoc's eyes widened slightly at this unexpected gesture. In his culture, a warrior's weapons were extensions of his soul, to return them to a defeated enemy was an act of profound respect, acknowledging him as an equal rather than a vanquished foe.

The war chief took his weapons slowly, his calloused hands closing around familiar grips with obvious relief. For a long moment, the two men stood facing each other in silence, enemies who had fought to mutual exhaustion, survivors who had tested their skills against equals and emerged with new understanding of their own limitations.

Finally, Cadoc nodded once, a gesture that conveyed more than words could express. Recognition, respect, and acknowledgment of a bond forged in blood and steel that transcended national allegiances or tribal hatreds. Then he turned and walked into the forest, his powerful frame disappearing among the trees as if he had never existed.

Falco watched until the last trace of movement vanished, then turned and walked back toward his brothers-in-arms. His wounds still pained him, his strength was far from fully restored, but his step carried the satisfaction of a man who had proven himself against the finest opposition the enemy could offer.

'Ready?' Seneca asked as Falco rejoined the group.

The former gladiator nodded in silence. Around him, the Exploratores were already mounting up, preparing for the long journey back to Roman territory. The brief respite was over, it was time to resume their extraction from hostile lands.

'So be it,' said Seneca. 'Let's go.'

As they moved out of the clearing that had witnessed such savage combat, none of them looked back. Behind them lay the evidence of their struggle, blood on the ground, disturbed earth, the lingering scent of violence. But ahead lay the path home, and for men who had survived the impossible once again, that was all that mattered.

The brotherhood of warriors recognized no national boundaries, no tribal allegiances. In the end, courage honoured courage, skill acknowledged skill, and warriors respected warriors. It was a lesson written in blood and steel, understood by men who lived and died by the sword.

Chapter Forty-Eight

Camulodunum

The medical tent at Camulodunum buzzed with activity as the garrison's medici worked to treat the various wounds the Occultum had sustained during their ordeal. The canvas structure was large enough to accommodate multiple patients, with wooden cots arranged in neat rows and supplies organized with military precision along the walls.

Seneca lay on his back while a Greek physician carefully cleaned a series of cuts along his ribs, the man's skilled hands working with the practiced efficiency of someone who had treated countless battlefield injuries. The wounds were not deep, but they required attention to prevent infection, a constant threat in the damp British climate.

Nearby, Marcus gritted his teeth as another medicus reset the bones in his left forearm, which had been fractured during the final desperate moments of their fight with the Shadow Walkers. The physician worked quickly, his movements sure and confident as he aligned the broken bones and began wrapping them in linen strips stiffened with tree sap.

'Hold still,' the medicus commanded in accented Latin. 'The bones must be properly aligned, or you'll lose the use of that arm permanently.'

Decimus sat on the edge of his cot, allowing a young assistant to stitch a particularly nasty gash across his shoulder blade. The wound was deep enough to require careful suturing, each stitch pulled tight to ensure proper healing. He bore the pain in stoic silence, though his knuckles showed white where he gripped the cot's wooden frame.

But it was Falco who dominated the tent's atmosphere

with his characteristic mixture of bravado and dark humour. Despite being arguably the most seriously wounded of the group, he seemed determined to regale anyone within earshot with increasingly embellished accounts of their adventures.

'And then,' he was saying to a wide-eyed medicus who was cleaning the arrow wound in his upper arm, 'this Shadow Walker, must have been seven feet tall, built like a siege engine, comes at me with an axe the size of a small tree. So I say to myself, 'Falco, this is just like the arena, except with higher stakes and no crowd to cheer when you die.''

The former gladiator gestured expansively with his free arm, nearly knocking over a bowl of antiseptic herbs in his enthusiasm.

'So there I am, bleeding like a stuck pig, facing this giant who's covered in tattoos and probably hasn't had a bath since the winter solstice, and I think, well, at least if he kills me, I won't have to smell him anymore.'

Several of the medical staff chuckled despite themselves, while his comrades showed the long-suffering expressions of men who had heard these stories grow more elaborate with each telling.

'Falco,' called Marcus from his cot, 'in your version, Cadoc gains a foot in height and fifty pounds of muscle every time you tell it. In a few days, you'll be claiming you fought a giant who breathed fire.'

'Details,' Falco waved dismissively. 'The important thing is that I faced him down and lived to tell about it. Not many men can say they've fought the legendary war chief of the Shadow Walkers to a standstill.'

'You're right,' Decimus observed dryly. 'Not many men are foolish enough to volunteer for single combat when they could have let someone else take the risk.'

'Exactly!' Falco beamed, apparently missing the intended criticism entirely. 'Which is why I'm a legend and you're all just... well, whatever you are.'

Sica shook his head slowly, his wounds being the least serious of the group despite his active participation in the fighting. A few cuts on his arms and a bruised rib were the extent of his injuries, testament to his seemingly supernatural ability to avoid damage even in the fiercest combat.

'Next time,' he said quietly, 'we let the big mouth fight all the enemies himself. Save the rest of us the trouble.'

The tent's entrance flap was pushed aside at that moment, admitting a figure that brought immediate silence to the previously jovial atmosphere. Talorcan entered, moving somewhat stiffly but clearly alive and relatively unharmed. His clothes were different from what he had worn during their mission, local garments that suggested an interesting story about his own escape from Silures territory.

'Talorcan!' called Marcus out in relief. 'We weren't sure you'd made it out.'

The Belgic hunter's face showed the strain of his own ordeal, but his eyes held the satisfaction of a man who had successfully completed an impossible task.

'Barely,' he admitted, settling onto an empty cot with obvious relief. 'That mud was colder than a Germanic winter, and I had to spend most of a day buried in it while they searched for me. But I managed to slip away after killing their leader.'

'You managed to kill their chieftain?' asked Marcus, obviously impressed. 'Tell us more.'

Before Talorcan could continue, the reunion was interrupted by the arrival of another figure, Senator Lepidus, his uniform somehow managing to remain pristine despite the muddy conditions that seemed to characterize everything in Britannia. His expression was carefully neutral, but there was something in his eyes that suggested this was not a social call.

'Gentlemen,' he greeted them formally, his gaze sweeping across the wounded operatives. 'I trust your injuries are not serious?'

'Nothing that won't heal,' Seneca replied cautiously, noting the tension in the senator's voice.

'Excellent.' Lepidus glanced around again, his expression exuding both authority and disapproval. 'I've received preliminary reports about your mission, but I'd like to hear the details directly from you.'

Falco, never one to miss an opportunity for an audience, immediately launched into a comprehensive account of their adventures. He described the infiltration of Silures territory, the discovery of both Rhiannon and the location where Mordred was hiding, the difficult decision to prioritize the political rescue over the military assassination, and finally their desperate extraction under pursuit by the Shadow Walkers.

His narrative was vivid and largely accurate, though characteristically focused on his own heroic contributions to their success. He spoke with obvious pride about the single combat with Cadoc, describing it as a contest between equals that had earned mutual respect despite their opposing allegiances.

'And so,' he concluded with evident satisfaction, 'we not only completed the extraction of Cartimandua's daughter, preventing a war that could have driven Rome from Britannia entirely, but we also gathered invaluable intelligence about enemy dispositions and capabilities. I'd say that constitutes a highly successful mission.'

He sat back on his cot, clearly expecting praise for their accomplishments. The silence that followed was therefore particularly shocking, as Lepidus's expression showed none of the satisfaction or approval that Falco had anticipated.

'Did you kill Mordred?' he asked eventually.

Falco blinked in confusion.

'Well, no, but…'

'Did you complete the mission as originally assigned?' Lepidus interrupted.

'We made a tactical decision to…'

'Yes or no, Falco. Did you complete the mission?'

Seneca intervened before his subordinate could dig them deeper into whatever hole they were apparently falling into.

'We made a decision in the field,' he said carefully. 'Based on intelligence gathered during the operation, we determined that the political extraction served Rome's interests better than the military assassination. We changed the plan to reflect changed circumstances.'

Lepidus turned his attention to the team leader, his expression growing colder.

'So the answer is no. You did not complete the mission. Mordred still lives.'

The weight of those words settled over the tent like a funeral shroud. After all their struggles, all their sacrifices, all their desperate efforts to serve Rome's interests, they were being told that their mission was a failure.

'Yes,' Seneca replied quietly. 'Mordred still lives.'

The tent fell into complete silence, the only sounds coming from the medical work continuing around them. The medici seemed to sense the tension and worked more quietly, not wanting to draw attention to themselves during what was clearly a sensitive military discussion.

'Come with me,' said Lepidus finally. 'We need to discuss this privately.'

As Seneca rose from his cot and followed the senator toward the tent's exit, the atmosphere behind him shifted dramatically. The initial shock of his men gave way to a rising tide of anger as the implications of Lepidus's words sank in. Falco was the first to explode, his voice rising with indignation.

'Failure? He calls that a failure?' The former gladiator struggled to his feet, his various wounds making the movement painful but not deterring his rage. 'We prevented a war! We saved the province! We...'

'Sit down,' Marcus commanded sharply, but Falco was beyond reason.

'That toga-wearing bureaucrat thinks he knows better than men who were actually there?' Falco reached for a gladius, his naked form presenting an alarming sight as he waved the blade in the air. 'I'll show him what failure looks like when I cut his balls off and feed them to him!'

'Falco!' Marcus barked, abandoning his own cot despite his broken arm. 'Put that down and calm yourself!'

The confrontation might have escalated further, but Decimus and Talorcan moved to restrain their furious comrade, physically forcing him back onto his cot while Marcus took possession of the sword.

'Think!' Marcus commanded, his centurion's authority cutting through Falco's rage. 'Getting yourself executed for threatening a senator won't change anything. Control yourself!'

Falco submitted to their restraint, but his fury remained evident in every line of his body.

'We made the right choice,' he hissed. 'We saved the province from civil war. We prevented an alliance that would have cost thousands of Roman lives. How is that failure?'

'Because we disobeyed orders,' Decimus replied quietly, settling back onto his own cot with obvious weariness. 'Because we were sent to kill Mordred, and we chose not to.'

'Because we used our judgment!' Talorcan protested. 'Because we adapted to circumstances that the planners never anticipated!'

They continued their debate in lowered voices, each man defending their actions while struggling with the growing realization that their superiors might not see things the same way. The argument went in circles, they had prevented a war, but failed to complete their assigned mission. They had served Rome's greater interests, but disobeyed explicit orders. They had saved lives, but allowed a dangerous enemy to escape.

No matter how they approached the problem, they always reached the same conclusion: they had made the right choice under the circumstances. The political ramifications of Rhiannon's death would have been catastrophic for Roman interests in Britannia so preventing that outcome was worth more than eliminating a single druid, however dangerous he might be. *Wasn't it?*

Epilogue

Camulodunum

The oil lamps flickered in Lepidus's quarters as shadows danced across the wooden walls of the administrative building. The senator sat behind his desk, scrolls and tablets scattered before him like the debris of a battlefield. When Seneca entered, Lepidus didn't look up immediately, his fingers drumming against the wood with barely contained tension.

'Sit,' said Lepidus finally, his voice carrying none of its usual diplomatic polish.

Seneca settled into the chair across from the desk, noting the way the senator's jaw worked as if he were chewing on words too bitter to swallow. The silence stretched between them, heavy with unspoken recriminations.

'Explain it to me again,' said Lepidus quietly, still not meeting Seneca's eyes. 'Your reasoning. Your tactical assessment. Make me understand why you chose as you did.'

Seneca straightened, falling back on the logical arguments that had seemed so clear in the forests of Siluria.

'The political ramifications were that if Rhiannon had died in captivity, Cartimandua would have been forced to declare war on the Ordovices to avenge her daughter's death. The Silures would have supported the Ordovices, seeing it as an opportunity to strike at our Brigantes alliance. Other western tribes would have probably joined, including the Deceangli, and elements of the Dobunni and we would have faced a unified opposition that could have driven us back to Gaul entirely.'

'And Mordred?' Lepidus asked, his voice dangerously quiet. 'Caratacus? Two of our most dangerous enemies, both vulnerable, both within your grasp?'

'We made a decision in the field,' said Seneca. 'It was obvious to me that…'

'Stop.' Lepidus finally looked up, his eyes blazing with suppressed fury. 'Just stop talking and listen to me, Seneca. Really listen.'

The senator rose from his chair and began pacing behind the desk, his toga swirling around him like a storm cloud. When he spoke again, his voice carried the weight of accumulated frustration.

'During your first mission to Britannia, your team had Togodumnus, one of the most dangerous tribal leaders we faced, isolated in a tribal hut. A clean kill would have saved hundreds of Roman lives in the campaigns that followed. But you didn't take it.'

Seneca opened his mouth to respond, but Lepidus continued without pause.

'When Veteranus was on Mona, embedded with the druids, he had close access to Mordred himself. Close enough to put a knife between his ribs and end the threat he represented. But he failed to act, and Mordred lived on to almost kill the emperor.

The pacing intensified as Lepidus's control began to slip.

'And now, now you had both Mordred and a wounded Caratacus in the same location, and instead of completing the mission you were sent to accomplish, you chose to rescue a single woman. However politically valuable she might be.'

'But the strategic implications…' started Seneca.

'I know the implications!' Lepidus exploded, slamming his hand down on the desk with enough force to scatter papers and send an inkwell jumping. 'Jupiter's blood, Seneca, do you think

I'm some toga-wearing fool who doesn't understand military necessity? I know exactly why you made the choice you did, and tactically, politically and strategically, you were probably right!'

The outburst left both men breathing hard, the senator's carefully maintained composure finally cracking under the pressure he had been carrying. He collapsed back into his chair and paused as he gathered his thoughts.

'But Claudius won't see it that way,' he said quietly, the fight draining out of him. 'All he sees is a pattern of failure. Three major opportunities to eliminate Rome's most dangerous enemies in Britannia, and three times the Occultum chose not to strike. He doesn't understand nuance, doesn't care about political ramifications. He sees results, and the results he wanted aren't the ones he received.'

Seneca felt a cold weight settling in his stomach as the full implications began to dawn on him.

'What are you saying?'

'I'm saying we're very close to being disbanded,' said Lepidus. 'The Emperor is losing faith in the Occultum's effectiveness. There are those in Rome who whisper that you've become too independent, too willing to substitute your judgment for imperial orders.'

The silence that followed was deafening. Outside, the sounds of the garrison continued, sentries calling out their watches, horses stamping in the stables, the distant murmur of men going about their duties. But inside this room, the future of Rome's most elite unit hung in the balance. Finally, Seneca spoke, his voice steady despite the turmoil in his thoughts.

'We'll go back in and complete the original mission,' he said. 'We'll kill Mordred and Caratacus both, however long it takes.'

Lepidus shook his head wearily.

'No. Not yet. Maybe not ever.'

He reached for a scroll sealed with imperial purple wax, its very presence radiating authority and urgency. 'This arrived this morning by the fastest courier Claudius could dispatch. We are all being recalled to Rome immediately. All of us, no exceptions, no delays.'

'Why?' asked Seneca, though something in Lepidus's expression suggested the answer wouldn't be comforting.

'I don't know,' admitted Lepidus. 'The orders are brief and provide no explanation beyond the urgency. Claudius wants the Occultum back in Rome as quickly as transportation can be arranged and given the context of our recent... *disappointments*... I can only assume it's not for commendation.'

Another silence fell between them, this one heavy with the weight of uncertainty. Years of successful missions, countless victories achieved through impossible odds, and it might all be ending because of well-meant choices made in the forests of a distant province.

'How long do we have?' Seneca asked finally.

'A ship leaves for Gaul tomorrow morning. We will be on it. Get your men ready, Seneca. Whatever comes next, you'll face it in Rome.'

The medical tent felt smaller when Seneca returned, the canvas walls seeming to press inward as he surveyed his wounded team. They looked up expectantly as he entered, their faces showing the mixture of hope and apprehension that came from not knowing their fate.

He settled onto his cot heavily, the weight of command suddenly feeling heavier than it ever had before. His men waited patiently, accustomed to his thoughtful silences but clearly sensing that something significant had occurred during his meeting with Lepidus.

Finally, Marcus broke the silence.

'Well,' he said, 'what's going to happen to us?'

Seneca sighed deeply, a sound that seemed to come from the very depths of his soul. He looked around at these men who had followed him through impossible missions, who had trusted his judgment even when it led them into the most dangerous situations imaginable. They deserved honesty, whatever the consequences.

'I don't know,' he said finally, his voice carrying the exhaustion of a man who had made too many hard choices. 'But get your gear packed. We're going home.'

The simple words hung in the air like a death sentence. None of them asked for clarification, they had all been soldiers long enough to recognize the difference between a temporary recall and something more permanent. The way Seneca had delivered the news, the tone of defeat in his voice, told them everything they needed to know.

One by one, without discussion or complaint, they began gathering their few possessions. The medical staff continued their work around them, but the atmosphere in the tent had fundamentally changed. Where moments before there had been the comfortable camaraderie of soldiers recovering from a successful mission, now there was only the quiet resignation of men who understood that their world was about to change in ways they couldn't control.

Outside, the British rain had started again, drumming against the canvas with the relentless persistence that characterized everything about this island province. Soon they would be leaving it all behind, the mud, the endless forests, the hostile tribes, and the impossible missions that had defined their existence.

The Occultum's war in Britannia was over. What came next would be decided by powers far beyond their control, in a city they had served faithfully but might no longer call home.

The End

Next Book

Follow the adventures of the Occultum in the next enthralling adventure deep in the heart of the African continent.

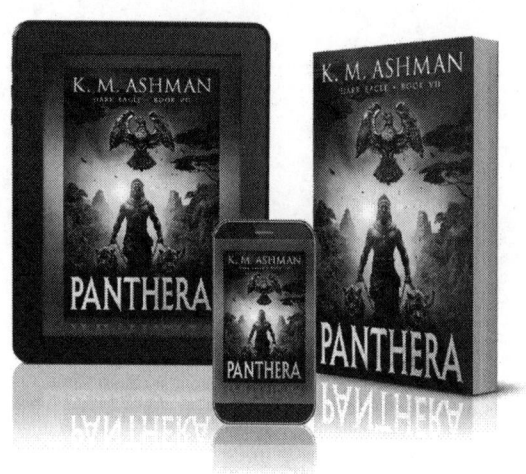

On the scorching fringes of the Roman Empire in Egypt, a patrol uncovers a half-dead man staggering out of the desert, emaciated, raving, and clutching a necklace of staggering beauty. A Roman eagle tattooed on his arm hints at a legion long thought lost, and with his final breath, he utters a single word: *Panthera*.

To the centurion, it's a mystery best left to Rome, but to Emperor Claudius, it's a warning. He knows exactly what the discovery means, and what he needed to do.

Summoning the secretive and deadly Occultum, Claudius launches a mission shrouded in secrecy, leading into the untamed heart of Africa. There, in lands uncharted and ruled by ancient powers, the truth awaits, and it could shake Rome to its core.

Authors Notes

The Roman Invasion of Britain (43 CE)

The Roman invasion of Britain under Emperor Claudius in 43 CE was a massive undertaking involving four legions and auxiliary forces totalling approximately 40,000 men. Led by Aulus Plautius, the invasion force landed at Rutupiae (modern Richborough) and fought decisive battles at the River Medway and Thames. The campaign aimed to complete what Julius Caesar had begun nearly a century earlier. Camulodunum (Colchester) became the first Roman capital of Britain and was where Claudius himself arrived to accept the surrender of eleven British kings, establishing Roman rule over much of southern and eastern Britain.

The Exploratores - Roman Military Scouts

The Exploratores were specialized Roman reconnaissance units that emerged during the Imperial period, particularly valuable in frontier warfare. These mounted scouts operated far ahead of the main legions, gathering intelligence on enemy movements, terrain, and tribal dispositions. Unlike regular cavalry, they were trained for stealth operations, long-range reconnaissance, and survival in hostile territory. Their skills included tracking, map-making, and the ability to live off the land for extended periods. They were crucial in Rome's expansion into Britain, where the dense forests and hostile tribes made conventional military intelligence gathering extremely difficult.

The Silures Tribe

The Silures were one of the most formidable and warlike tribes in ancient Britain, controlling much of what is now South Wales. They were renowned for their fierce resistance to Roman rule and their mastery of guerrilla warfare tactics. Unlike tribes that favoured open battle, the Silures specialized in ambush attacks, melting into their mountainous terrain after striking Roman forces. Tacitus described them as having 'swarthy faces and curly hair,' distinguishing them from other British tribes. They successfully resisted Roman conquest for over 25 years, making them one of the last tribes to be fully subdued, finally falling around 78 CE under governor Sextus Julius Frontinus.

Caratacus - The British War Leader

Caratacus (Caradog in Welsh) was the most significant British resistance leader against Roman invasion. Initially a prince of the Catuvellauni tribe, he fled west after the fall of his territories and united various Welsh tribes against Rome. For nearly a decade, he led a highly effective guerrilla campaign from the Welsh mountains, becoming the embodiment of British resistance. His tactics included avoiding pitched battles, striking at Roman supply lines, and using the difficult terrain to his advantage. He was finally defeated in 51 CE and brought to Rome, where his dignity before Emperor Claudius reportedly saved his life and earned him a pardon.

The Brigantes and Queen Cartimandua

The Brigantes controlled the largest tribal territory in Britain, covering much of northern England. Their queen, Cartimandua, made the controversial decision to ally with Rome rather than resist, making her a crucial Roman client ruler. This alliance provided Rome with a buffer against Scottish tribes and secured their northern frontier. However, her pro-Roman stance caused internal strife, particularly with her husband Venutius, who favoured resistance. The tribe's strategic importance meant that maintaining Brigantian loyalty was essential for Roman control of Britain, making political marriages and diplomatic agreements vital tools of imperial policy.

Celtic Druids and Roman Suppression

Druids held immense power in Celtic society as priests, judges, teachers, and political advisors. They maintained oral traditions, conducted religious ceremonies including human sacrifice, and often led resistance against Roman rule. Rome viewed them as a serious threat to imperial authority, not just for their religious practices but for their role in uniting tribes against Roman expansion. The systematic suppression of Druidism culminated in the assault on Anglesey (Mona) in 60 CE, where the Romans destroyed the sacred groves and slaughtered the Druids. This campaign was part of a broader Roman policy to eliminate potential centres of resistance and replace Celtic religious structures with Roman institutions.

Iron Age British Hillforts

British hillforts were sophisticated defensive settlements that dominated the landscape during the Iron Age. These weren't mere military installations but thriving communities that served as political, economic, and religious centres. They featured multiple defensive rings with elaborate entrance systems designed to channel attackers into killing zones. The largest could house several thousand people and included areas for livestock, grain storage, workshops, and elite residences. Their strategic positioning on prominent hills provided excellent visibility and defensive advantages. When Romans encountered these fortifications, they often found them more challenging to assault than traditional Mediterranean-style walls, requiring adapted siege tactics.

Roman Military Medicine and Field Surgery

Roman military medicine was surprisingly advanced, with professional medici (doctors) attached to legions and specialized medical corps for treating battlefield injuries. Military hospitals (valetudinaria) were established at major bases, featuring surgical instruments, pharmaceutical supplies, and systematic treatment protocols. Field medicine included techniques for treating arrow wounds, setting broken bones, and performing emergency surgery under combat conditions. Roman medical knowledge, heavily influenced by Greek practices, included understanding of anatomy, the use of opiates for pain relief, and antiseptic practices. This medical expertise gave Roman forces a significant advantage in maintaining combat effectiveness during extended campaigns.

Celtic Warrior Culture and Single Combat

Celtic warrior culture placed enormous emphasis on personal honour, individual prowess, and the glory of single combat. Warriors often fought nearly naked, decorated with woad and ritual tattoos that proclaimed their achievements and tribal affiliations. Single combat between champions was a recognized way to settle disputes or demonstrate courage before major battles. These encounters weren't merely displays of skill but religious rituals that invoked divine favour and established the moral authority to lead. Roman observers noted both admiration and horror at Celtic courage, describing warriors who seemed to welcome death in battle as a path to immortal glory among their ancestors.

Roman Intelligence Networks in Britain

Rome's success in conquering diverse territories relied heavily on sophisticated intelligence gathering. In Britain, this included recruiting local informants, establishing trade relationships that provided access to tribal territories, and using diplomatic missions to gather political and military intelligence. The Romans were skilled at exploiting existing tribal rivalries, offering alliance terms to some groups while targeting others for conquest. Merchants often served as unofficial intelligence agents, mapping territories and reporting on tribal movements, fortifications, and political situations. This intelligence network was crucial for understanding the complex web of alliances and enmities that characterized Celtic Britain.

Also by K. M. Ashman

The Exploratores
Dark Eagle
The Hidden
Veteranus
Scarab
The Wraith
Silures
Panthera

The Brotherhood
Templar Steel
Templar Stone
Templar Blood
Templar Fury
Templar Glory
Templar Legacy
Templar Loyalty

Seeds of Empire
Seeds of Empire
Rise of the Eagle
Fields of Glory

The India Summers Mysteries
The Vestal Conspiracies
The Treasures of Suleiman
The Mummies of the Reich
The Tomb Builders

The Roman Chronicles
The Fall of Britannia
The Rise of Caratacus
The Wrath of Boudicca

The Medieval Sagas
Blood of the Cross
In Shadows of Kings
Sword of Liberty
Ring of Steel

The Blood of Kings
A Land Divided
A Wounded Realm
Rebellion's Forge
The Warrior Princess
The Blade Bearer

The Road to Hastings
The Challenges of a King
The Promises of a King
The Fate of a King

The Otherworld Series
The Legacy Protocol
The Seventh God
The Last Citadel
Savage Eden
Vampire

Printed in Dunstable, United Kingdom